Barefaced Lies and Boogie-Woogie Boasts

JOOLS HOLLAND

with

HARRIET VYNER

PENGUIN BOOKS

PENGUIN BOOKS

Published by the Penguin Group
Penguin Books Ltd, 80 Strand, London WC2R ORL, England
Penguin Group (USA) Inc., 375 Hudson Street, New York, New York 10014, USA
Penguin Group (Canada), 90 Eglinton Avenue East, Suite 700, Toronto, Ontario, Canada M4P 2Y3
(a division of Pearson Penguin Canada Inc.)
Penguin Ireland, 25 Sffi'tephen's Green, Dublin 2, Ireland
(a division of Penguin Books Ltd)
Penguin Group (Australia), 250 Camberwell Road, Camberwell, Victoria 3124, Australia
(a division of Pearson Australia Group Pty Ltd)
Penguin Books India Pvt Ltd, 11 Community Centre, Panchsheel Park, New Delhi – 110 017, India
Penguin Group (NZ), 67 Apollo Drive, Rosedale, North Shore 0632, New Zealand
(a division of Pearson New Zealand Ltd)
Penguin Books (South Africa) (Pty) Ltd, 24 Sturdee Avenue, Rosebank, Johannesburg 2196, South Africa

Penguin Books Ltd, Registered Offices: 80 Strand, London WC2R ORL, England

www.penguin.com

First published by Michael Joseph 2007
Published in Penguin Books 2008

006

Copyright © Helicon Mountain Ltd, 2007
All rights reserved.

Typeset by Rowland Phototypesetting Ltd, Bury St Edmunds, Suffolk
Printed in England by Clays Ltd, St Ives plc

ISBN: 978–0–141–02677–0

www.greenpenguin.co.uk

To George, Rosie, Fred and Mabel

Acknowledgements

The person who I would most like to thank in the creation of this autobiography is my co-author, Harriet Vyner, without whom no book would have been possible. Furthermore, if anybody has been left out of this book or is in anyway misrepresented, I would like to lay the blame firmly on her shoulders.

I am further enormously grateful to Paul Loasby, Valerie McCartney, David McCartney, Christabel Holland, Mother, Father, Richard and Christopher Holland, Gilson Lavis, Dave Swift, Mark Flanagan, Phil Veacock, Michael 'Bammi' Rose, Lisa Grahame, Derek Nash, Nick Lunt, Roger Goslyn, Winston Rollins, Rico Rodriguez, Fayyaz Virji, Jason McDermid, Jon Scott, Chris Storr, Andy Salmon, Ron Burrow, Pete Dawson, Paul Reynoldson, Simon Chandler Honnor, Richard Hutton, Nick Darton-Bigg, Vicky Hooper, Fred Heffer, Mike Chaplin, Edgar Lustgarten, Uncle David, Mary McCartney, Cathy Coleman, Clare Conville, Tom Weldon, Katy Follain, Carly Cook, Sarah Day, Debbie Hatfield, Natalie Higgins, Lesley Hodgson, Helen Reynolds, Laurie Latham, Garry Cooper, Martin Pugh, Mark Smith, Nicky Armstrong, Lawrence Impey, John Lay, Elena Bello, Mario Warner, Jimmy Mulvoy, Nick Phillips, John Reid, Bernard Doherty, Doug Wright, Grant Eskriett, Ben Ward, Andy Murray, Peter Price, Miles Copeland, Graeme de la Terre, Nick Fleming, Chris Hession, Niki Sanderson, Stuart Kenning, Mark Cooper, Alison Howe, Glenn Tilbrook, Chris Difford, Keith Wilkinson, Paul Gunn, Harry Kakoulli, Pino Palladino, Martin Deegan, Mike Paice, Kim Lesley, Maz Roberts, Louise Marshall, Sam Brown, Ruby Turner, Edna Hales, Sandra Grove, Kathy Syplywczak, Roger Brown, Paul and Juli Collins.

I'd also like to thank all the people who I mention in this book, and all the people who haven't been mentioned in this book but who have, nevertheless, made it possible to have a life to write about. Cheers.

And finally, thank God for the gift of music.

Contents

List of Illustrations

Mike Paice (lying down), Maz Roberts, Martin Deegan, Taif (© Pino Palladino/Kim Lesley)

25. The Millionaires, Caracas, 1981
26. Pino Palladino (standing), Jools and Martin Deegan (inside house)
27. Jools wearing his custom-made piano suit (© ITV/Tyne Tees)
28. Jools, chequered floor and grand piano (© Barry Ord Clarke)

Inset Two

1. Jools Holland and Paula Yates (© Joe Bangay)
2. Jools, Mary Leahy, their baby son George, and Paula Yates, 1985
3. Jools and Lesley Ash, New York (© ITV/Tyne Tees)
4. Stephen Fry, Jools Holland, Stanley Unwin (seated), member of the Tyne Tees production crew, Portmeirion
5. Jools and George Harrison, Hong Kong, 1985
6. Jools and Fats Domino (© ITV/Tyne Tees)
7. Jools and Stevie Wonder (© ITV/Tyne Tees)
8. Jools and Van Morrison
9. Jools and Ray Charles
10. Jools and BB King (© BBC)
11. Jools and Joe Strummer
12. Jools and President Bill Clinton, Birmingham, 1998
13. Mark Flanagan, Laurie Latham, Christopher Holland, Jools Holland, Dave Swift, Eric Clapton and Gilson Lavis at Helicon
14. Jools and Amy Winehouse (© BBC)
15. The remains of the crushed Vauxhall Cavalier (© Marsha Lay)
16. Jools and Christabel Holland
17. Rosie Holland, aged three (© Mary Garland)
18. Jools and his youngest daughter, Mabel, on a Velocette Venom 500
19. Jools in front of one of his buildings
20. Rhythm and Blues Orchestra, Glastonbury, 2000 (© Mary McCartney)
21. Rhythm and Blues Orchestra on stage at the Royal Albert Hall
22. The Rhythm and Blues Orchestra line-up (© Mary McCartney)
23. Jools and Christabel's wedding day, August 2005 (© Julie Adams)

Unless otherwise noted, pictures courtesy of the author's own collection. Every effort has been made to trace copyright holders and the publishers will be pleased to rectify any unintentional omission in subsequent editions.

Sex and Jazz and Rock and Roll

I was born on 24 January 1958, shortly after Prime Minister Harold Macmillan announced to the British people that we'd 'never had it so good'. I would ask you at this point to refer to the photograph of the newly born me, the embodiment of his optimistic view of Britain.

There was a huge thunderstorm the night I was born. My mother, June, was very beautiful and only twenty-one years old. My father, Derek, the same age, had not long finished his national service in the RAF. He had met my mother by chance, on a Southern Region train travelling into central London from Greenwich, and shortly after this first meeting had invited her to go dancing at the Hundred Club in Oxford Street, where Humphrey Lyttelton was playing. It's a well-known fact that jazz, played in the right way, can heighten feelings of love and desire, and there's little doubt that on that particular evening Humph's band had this effect on my parents. Many years later I was to give Humphrey Lyttelton an award for his outstanding achievements in jazz. I shook his hand firmly and thanked him for the role that he'd had in the conception of the Boogie-Woogie Boaster.

At the time of my arrival, my parents had a small flat in Pimlico. I was the first grandchild for both sets of grandparents, which meant that I was on course for plenty of spoiling. Shortly after I was born we went to live with Ena and Percy, my father's parents, who had moved from a comfortable house in Winchmore Hill to Eltham. They were the epitome of 1950s respectability and kindness. Percy had always been good-looking and resembled Superintendent Lockhart from *No Hiding Place*. To add to his appearance of gravitas and stability, he owned a large black Wolseley, identical to the ones at Scotland Yard. Beneath this façade, however, he was an infamous joker, apt to play the giddy goat at Christmas, weddings and other family gatherings. My father had an older brother, Brian, and younger sister, Barbara. Teenage Barbara was a huge fan of Cliff Richard, who in the late fifties was one of Britain's first pop stars. One evening she went to one of Cliff's concerts. Percy, in his usual kindly way, dropped Barbara and her friends off at the theatre, saying he'd pick them up at the stage door when the show was over. He sat waiting in his official-looking Wolseley as the show finished. Hordes of teenage fans surged on to the street, making for the stage door. Impressed by the car and my grandfather's demeanour, one young girl asked him who he was. For some reason, he thought it would be amusing to say that he was Cliff's driver and was waiting for him. This announcement turned the already excitable young women into a frenzied mob. By now there were hundreds of them, and they started rocking his shiny black car from side to side until, eventually, their brute force turned it over.

After a while living with Percy and Ena, my parents decided to take a house at 5 Myddleton Gardens, Enfield, with their friends the Gadstones, as all four of them were in their early twenties and quite bohemian. John Gadstone was an academic and Michele, like my mother, was ravishingly beautiful. Fortunately, we didn't have a television, so I was quickly exposed to other, more interesting activities. The first real song I remember hearing was 'Careless Love', the blues song based on an old Scottish folk song, sung by my mother. In the evenings we would all play games, with background music of opera and Bessie Smith and Mr Jellylord, Jelly Roll Morton. I was generally the centre of attention and allowed to join in with whatever the grown-ups were doing.

It was in this house that my father started to read to me every evening, and he continued to do this for many years. His choices would include Greek mythology, *The Lord of the Rings*, biographies of Mozart. I was taken to see films such as *Henry V*, starring Sir Laurence Olivier, and encouraged to adopt Horatio Nelson as my hero. All of this must have had some effect on me, even though I was still only four.

The young Gadstones and Hollands were a great household,

filled with culture and high spirits, but they didn't have my grand-parents' good husbandry skills and were a bit vague about organiz-ing bills and paying the rent. After a while, the electricity was cut off, but we all enjoyed this, as it meant we could use oil lamps and light the log fire. Unfortunately, one evening, one of the logs fell out of the grate, burning a great big hole in the floor – the whole house nearly went up in flames. A few days later the landlord, who had a little Alfa Romeo, pulled up outside, as the rent was late. We decided not to let him in in case he saw the damage, and we all hid below the window of the front room, trying to suppress our giggles and ignoring his repeated knocks.

But our days were numbered at 5 Myddleton Gardens and by the summer of 1963 the time had come for us to move. My father found us somewhere to live, presenting it as the latest style in modern living. It was a top-floor bed-sitting room in Coleherne Road, on the edges of Earls Court. The set-up was quite different to Myddleton Gardens: instead of safe suburban streets with well-kept front gardens and sensible neighbours living next door, Coleherne Road had more of an edgy feel. It was a terrace of tall, thin early Victorian houses, far more urban than suburban. The house itself had been divided into one-room flats, the others inhabited by students, one junky and a couple of fly-by-nights, including one on the ground floor who could have been a dubious villain from an Edgar Wallace mystery. My mother wasn't so keen on these neighbours but my father felt the location was going to be more beneficial for us, a way to plug into London life.

One of the reasons my father had thought it a good idea to live in central London was for what he perceived to be the better educational opportunities for me. There was a modern and highly regarded state school near the Boltons in Chelsea, where he immediately went to enrol me. Although we lived very close by, he was told there was no room for me there, and I had to be sent instead to the scrottier Park Walk school. A short while later, there was a feature in the local paper about the new American ambassador who had been appointed to London; his children had been accepted at the Boltons school. My father was furious about this and went to see the headmaster, demanding that they find a place for me too. A place could not be found. He got into a heated educational debate with the headmaster and ended up saying, 'If you refuse to educate him, I shall have to do it myself.' He was a man of his word and took me out of school straight away and drew up his own timetable for my education. Each morning we would visit a different place of interest, some landmark or museum in London. One morning you'd find us in the British Museum, the next we'd be scampering up inside St Paul's Cathedral and marvelling at Wren's dome. In the afternoons we'd read from the classics. At one point during this period of home schooling, my father and I passed the huge smart villas around Regent's Park and, arriving home, our bedsit looked a bit drab in comparison. I asked whether we couldn't go and live in one of those houses instead. And it was explained, not just at the moment. After a couple of weeks of this, quite understandably, my father felt rather exhausted and I was sent back to Park Walk.

Meanwhile, I was looking forward with excitement to our landlord's first visit and the ploys of avoidance we'd have to think up this time. On the morning of his arrival, we looked down from our top window to see a sharp-looking man in his late teens driving up in his Alvis. Far from menacing us for our overdue rent, this stylish slum landlord and jazz drummer, Colin Strickland, instead became our great friend. I was a bit disappointed not to have to resort to hiding or disguising ourselves, but Strickland and my father were to enter into various business ventures that would make up for this. Their first was a sea-food restaurant, the Sea Net, situated at the foot of the Admiralty building and decked out with fishing nets and shells. How could it fail? It would have the added bonus of myself dressed as Horatio Nelson sitting on the counter. This last attractive proposition, put forward by Colin and my father over a long lunch, never materialized. I would often be sat on the counter, but in my normal clothes, and only two or three people ever came in and the Sea Net soon closed.

That Christmas, we put a tree up in the dormer window and, what with the fairy lights and the smell from the one-bar electric fire, our room felt very cosy. Colin brought some fine claret for the grown-ups and I was given a policeman's uniform, including hat and truncheon. Desperate to show it off, I left our room on the top floor and peered over the banisters to the hall, four floors below. The fly-by-night on the ground floor happened to be going into his flat, and he looked up and saw me through his thick glasses. For whatever reason, he was so ready to feel the long arm of the law on his collar that he immediately ran from the building and was never seen again. Colin Strickland tried to rent us his room, saying it was superior to ours but, by this time, my mother had had enough and wanted us all to leave the 1960s high life of *Darling* and *Performance* and return to the pre-war Ealing film world of comfort and security of her family in Greenwich.

Greenwich

My mother's family had always lived in south-east London. Her father came from a huge family that had all lived together in a tiny house in Orlop Street, at the back of the Cutty Sark pub. As a boy, he would swim in the Thames and played in Greenwich Park when the deer still roamed free. The street in which he lived is now used when period feature films are being made and the location people need a perfect example of a London slum.

My grandmother Rosie was born in Deptford. Her mother, Britannia, had lived the exciting life of a Dickensian heroine and brought up her children almost single-handedly with very little money. She made sure they were always perfectly turned out and well-behaved. By the 1930s the family had moved to Greenwich, a step up, although it would have been hard to step down from Deptford. By the end of the decade Rosie and her brothers and sisters, Nelson, John, Albert and Daisy, had set up a greengrocer's business, and they all lived in the same small streets of Victorian terraced houses, with Britannia living above the shop. This was the cosy pre-war world that still existed when my father, mother and I moved in to 19 Couthurst Road in 1964.

The house had a small back garden but no bathroom, and I used to have to go round to my nan's for a bath once a week. This arrangement had many advantages, as not only did I not really like baths but even now I have the amazing complexion of a gypsy prince, a tribute to that early period of not being scrubbed properly.

Our house was all right, but my nan's, at 7 Hassendean Road, was by far the loveliest place in the world. There was a kitchen with a scullery at the back with a large valve radiogram, mismatching, well-polished Victorian furniture, 1930s armchairs and a budgie in a cage. In the front room there were flying ducks on the wall and, most importantly, a piano. My nan told me that it had been a wedding present from her mother. She said that they had always had singsongs around it at Christmas and showed me how the pianola part of it worked, putting on piano rolls and pedalling the bellows. The piano then sprang into life with 'Red Sails in the Sunset'. She said she was sorry it was a bit out of tune, but she blamed Hitler. In 1940 her street had been bombed and all the windows of the house blown in. She pointed out how the outer case was blackened and slightly charred whereas, when you lifted the lid, there was beautifully preserved rosewood lacquer with gold letters saying, 'W. H. Barnes, London'. I didn't mind the piano not having been tuned since the war – piano tuners, like butter and fresh meat, were probably hard to get hold of – and it didn't detract from the pleasure I took in hearing the lovely old tunes played from the piano rolls.

As I listened, I thought how lucky it was that the Luftwaffe hadn't destroyed the piano and my nan's lovely house in their raid, and felt lucky, too, to be living now, in improved circumstances, being given endless treats such as helping out in the family green-grocer's or being bought ice creams by numerous kindly rellies. Much as I'd enjoyed my louche days in Enfield and Earls Court, I found myself at home in these more old-fashioned surroundings. I rather liked the way the nans, granddads, uncles and aunts all seemed to act like proper grown-ups, with an air of practicality. And I liked the look of the area; it seemed to lend itself to *Boy's Own* activities. I have often described to my wife, Christabel, happy memories of playing in war-damaged buildings, like those children in 1940s films who wear big shorts and find a Luger in the rubble or a hiding Luftwaffe pilot. Christabel, not realizing perhaps that Greenwich and Blackheath weren't regenerated as quickly as the London she knew, sometimes suggests that I might somehow be borrowing the memories of a child from an earlier generation, or have taken them from one of those war-time films. But I will take a moment here to reassure my readers that, while some people can't recall anything before the age of eighteen and resort to fantasy, I can recall all the early parts of my life and details of childhood pastimes quite clearly, and I was very much there, playing in the rubble. In fact, shortly after having moved to the area, I remember climbing into a bombsite with a slightly older friend. It was just basically a basement, the shell of the building around it boarded up with posters for Bovril, Cadbury's and Ever Ready batteries, and it was flooded at the bottom. There was a cooker right in the middle, sticking up like an island. I climbed across to it and thought, 'Oh, this is fun.' And my friend said, 'Right, I'm going now, see you later,' and scampered over the wall. When I got to the wall, I couldn't get over it, so I was stuck in this cellar, exposed to the sky, with the water about a foot deep all around, the cooker in the middle. I managed to climb over all the rubbish to perch on top of it. I waited there for ten minutes, beginning to think, 'Oh, no . . .', then I found I really wanted a crap. Eventually I realized there was only one thing to do: I started to crap in the cooker.

At this point, a policeman peered over the poster boards. 'You're disgusting! What are you doing?' he said, and all I could say was, 'I'm so sorry, I'm stuck here.' So he said, 'Well – you've got to get out of there,' and reached out his hand through the great big blue cuff with the official stripy band. So I stopped crapping half-way through and waded towards him. As I drew up, he said, 'And you haven't even washed your hands, have you?' I just hung my head. 'No. Sorry . . .'

He pulled me up and I grabbed his cuff so tightly it nearly came off. Once I was out, all he said was, 'All right. On your way, sonny . . .'

After that I half considered a future career in the police. I imagined tearing around in a Wolseley pulling trapped people from bombed-out buildings, although not people like me. I never fancied being a fireman so much, in spite of the fact that I would quite like to slide down a pole in an emergency, because even driving a fire engine – well, it's not a Wolseley, is it?

Rudiments

My first school in Greenwich was the Invicta infant school. I didn't like being there and, really, I felt there was no need for any more education as I already knew it all. I remember being in the playground and staring hard at the sun as they warn you not to do so that I could be blinded and leave. However, that having failed, I stayed there until 1965, when it was time to move to Sherrington junior school, one of those state schools where well-educated people sent their sons in order to improve them by mixing with scrotty people like me.

Glenn Tilbrook attended both of these schools and there began to make his legend: he was famous for being so accident-prone, having managed to break both his arms, or both his legs – or both. I didn't get to know him at this point, but when I did he said that he remembered me from Sherrington because I sometimes wore an absurd posh bow-tie and looked very annoying. Now I had nothing to do with this – my mother had dressed me in this bow-tie, probably to make me look more academic. I hadn't been aware of it at the time, but it obviously made an impression.

At Sherrington, there were huge classes of forty-five and some rather nice teachers. There was an attractive teacher called Miss Taylor who used to join in our little cricket games and the octogenarian Mr Charman who had taught my mother and her cousin Valerie. He must have done a good job on them, since they are the only two people I know in England who can still spell. He always wore a blue pin-striped suit in summer and a brown tweed one in winter. Every Friday afternoon, instead of work, he would give us the *Daily Telegraph* crossword to do and hand sixpence to whichever boy had the most words right. I used to make words up to try to win. I miss teachers like that.

One of the great friends I made there was Simon Ellis. One day, these bigger lads were playing a game which involved knocking over the smaller kids, and they did it to us. Simon said, 'Watch it!', and the biggest of the lads, who had a thick tuft of black hair and was wearing shorts which didn't really suit him, turned round and snarled, 'Are you trying to make trouble?' Simon Ellis turned and gestured to me, saying, 'Yeah, what do you say to that, Julian – are you?' I said, 'I dunno,' and the big lad jabbed me with his finger and said, 'Well, you – *don't*,' gave me another big shove and went off. And that was my first introduction to one of the greatest actors the cinema has ever known, Daniel Day Lewis.

His father, C. Day Lewis, was Poet Laureate then and one of those who thought that mixing with my type would somehow better their children and, of course, he was right. As the Ellises and Day Lewises were neighbours, they used to take it in turns to collect their children from school. Because I was a friend of Simon's, I would sometimes go back to his house for tea, and the Day Lewises would pick me up too. So, despite this jabbing-finger incident, Dan and I became, if not close friends, then on jolly speaking terms.

We would all jump in the Poet Laureate's car, a lovely air-force-blue Mercedes-Benz 220. I'd never been in a Mercedes-Benz and the first time I got a lift I was struck by the fact that the Mercedes symbol looked like a gun sight. I remember saying to C. Day Lewis and Dan, 'Cor, you could just imagine shooting a load of Nazis through that – *Er! Er! Er! Er!*' (making the noise of a machine gun). After this, there was just a sort of silence in the car.

But they were always very nice and got us home safely. I don't think Dan had a very happy time at the school, and eventually he moved on. Whenever we meet now, although neither of us particularly liked Sherrington, there is always a warmth between us because of it. And I do have some rather happy memories of the place – particularly of Miss Taylor. Simon and I worked out that if we lay on our coats when she was bowling you could see the tops of her stockings, which women still wore then. We suggested to Dan that he might want to do this too, but he was still playing the running around the playground shoving people game and hadn't cottoned on to that form of pleasure yet – I think he has now.

Finding the Keys

My Uncle David and my mother's cousin John were already exciting figures, not only because they were older than me but also because they had snazzy sports cars – Lotuses and Jags, that sort of thing. They had a lorry business too and occasionally brought some Bedford or Albion tractor units home, which was a real treat.

My Uncle David also had an R&B band called the Planets. They had a lovely wooden sign, which I kept for a long time: 'London's top rhythm and blues group – The Planets'. When I was about eight, I heard him rehearsing with his band for the first time, in my grandparents' front room. I'd never really heard that type of music before and I loved it immediately. They were all playing so loudly it was deafening the whole street, and they were asked to stop after a while.

My uncle was the bass player but he knew this piano piece, 'St Louis Blues', taught to him by my mother. That same afternoon he played it to me and I was instantly fascinated, going over and asking, 'Hey – how did you do that?' He encouraged me to try it myself and I found I could copy him straight away. It felt like all the elements of the universe had come together for the first time, making order out of the chaos.

I was obsessed with it after that, would just sit there playing in my grandmother's front room for hours on end. 'St Louis Blues' had a left-hand riff – a boogie-woogie riff played with the left hand on the piano, in both major and minor key at the same time. (Coincidentally, I've since discovered, having talked to them, that Ray Charles, Ringo Starr and Mark Knopfler all had uncle figures who introduced them to exactly the same riff as children. Dr John too – but the aunt who taught him it as a child told him it was called 'Texas Boogie'.) It was definitely the sound that attracted me to boogie music. It is one of the great and most enjoyable musical forms. When my uncle first played the piece, I was instantly able to appreciate that the music hit you in two places at the same time and that there was a contrast between the two. The left hand played the major and the minor key figure as the right hand played the improvisation melody or riff. That he was hitting them together at the same time really got me going. The contrast between the left and the right hand was like an orchestra in itself and it also had a bit of swing and boogie in it and just made me want to jump up. It was so exciting – I would have run across a road to hear it, and I wanted to leap around.

Back in 1964, on a bus with my father, I had heard the Beatles' 'All My Loving' playing on someone's radio and had found myself excited by that too – so excited that I went on thinking about it for days afterwards. My mother had a 78 record of Sister Rosetta Tharpe singing 'Up above My Head I Hear Music in the Air', which I used to ask her to play again and again, as I did her Bessie Smith 78s and the music-hall records of comedian Sandy Powell. Then, a few years later, I was sitting at the window of Couthurst Road and I heard 'Oh Happy Day', the Edwin Hawkins song, and wept because the chord changes were so incredibly beautiful. There's one bit where they go into a certain chord and I just kept waiting for it – and then, aahh! It's amazing! Good music of any type has such a physical effect; it often makes you want to cry, or to skip around. Maybe then I didn't identify quite what it was that made me want to react like that and I'm not sure I even do now. It was then, and still is, a beautiful mystery.

I had already saved up and bought two records – a Beatles LP, and 'For Once in My Life' by Stevie Wonder – which I played on our 78 record player by slowing down the turntable. I listened to them so often the records were ruined by the oversized needle. But now, having copied my uncle's 'St Louis Blues' boogie-woogie riff, I was desperate to hear more music like that. I still enjoyed listening to the songs on the radio, but this was different. Not only had I enjoyed its sound and wanted to jump up on hearing it but, more importantly, I was able to reproduce this sound myself. It was like suddenly learning to fly or do magic and I became an obsessive. I now wanted to go and get recordings of exactly the sort of music I was trying to play; nothing else would do. My father agreed to buy a modern record player and I was given some record tokens, but it was hard to find such specialist music in those days. Nowhere near by sold any boogie-woogie records and I didn't even know which artists to ask for or where to start. My father gave this some thought and then suggested I should go to Dobell's, a famous jazz and blues shop in Soho. Nowadays, it might be thought unusual for a child of eight to go alone into Soho in search of an address scribbled on a bit of paper, but my parents weren't the restrictive type.

In the mid-sixties, you could get something called a Red Rover, a ticket that allowed you to go anywhere on a bus, three bob for the day. I bought one and, sitting and looking out from the top deck of a number 53 travelling up Deptford Broadway that summer's afternoon, I thought that London seemed the most romantic place in the world. The Old Kent Road and the Elephant and Castle were different to St Paul's Cathedral and the London museums but no less thrilling. I imagined police inspectors and spies lurking up every alley.

Arriving in the West End at noon, I skipped along the Soho streets in my great big shorts and stripy school tie, mop of hair, ignoring or ducking round the prostitutes and drug users in the doorways, like a cross between *Expresso Bongo* and *Oliver Twist*. At the shop, I explained to the man behind the counter that I had enough record tokens to buy one record and asked him what he recommended. With some thought, he picked out twelve records from which I could choose. In those days there were listening booths in record shops, and so I took my pile into one and closed the door and listened to each record the whole way through. At about five o'clock there was a tap at the booth door, telling me that the shop was about to close.

It was a very hard decision, because I wanted them all, but the record I finally decided to buy was *The Kings of Boogie-Woogie* by Albert Ammons, Pete Johnson and Jimmy Yancey. Taking my record token, the proprietor said, 'I think you've made the right choice.' A very nice man – so many people wouldn't have given me the time of day and certainly wouldn't have let me take up so much time in the listening booth. Clutching my new record, I went skipping off down the streets, once again passing by the doorways of beckoning sin.

The man in Dobell's was correct; it *was* the right choice. I've still got that record and I listen to it even now. I've got it on CD too but, apart from the scratches, it sounds clearer on record than on CD – probably because it's closer in time to the real thing.

The wonderful thing about great music is there are always new discoveries to be made within it. I listen to Albert Ammons, Pete Johnson and Jimmy Yancey now and still find something new in the tempo or in the fluid way they're playing that makes me think again about my own playing.

One of the things I knew even at that age was that it was the music, not the fashion or the style, of the musicians and bands that interested me. I could see how the Beatles were great and, of course, I wanted to be a Beatle. People told me that Elvis looked sexy, but I couldn't care less. What I was interested in was the musical content – it didn't bother me if the musicians themselves were old or young. What I noticed too was that the people in the blues seemed to have a more adult perspective – they weren't whining, which I rather appreciated. And the music didn't seem to be of any particular time; it seemed to be of all time.

Some music is fashionable and of the moment, but that moment doesn't always last. Other music transcends its time and place, and that's certainly true of *The Kings of Boogie-Woogie*.

Parking Mad

My gift of being able to play music by ear and copy what I'd heard was a very important element in my lifelong devotion to the piano. Genetically, the fact that my two grandmothers, my mother and my uncle played the piano may have had something to do with my ability. And I loved playing more than anything. Unfortunately, my parents couldn't afford a piano. Second-hand ones for £10 would come up but even that was out of the question so I spent hours in my nan's front room pounding away on hers, trying to figure it all out.

As a break from this devoted practising, I'd sometimes go round the corner to a friend's house in the next street and play toy cars on his landing. The gap between the skirting board and the carpet provided the perfect Dinky-sized road and parking area. On one of these occasions my friend's mother came out of the bathroom, her towel dropped off and I observed her slightly quivering buttocks, her beautiful form, as she stepped over our parked cars and crossed the landing to disappear into her bedroom. I was just mesmerized. I kept thinking, *why* is that so interesting? And then my friend nudged me. 'Go on – it's your turn to park.' I really had little interest in toy-car games now, but I went round to this same friend's house even more after that. I would say to him casually, 'Shall we play cars up on the landing again then?' And he'd agree. Then after a while I'd say 'So . . . your mum not having a bath today then?'

'Dunno. Why?'

'Just wondered.'

For about a month I kept going back – but never again was I to be treated to such a thing, such an amazing vision. It really did make me look at girls in a whole different way.

Shortly after having found this new interest, it was suddenly given an unexpected boost, and one that tied in perfectly with the amount of time I was spending at Nan and Granddad's and added to my enthusiasm for perfecting my art. A couple moved into the house next door to theirs, and they had a very attractive teenage daughter. She would sit in an upstairs window, like a damsel in a Victorian painting of a fairy-tale scene, with her bleached blonde hair and her enormous dog – an Alsatian called Sheba.

At that time the film *Zulu* had just come out and my friends and I would all play Zulu in the street. This involved shouting out (I took the officer's role), 'RE-RANK – FIRE!' Then one lot of children would pretend to be the Zulus and the other lot the British soldiers from the Royal Engineers. I was shouting 'RE-RANK – FIRE!' with great authority, then suddenly I caught sight of her through her window and she was looking at me with such disdain . . . Meanwhile, my troops were waiting for my next order – but I lowered my voice after that, from a barking Michael Caine to a much quieter Alastair Sim.

I thought that if I learned to play the only piece I knew really well, maybe it would cancel out this episode and she would pay attention to me. Of course, what I didn't realize was the walls were so thin she could hear all my endless practising. In fact, the neighbours must have been very good to put up with my relentless pounding. But that's all I could do – just play, day and night, day and night, every moment I could – until, finally, like my Uncle David and his band before me, I was told to stop.

However, had it not been for my uncle introducing me to the particular excitement of these boogie-woogie rhythms I wouldn't be here writing this now. It was almost certainly the biggest and most significant thing that happened in my childhood. The other things – being introduced to the mysteries of girls and sex – would, I think, have happened anyway. But being introduced to the thrill of playing the piano changed the course of my life. Instead of running MI5 or a greengrocer's shop, it brought me to where I am now. It's really only one element, but clearly the most important element for me.

Augmented

In September 1966, my twin brothers were born, and they were the sweetest babies you would ever lay eyes on. When my mother brought them home, I asked what she was going to call them and she said Richard Edward and Christopher William. They were charming and I didn't mind them getting the attention – but there was the question of cash as well. They cost a lot to keep so a piano was even more out of the question after that. Apart from anything else, there wouldn't have been room for a piano. As it was, my mother now slept in the back room with the twins and I shared the front bedroom with my father. It was hard work for my mother bringing up two small babies in this bathless dwelling and made even more difficult because she was terrified of mice and the house seemed to be overrun by them, and by stag beetles. One time when my father was away working my mother said she was so frightened of the mice that urgent measures had to be taken. She read a book on the subject, which explained that mice were very scared of salt. Before going to bed, we emptied a large containerful in a circle around her bed. We then all got into it together and lay there cosily, hearing the occasional pitter-patter of mice feet but quietly confident that they wouldn't dare cross the charmed line of salt dividing us from them. I can recommend this to any reader today as a way of repelling mice.

Two small babies are quite a handful. They'd be fed, bathed in their tub, have their nappies changed, both simultaneously. At Christmas 1966, my brothers' first, I got some wooden stilts and a Minic motorway and my first game was to lay Richard or Christopher across the track and crash oo scale lorries and cars into them. I was stopped from doing this after a while as it was time for them to be fed. Then my mother cradled them on her lap, one in each arm, rocking them to sleep after their feed. At the beginning of this process, I'd started trying the heavy wooden stilts out in the corner of the small room. Occasionally I'd hear my mother's gentle admonishing tone saying, 'Don't play with those in here, dear' or 'There really isn't the space for those in here, dear, take them outside.' However, I was so thrilled at discovering the art of stilt-walking I was oblivious to it. Then, at last, just as my brothers had fallen asleep, the fantastic moment came when I discovered I could walk three feet taller. I gasped, 'Mum – look at me!' and, having taken one giant step across the tiny room, immediately slipped and fell off, watching in slow motion as one stilt plummeted heavily on to Christopher's sleeping head with an ominous crack. There was a silence. I assumed I'd killed him. Would I be put into care? Prison? Or worse? Then, to our relief, he opened his mouth and started screaming. This woke his twin, who followed suit. I said to my mother, 'That's good. It's not dead.' Then, as kind and patient as ever, my mother said, 'Well done. Now, could you play with those elsewhere.' I took my stilts off to the front room and, listening to the noise and commotion from my brothers in the back room, lit up a cigarette. I don't think there's any connection, but I had taken up smoking just after their birth. My mother may not have liked this habit but she didn't say anything. A friend did ask her whether I should be sitting there, aged eight, chain-smoking Player's No. 6. But she didn't want to seem censorious or cross.

Now that attention was no longer focused on me as an only child, I soon noticed the benefits, one of which was freedom. Everything I'd done had been watched and doted upon but, in spite of general contentedness and the liberal atmosphere, I still had the occasional urge to break free and experience the call of the wild, as most children do. In 1967, the summer of love, my friend Carl and I planned to run away and live in Greenwich Park, hunt the deer and eat them and live off the wild berries in the flower garden. But when it came to the day, I didn't bother and he did. The police were called. Eventually, they found Carl, but when I first told them our plan, they didn't seem to be too concerned about his whereabouts, more interested in telling me that it was an offence to kill the deer.

My other dear chum was Martin Pugh, and when we went to his house for tea, I couldn't help but notice that his parents had a more orderly side to them than mine, being closer in age and character to my grandparents' generation. His father's shed was a good example of this, nails sorted and everything hung up in its place, and the set-up at Martin's house was very comfortable – you would be sitting in his small front room after school and there would be a knock on the door. It would be half opened and a hand would appear holding a tray of tea and biscuits. We'd help ourselves and the hand and tray would disappear again. I never knew which of the kindly relatives this hand belonged to and never found it necessary to ask. His mum and dad were lovely and of the generation who had to make do and mend; they'd been through the war and were a bit more organized in their ways. I was perfectly happy with the set-up at my house though, and I didn't yearn for his since there were drawbacks to it, such as not being able to stay up late or swear.

Meanwhile, back at Sherrington school, I was finding that I rarely shone in any subject. That was until Mr Sanders, the form teacher, announced at the start of the 1968 spring term that, once a week, pupils would give a one-minute talk on a subject chosen by the class. Various boys got up and stumbled through this ordeal but, when it was my turn, I discovered that I really enjoyed making up bogus facts and boasting of my knowledge of subjects that in reality I knew little about. I'd have the whole class howling with laughter with subjects like Field Marshal Montgomery's strategy in the Second World War or the Roman occupation of Britain. In my school report of 1968 Mr Sanders noted that it would be better for me to try harder at my academic studies and spend less effort on thinking of ways to entertain the class. However, my showing-off tendencies had been awoken.

My older cousin, Robert, was an early skinhead and he and his friends would listen to Jamaican reggae and ska in the room above his parents' shop. I was allowed to join them there and it opened a door to a kind of music which I hadn't previously come across – Skatolites, Rico Rodriguez, Desmond Dekker and Prince Buster, legendary musicians, some of whom I would later have the privilege of working and being in bands with. The only disappointment was that there were never any girls present. We also used to go to a youth club called St John's together, round the corner from their house in an old red-brick church hall. This turned out to be where the Hells Angels from all over England used to meet. It was rather odd, quite sinister, this youth club with all these Hells Angels milling around but, admiring the lettering they used and their American Harley-Davidson motorbikes, I started acting like their mascot, hanging around and getting in their way a bit. There was a piano I used to tinker on to show off my playing alongside the records they'd put on and one time, frustrated because I couldn't manage the chord changes to 'Band of Gold', which they were dancing to, I ran around pushing them. I was just horsing around a bit but the next thing I knew. I was flying through the air off the stage, landing on my head and getting concussed. When I came to I was giddy, and my cousin Robert took me back to his house. His parents were away, but he said, 'There you are,' and gave me some toy cars. As I looked at them, I realized one of them was mine and he'd repainted it – really annoying, but my head was spinning too much to bother with ownership issues. Robert thought that I should sleep, so he left me, occasionally returning to pat me with a cold towel. By morning I was fine again and unaffected by the whole incident. I went running back to the club the next weekend and continued tinkering on the piano, showing off and generally having a good time.

In 1969 there were some big changes. My parents separated and the rent stopped being paid on our little house. My mother was friends with a woman called Roz, who had also just separated from her husband, and they were given shared temporary use of a house in Blackheath that was due to be demolished to make way for a road. This was from a charity housing association, the sort that would be described now as providing sheltered accommodation. My brothers and mother and I moved in with Roz. It was freezing cold, there was a pay phone in the hall and a bathroom that we had to share with Roz and her small children. *Abbey Road* had just come out and we played that in the house all the time. I enjoyed listening to it, but I still wasn't very happy to be there, not only because we'd been in our last house quite a long time but also because, there, I had had access to my grandmother's piano, just round the corner, a most important thing for me.

A kind friend of my mother's called Julia let me use her piano, and there was a piano in the local St James's church, which the vicar let me play when the church was empty. However, overall, the situation was unsatisfactory. During this time, I'd wake up in the morning and think, 'Well, I could go to school or, with my lunch money, I could go up to the West End and have some fun . . .' I did that for a bit but was eventually found out and, without too much stress, sent back to school again.

My parents were trying to sort their lives out and in the end they decided my mother would relocate to Kent with my brothers and I would move into a flat with my father so I could remain at the same school. While he was organizing it, it was decided that I should live with my maternal grandparents.

Nan's

Life was very comfortable at my nan and granddad's house. My mother always said that when she was growing up her brother, the boy child, had been spoilt and given preference over her. I found that this spoiling extended equally to me, and I grew quite used to it. Each morning I would be woken up with a nice pot of tea and then my grandmother would go off to work at the family greengrocer's, having been out already to bring me back a fresh loaf from the baker's.

Martin would arrive to find me sitting in their back parlour eating the full English breakfast that had been cooked for me. I would offer him some sausage or bacon and we would take our time, finishing it together before going to school. Every morning the same: sausage, tomato, bacon and egg, big crusty white bread and butter, mug of tea, all on stripy blue and white crockery. No grand furnishings, but an ironed white tablecloth and a solid 1940s radiogram sitting in one corner, which I'd tune to Radio One, turning it up if Gladys Knight or Barry White came on. The window looked on to other terraced houses and my grandparents' back garden. Squashed into this postage-stamp-sized area were lots of beautiful highly coloured flowers, tomato plants and runner beans. There was also a Victorian sink which served as a pond for goldfish, an outside toilet and, of course, my grandfather's maroon-and-cream-coloured shed, more tomato plants growing up the sides of it. It was stuffed full of useful things he had hoarded there immediately after the war – radiophonic devices from submarines or spark plugs from Rolls-Royce experimental engines he thought might come in handy one day. I've still got some of his tins and, to this day, if I see a tobacco tin I think what a useful receptacle it is. The shed was pretty standard, but to me it seemed like a place of mystery and delights, and I still think you can't beat the idea of a shed in the garden. My one regret is that my grand-parents never got to see the garden I have now – I think they would have liked it.

By this time, I had started at Shooters Hill school. It was a sort of half-cut measure to be sent there: if you were clever you went to a grammar school, and if you weren't that clever but your parents had pretensions you went to Shooters Hill. It had been a grammar school until recently and was in the process of being turned into a comprehensive, so I was able to see what both educational worlds were about and get the benefit of neither. But what was marvellous was that it was very small and everyone got to know one another. I made many friends there, some of whom I still have, such as my very good friend Mark Smith.

In my second year, aged twelve, we were told we could pick a subject to focus on, and I picked music, partly because I thought that it would be an easy option. I imagined a classful of people making a noise and no one having to do any work. But arriving at the first lesson, I found I was the only pupil present. The classroom was empty other than a teacher to whom nobody had ever paid any attention whatsoever, Mr Pixley. It tells you some-thing about the artistic aspirations of the pupils at that particular school; nobody round our way had anything to do with anything like music lessons.

And so Mr Pixley took on the responsibility of drumming into me, his only pupil, the theory of music. And these music lessons mostly consisted of learning the history and theory of music. As for playing the piano, I wouldn't particularly have wanted to play the sort of pieces he tried to teach me. However, the one very useful thing he *did* teach me was to keep my nails cut short; I hadn't realized how impractical for piano playing my long nails were.

The history of music was interesting because we'd talk about the records we'd listened to – Haydn, Handel, Mozart and Bach, and then I'd have to write things out, but the bit that was really amazing was learning the theory, getting to understand what chords were or how to recognize a relative minor and a key signature.

I didn't know it then but what Mr Pixley taught me would be of more help than anything else I ever learned. Years later I was in New York making a TV show and the music director of the show sent out a chord chart. I found I could understand and read it perfectly because of my lessons with him. But back then what really brought it together was that I had bought a Beatles songbook and a Tamla Motown songbook for the lyrics, and suddenly I found I could look at these songbooks and could play the chords in them too. I realized his lessons had suddenly opened up a world of possibilities to me. It was a big turning point and I really was very fond of Mr Pixley.

Martin and I would look out for his car as we waited at the bus stop, opposite which the singer Sandie Shaw and her husband, the fashion designer Jeff Banks, lived. They'd come out looking very glamorous and swish off in their Bentley Continental into London's fashionable West End, then Mr Pixley would come along in his pale blue Ford Anglia and head for the unfashionable Shooters Hill school. And we'd wave and he'd wave and drive past; it would have been inappropriate for him to give us a lift, even when it snowed.

I thought the world of him, he was fantastic. Putting this new academic knowledge together with the instinctive feeling I already had spurred my musical progress on and it's enabled me to do so much since. My sort of music may not have been his sort of music, but whether you're playing Bach, Duke Ellington or Nirvana, a minor is a minor. And if you play it so that it sounds great, people love it.

Then, when I got home, I can't describe how happy I felt in Nan's front room, where the sun shone in, and I would play the piano, trying to figure out what I'd just learned from Mr Pixley, smelling the huge roast dinner cooking in the kitchen. There would be the freshest seasonal veg that you could get, mashed or roast potatoes, gravy but not a single sauce in sight, and the choicest cuts of meat from her friend the butcher. And all perfectly cooked by somebody who knew what she was doing. And still now, when I see things like pasta or rice, I'm rather suspicious of them, other

than as fun holiday food, avoidable in those days, since we didn't
go on holidays. When my mother brought such dishes to the table,
I used to complain and ask why she couldn't prepare delicious
roasts like my nan's. But my mother didn't have any money and
was having to bring up three sons, two of them small twins. Quite
hard, and certainly not helped by my reproving remarks.

I've found that the only places that have almost reached Nan's
standard have been very grand country houses or royal residences,
and I have to say that her food was as good as any of theirs. Better
actually. The only other difference would be, of course, that in
those days I would just have a bottle of pop with my tea. My
grandparents didn't really drink and, anyway, I wouldn't have
appreciated a magnum of Petrus with my dinner aged thirteen.

I was pleased to be in this cosy world after that of temporary
housing and truancy. But it didn't last that long. Soon I was back
off the rails again.

Bus Greaser

For me, music had started to change by the time of my lessons with Mr Pixley at Shooters Hill. Up until that point, I'd heard records but hadn't known that different music had different names. I hardly knew the difference between Little Richard, say, and Oscar Peterson. It was all music to me. But when I became a teenager, for the first time I began to recognize the different types and styles of music. I'd always loved Stevie Wonder records, but now I appreciated that his sound was developing in a more adult direction, which really excited me. Then I'd make a point of buying all the Motown chartbuster collection LPs, because I knew I'd probably like most of the songs on them. At school there would be rumours of the Motown record pluggers knocking the middles out of these records and sending girls round to the radio stations to give the DJs blow jobs through them. I thought, 'What's going on – is this all part of the record business? As well as the great music, there's all this too? This is the business – I've got to get into it!'

I used to listen to them all (the Four Tops – ah!) and I thought how much I'd love to be at a party – there'd be the Beatles, the Supremes, the Four Tops, and we'd all be having a laugh . . . It did occur to me though that, even if that did happen, I would be this thirteen-year-old white kid from London and some of the guests wouldn't understand a word I was saying. But it wouldn't have bothered me, I would have been very happy listening or chatting to the Beatles, who were English, had once lived in the sort of house that I lived in and knew who the Queen was.

Like all music lovers, I'd play the same records again and again until I'd learned them and then try to play them back myself on the piano. However, I was suffering because there were so few records with piano parts for me to copy; they all featured guitars.

I remember buying 'Hitching a Ride' by Vanity Fair because that had a small eight-bar piano bit in the middle – but what a boring record! Other songs, such as 'O Happy Day', were so beautiful though, and I liked that in it they sang of God with such sincerity. The lyrical content was such a contrast to the pop songs of the time, which could often be a bit lovey-dovey and got on my nerves. The Beatles' lyrics, on the other hand, were original and witty, and I listened to 'Revolution' until I wore it out. And then there were the attractively tough lyrics of blues songs such as Big Joe Turner's fantastic 'Shout for Joy', in which he sings 'You're so beautiful, but you've got to die some day, let's make a little loving, before you pass away.' Hearing that, I thought, 'Hello! That's more like it. How much better than the soppy "You don't love me, oh, this is so sad" songs.' Suddenly I was becoming aware of the poetry in music.

I didn't really share an interest in the sort of heavy-metal sound my school friends liked at that time. What I wanted to hear were Chuck Berry, Carl Perkins, Ray Charles and Big Joe Turner – all the rock and roll stuff. That really got me going. Fortunately, the Church of England was very good at supplying church halls named after patron saints where the great unwashed like myself could gather, play rock and roll music and be kept off the streets. I don't think this goes on any more and I think that's a great shame. At St John's, the church hall near my grandparents' house, a motorbike gang called the Outlaws used to meet and play the Rolling Stones and other good records of that sort, so I liked hanging out there. My friends and I would affect the same leather-jacket look as the Outlaws, although we didn't actually have any motorbikes since we were only thirteen or fourteen. We were what were known as bus greasers, because we had all the get-up but travelled round on buses. We would join line dances, bopping to these records, and try to make ourselves attractive to the girls. I'm not sure how well it worked; the girls seemed to prefer dancing with each other to 'Band of Gold'. I almost had my first snog in the rooms there, with a girl called Deborah Henning. She said to me, 'I bet you've never kissed anybody before,' and I lied, said, 'Listen, babe, I've kissed more people than you've had hot dinners – get in the queue.' She didn't believe me. 'Come on, give us a kiss then,' she said. And I closed my eyes and put out my tongue and nothing happened. I opened my eyes and she was laughing and pointing, saying, 'Look at him! Look at him!' I didn't see much of her after that.

At this point, I started inviting my teenage friends round to my grandparents' house. It got so out of hand that my grandparents, instead of saying anything, being too kind for that, took the door from the front room off its hinges so my grandfather could walk past and see what was going on. I just came back one afternoon to find the door gone, and the subject was never mentioned again. My grandmother did once see me trying to go up the stairs with a girl and she just said, 'No. Down. Down here, you.' Again, there was no tiresome explanation or arguments, and down I came.

I had a collection of *Penthouse* mags I'd cadged from somebody and hidden in a cupboard. One day I went to the cupboard and they were gone. I then had tea and Nan and Granddad were sitting there. I thought, 'Well . . . they know they've taken them and I know they've taken them, but they're not saying anything and I'm not saying anything – none of us are saying anything and so that's how we'll carry on.' It was a good formative lesson: button it up, keep your feelings to yourself, carry on and everything will be all right – as indeed it was here. Rather than confronting this type of situation, I still feel that the best solution is to go away and concentrate on a bit more boogie-woogie until the turbulence passes.

Theory and Practice

A lot of people write to me saying that their son or daughter is a keen musician and asking for advice. This book will be a very useful means of providing all the answers and, from now on, I will simply direct all questioners towards the bookshops which stock it.

I will start off by informing these readers how very difficult it is to get going in the music business but, should anyone wish to persist, here is the first music-biz tip gleaned by experience: after you have learned how to play an instrument, it's very important that you are able to play with as many people as possible. At this stage, you will learn much more by playing with people, especially in public, than you can from any musical lesson. There's nobody, better or worse than you, that you can't get something out of it. Some people, though not technically great, may have a certain feel of their own and can get into the groove with you. Or there may be those who don't have much of a feel but are technically great, so it's interesting to play with them for that reason.

I've played with a lot of people now, but when you're twelve or thirteen, the difficulty is that older musicians don't really want you playing with them, and people of your own age tend not to be very good. There would be various people of around my age who'd say, 'Come on, let's get a band together.' Of course, at first there would be great optimism – 'This is going to be great.' But then the main bloke would arrive, wearing a great big greatcoat to look the part, there would be a lot of trouble and fuss getting the guitar out and they'd drown me and my piano out anyway, just playing the one riff they knew, usually a Deep Purple lick. I mean, I like a Deep Purple lick – but that's often all they would know. They couldn't play anything else and wouldn't know anything about the blues, or the music I'd naturally grown up with.

Now, my view is never look down on anyone unless you're helping to pick them up, and even if they couldn't hear what I was playing on the piano, it would have been hard for them to play alongside me, whatever the song.

I did, however, know a very nice bloke called Little Pete who played the blues harmonica. His girlfriend was called Becky and she was the sister of Albert Lee, the great country guitarist. In fact, he is one of the most amazing guitarists there are – and he happened to live in the Greenwich area. One New Year's Eve, Pete invited me round to Becky's house, to a small family party. There was quite a grand piano in one corner and, encouraged by Pete, I started playing alongside Albert Lee. From time to time he would say, 'Yeah, that's good – go on, play a solo over this one,' then he'd play some changes. Obviously he was miles ahead of anything I could play, but he was really encouraging, which meant my confidence was up. If I got something wrong, he didn't tsk and throw his guitar down – maybe because it was New Year's Eve. And although it had only been in someone's front room, by having played with someone like that, my whole game had been lifted and I found that I had improved considerably from that one evening.

Snapping forward to some years later, and we were both playing in Eric Clapton's band for George Harrison's memorial concert at the Royal Albert Hall. And we reminded each other of that New Year's Eve party.

Albert Lee was one of the first proper musicians I played with, and I learned from him the principle that it doesn't matter how old the person is – I was a spotty fourteen-year-old lad at the time – you can always hear if somebody plays all right or will soon be able to, which is what he could probably hear in me.

At this time, I moved back in with my father, who had taken a comfortable modern house in Rangers Square, Greenwich. I would still get the bus from school back to my grandparents' house first, eat the big roast dinner they'd cook me, and then I'd catch the bus at the end of their road for the second part of the journey home. My father would often not be back till quite late, and I would have the run of the place. Since it was rented, it was all somebody else's seventies-executive-style soft furnishings and modern Swedish dark-wood cabinets bolted to the walls. It had a large television, rugs and glass coffee tables – a lot of luxury items which my grandparents had never had, being more traditional in their tastes. Most importantly, my dad, now better off and having seen that there was talent, had bought me a small upright piano. So, suddenly, I was in a modern house with a piano, no adult supervision, able to treat it as my own. Occasionally I would invite round some of the local herberts I'd made friends with, but the person I really wanted to have over was Lesley, the paper girl, who wasn't really interested.

My friend Simon Ellis lived down the road and he knew this girl called Kaethe Fishdrom. Kaethe knew that I played the piano and kept mentioning her schoolfriend Glenn Tilbrook – she was quite insistent: 'You've got to meet my friend Glenn who plays the guitar.' I'd make some joke – 'Oh, he hasn't got a greatcoat has he?' – thinking, 'Here we go, another one . . .' and she would answer, 'Yes, he has – but he's not what you think.' Anyway, a meeting at my father's house was eventually arranged, but all I could think of was Lesley, who I'd finally managed to persuade to come round that same evening. Lesley had blonde hair and an attractive face – a full face but attractive nevertheless – and she wore a Crombie coat with a velvet collar, high heels and bare legs, which I also thought was rather attractive. However, when I opened the door on the night, there were a load of her skinhead friends she'd invited along too. So what I'd hoped would be just her and me having chit-chat in executive surroundings in fact ended up as a big load of people sitting around the place. I gloomily realized I was going to have to share out my No. 6 cigarettes with them and make friends.

Then, just like at the beginning of *The Hobbit*, when all the people keep coming in, there was another knock at the door. I'd forgotten that Kaethe was coming but there she was with Simon Ellis, Glenn and his girlfriend, Max, all getting out of a taxi, all very hippy-esque, which warned of a potential clash of cultures. I fitted somewhere in the middle of these two groups, unwashed and really only interested in trying to get Lesley's Crombie off. I wasn't sure whether to pretend that Lesley was my girlfriend but when I saw that both groups were eyeing one another with suspicion, I decided I wouldn't in case it all went horribly wrong and they all thought, 'What a dur . . .' And, anyway, my thinking went, this new group might have new hippy girls in their circles whom I could meet, and then I could forget about poor Lesley altogether.

Glenn had with him his Vox AC30 amplifier and his Guyatone guitar, which was much later nicked (a diabolical theft, and I urge anyone with any information to come forward). He got this guitar out and started to play. I think we started off with relatively simple things, Chuck Berry or Beatles songs. And it was great, because at last there was somebody who could pick up things at the same speed I could. He could play the piano too – a Little Richard-style piano. He could play the guitar well, sing well and he was really quick – he was just clearly brilliant, flowing with music. He could see that I could cut it too; we were both really pleased with this encounter. And our playing seemed to silence the hippies and the skinheads, although I can't say it quite went so far as to unify them, since I didn't look round to see them all shaking hands or cuddling. In fact, they all still looked a bit suspicious of one another.

Glenn and I agreed that we must meet again. There was a disco he said he was going to go to on Thursday night with Max. I agreed to go too, secretly amazed that somebody actually had a girlfriend. And he seemed to live with her half the time as well, amazing at fifteen – what a legend! But Glenn always had legendary status, not only for breaking all his arms and legs at Sherrington school, having a girlfriend and playing the guitar really well but also because when his last school told him to cut his rather long hair, he announced, 'No, I'll just leave, thanks.' And was expelled. So – a gifted rebel guitarist with a girlfriend. Despite a slight twinge of jealousy, I already liked everything about him.

When they had swept out into a cab, I was left with the

skinheads. I tried to sift it so that Lesley stayed on, so I could chloroform her or whatever my chosen method of seduction would have been – but that didn't work, and off they all went too.

Sharp (Looks)

Up until this preliminary meeting, Glenn had come across the same problem as I had, that of not finding people he could play with. He had been just as desperate to play and would play with anybody at all but had always ended up with people who couldn't play that well. Not long after we met, we did our first couple of gigs, the two of us together. We did the first at his new school, Crown Woods, which was quite nerve-wracking because at the last minute they suddenly announced that we couldn't have any amplification; it was too dangerous to have any electricity involved. So with his acoustic guitar and an acoustic grand piano we sang as loudly as we could without microphones to about five hundred people, all standing up and surrounding us. It taught us a valuable lesson: the importance of having a PA.

Still, that went quite well, so then we did another one, the teachers having realized that we were quite a good little catch. We tried to write songs together but that didn't work out so well, and we had a limited if ambitious repertoire. We would do one song of mine and one song of his and then some rockabilly and Ray Charles songs, a western swing boogie-woogie number, 'Red Light' by Merrill Moore, sometimes a Beach Boys song, and 'Little Wing' by Jimi Hendrix. Although Glenn has always had the most amazing ear and a great gift for melody, at that stage he didn't know what the chords were called. I was still learning from Mr Pixley, so I had the benefit of being able to write them out.

Glenn came round to my nan's house once to rehearse with me but, unsurprisingly, there were complaints from the neighbours who, having suffered my poundings on the piano for years, now had Glenn's guitar joining in. And so I realized that we were going to need to find somewhere to rehearse.

*

By now, both Glenn and I were beginning to think that music
was a better bet than school. Glenn spent most of his time at Max's
house in Kent, and I began to spend a bit of time there too. Her
parents were very easygoing, her father, Felix Barker, was a theatre
critic and was charming and very funny. And her mother had been
involved in the theatre too. Max herself was very perceptive,
brought us a different angle and made us a bit less like young thick
blokes, which we basically were at that time. Not only would she
keep us away from those tendencies but she would also introduce
different influences and ideas. She, Glenn and their friends had
already thought up all sorts of hippy names for themselves, which
seemed rather exotic to me, and it was they who abbreviated my
name to Jools. This was a great relief. Up until then, I had never
been able to bear to tell my skinhead friends that my name was
Julian, would call myself 'J' instead. But if they ever came to the
door and asked my father for J, his big booming voice would reply,
'DO YOU MEAN JULIAN?' So embarrassing. So I was grateful now
to have a name that suited everyone.

Max had lots of parties down in Kent and since I'd hardly been
to the countryside, seeing things like trees was very unusual for
me. And in this exotic environment, I found myself among a most
talented and interesting group of people. There was one very
clever fellow who, when all the lights went out one evening,
climbed on top of a set of steps and lit his farts for a lantern effect.
There was another man called Strider, after the bloke in *The Lord
of the Rings*. We all used to hitch to get down to Kent and once I
said to him, 'I'll hitch with you.' And Strider said in rather a
poignant way, 'No, man. It's best if I travel alone . . .' And, as it
turned out, it was. He went off on his own and on that journey a
transit van smashed into his outstretched hitching hand.

Another time my friend Steve Springham and I got a lift on a
motorbike with a sidecar. At midnight that night a law was to
come into effect which made it compulsory to wear a crash helmet
so, although he was going right to our destination, on the dot of
midnight the driver stopped and made us get off. We got a bus the
next three miles and walked the rest of the way. We arrived at

dawn, thinking everyone would be pleased to see us, but they were all asleep and annoyed to be woken by our travel story.

In those days Glenn never wore underpants because he thought them too restrictive and he also refused to wear shoes or socks, explaining that early man didn't have shoes and modern man had weakened his feet by wearing them. His own were tough, like hobbit's feet, coming out of his own stylish satin flares. Appreciating this interesting theory, I decided to try it for a day or two. But I hurt my foot after about five minutes, trod in some dog shit and I soon realized why early man had come up with one of the first inventions – predating the wheel – the shoe.

Max and Glenn were great as a couple, and it was very good to find myself with an abbreviated name, somebody to play music with and a whole circle of friends, all a few years older and in the hippy vein of things. The people in my school were more in the rocker vein and were completely out of step with everything, hopelessly old-hat old rockers as I now thought. To fit in with these new friends, I even got rid of my greaser gear for a time. I bought a pair of loon pants about four inches too short on the leg and a silk jacket which wasn't really warm enough but made me look very attractive. Not having come from a mixed school like everybody else, I was initially worried I would be at a bit of a disadvantage with the new girls I was meeting down there, but after two or three minutes, I realized that that wasn't what it was about. Some people were just pushy and others weren't. And I was pushy.

Flat (Frank Sinatra at Ours)

By now, my mother had moved with my brothers to Kent, just outside London. I did cycle down there once, with my friend Simon Ellis, but it's quite a long way on a bike. However, every weekend, my father would drive down and pick up my younger brothers and we'd have them to stay with us in Rangers Square. And every Sunday morning they would ask to go and see the Changing of the Guard at St James's Palace, dressed identically as little guardsmen.

My father now worked as a marketing consultant with Sales Force, a company which would be hired by big corporations who were launching products and wanted them introduced all over England in a hurry. He was in charge of getting valuable accounts and coming up with new marketing strategies. He must have been good at this as he was made director, which meant he had a new car every year and we were much more comfortably off.

Now that he was earning good money, my father decided to buy a flat. In early 1972 he bought one on Shooters Hill Road, the idea being that he and I would live in it. But that never seemed to happen. My father decided a new kitchen needed to be put in and, instead of using registered contractors, he enlisted the services of his friend David Reardon, known to us simply as Reardon. Reardon had been brought up in India and had the gait of an officer in the Coldstream Guards. He was slim and distinguished-looking, with black eyebrows and thick snow-white hair, slightly bald on top. He had been a colleague of my father in the 1960s and whenever we needed any help on any new project Reardon became a great expert. Encouraged by my father, he would spend large sums on all the specialized tools and equipment and they would stay up late together making plans. In this instance, the floorboards in my bedroom were mysteriously taken up for use in his plans and were never replaced. I moved back to my grand-mother's.

Reardon was slightly more successful with the hifi. My father decided money was no object since, apart from enjoying listening to a good quality hifi, he felt it would also be of benefit to my musical development. Huge recording-studio-sized speakers were delivered and a wonderful valve Quad amplifier, followed by a specially weighted turntable. There was a lot of wiring and even soldering that had to be done before this monster hifi system would work. Reardon set about getting the highest quality tools and solder. My father, in preparation, got me some records which he thought would expand my musical horizons. One of these was Oscar Peterson live in Russia, which featured the fantastic 'Tend-erly', still my all-time favourite version of that song. He also got a record by a German concert pianist called Friedrich Gulda, who had given up being one of the greatest interpreters of Beethoven to play jazz and avant-garde music. Finally, there was a copy of *Sinatra at the Sands*, which Reardon had bought because he had read that, sonically, it was one of the best live recordings to date.

One blustery March Saturday afternoon, I sat in the unfinished flat waiting as my father and Reardon set to work on wiring everything up. By teatime, they didn't seem to have got much further and my father announced that he had to go out. I was making the tea in the half-finished kitchen when I heard this yelp and a booming 'Bloody hell!' Poor Reardon had dropped solder on his hand and had to go to hospital to get bandaged up. We gave up for the day and started again first thing Sunday morning. By midday, it still wasn't completed, as Reardon's bandaged hand had slowed them down, so I announced, 'I've got to go round to my nan's for lunch now, but she's not expecting you two, so I'll see you later.' After one of my nan's delicious Sunday lunches, I came back and, by early evening, the hifi was working, if only on the left-hand side. At last I was able to hear these new records. We put on Oscar Peterson, which I started to enjoy, but Reardon kept fiddling with the equipment to get the right side to work. My father spotted a button and pressed it, after which both sides seemed to work. Reardon then announced, 'Derek. We must listen to *Sinatra at the Sands*. The sonic quality is so fantastic that when you hear the cocktail glasses clinking in the background, it's just like you're in the room.' So on went *Sinatra at the Sands* and we all listened intently and, indeed, the stereophonic recording had brought the sounds of cocktails and the general hubbub of the Sands nightclub in Las Vegas to life in our building site of a flat. I was then hoping to hear Frank Sinatra doing a number with the Count Basie Orchestra, but Reardon kept playing the clinking-cocktail-glasses bit and saying in a hushed reverential tone, 'Bloody hell, Derek. That really is good hifi.' Some time after this, Reardon decided that some improvement needed to be made to the system – which meant it no longer worked. I can't remember it ever working again, so I had to return to playing records on my nan's more modest Dansette.

That night, as a thank-you, my father took us both to Dick Moy's Spread Eagle restaurant in Greenwich. Reardon told us about the new camera he was getting, which could take photographs of very tall buildings without them appearing to be out of perspective. He needed specialist equipment and printing paper for it too. My father then rather surprised me by announcing that it was very likely that my mother and brothers were going to move back with us and he was planning to buy a substantial property in which to house us all. Reardon said, 'Bloody hell, Derek! That's wonderful! Once you've chosen a house, I will be able to come and take photographs of it with my new equipment.'

The next day, I spoke to my mother, who confirmed it. We were all delighted. After a short while, we found a detached house with a large garden in Blackheath. My mother had agreed to come back so long as Reardon wasn't involved in any of the building work. Everything worked out – apart from Reardon's picture, as he decided that our house wasn't tall enough as a subject.

Around that time I'd realized that music was going to be the thing, and I had been going to school less and less. I felt that music had been the one subject I'd needed to learn and, once I'd got hold of that, the rest of school didn't seem to matter so much. And there had been one or two incidents – one, for example, involving a coin that had rolled underneath a teacher's car. Somebody had said that the only way to get it back was to bounce the car out of the way. If there are three of you pressing up and down on a car it will bounce eventually – a useful tip if you're blocked in a car park somewhere. That's what we did to retrieve this small coin. Yes, it might have been easier just to reach underneath and get the coin, but that wasn't the method we chose to employ. It was the final straw for the school and now, aged fifteen, shortly after the move into our new house, Martin, Mark Smith and myself all had to leave. I won't say expelled. A strong word, 'expelled'.

Since I'd done a lot of work for my music O level, the school said I was allowed to go back to sit the exam. But I was too big-headed to bother, as I felt I had learned what I needed to learn and now needed to go out and do it. I didn't feel I needed any official qualifications.

I had definitely been drifting at school and wondering where it was all going. But then, meeting Glenn, getting girlfriends and making new friends in the country had made a big difference to me. I think a great many teenagers, unless they've got a lot of friends and can see where they're going, can find those years a disheartening time. I was lucky to have a dream which actually came to something. My dream had led to me hooking up with a fellow musician with whom I could play. It lead to meeting wonderful and attractive girls. All the things that I'd hoped were going to happen did. This gave me an optimistic outlook which in turn allowed further good things to happen, and one of them was leaving school.

I think a lot of people get sucked into gloomy thinking; if one thing goes wrong, well, it's always going to go wrong, and by thinking that, it does. It's hard, but if you get into a cycle of things going well, it's easier for them to continue to go well. However, I do think optimism is genetic to some extent and so, again, a matter of luck. In this I have been quite fortunate, in that my mother has always been extremely optimistic. When she was twenty she went out with somebody who had an AJS motorbike, and they were going along Fleet Street, having had a night out in the West End. In this 1950s London street scene, in front of the gleaming *Daily Express* building, an *Evening News* Morris van with a whining gearbox pulled out in front of them. Her boyfriend was going too fast, panicked, braked and hit a car. My mother was thrown off the motorbike. She said the one thing she could remember thinking as she was flying through the air was, 'Oooh! This'll get me a day off work tomorrow . . .' I think that's the embodiment of her positive way of thinking – and, to some extent, I have inherited this trait.

Uptown Ton Up

After I had to leave school, my father told me that, as he didn't think that I would be able to do anything else except music, he would support me financially until something happened for me in this area. This was amazingly generous – so many parents would have said, 'Go out and get a job' – but it was characteristic of his unwavering support. He had seen there was clear talent and a complete commitment to music, and now that he was able to afford one, he bought a Broadwood grand piano for £25 from a lady whose house in Westcombe Park Road was being demolished. I would now spend my mornings playing this piano, not a moment of which was hard work. It was a pleasure. And any musician will tell you the same story: the more you play the more you discover, and the more you discover the more of a mystery it becomes.

My father continued to be artistically encouraging in all sorts of ways. He would get a variety of records for me to listen to in order to broaden my horizons and sometimes show me slideshows at night after I'd got back from the pub, of German Abstract Expressionists or other artists he thought might interest or startle me. And all this took me off into quite different directions, made me realize there was more to music than what I was hearing on the radio.

It was a time of great development for me. I had a piano to play, was being fed new ideas and had many other hours to fill. It was before Squeeze had formed and started on gigs – once we started that, there was no time for my old friends. But just then, with no school and no job, I had plenty of time on my hands, even if I didn't have any money. Having an interest in motorbikes as well as music, I formed a gang with those friends who liked them too and who, like me, had nothing much to do. Styling ourselves on Marlon Brando and Lee Marvin in *The Wild Ones*, we called ourselves the Speed Freaks and went on a couple of runs. We were going to get proper colours done, but rather lost interest after a bit.

Of course at that time our transport was old British motorbikes, and it meant there was ever such a lot of breaking down. We didn't have them because of some romantic idea of having classic motorbikes, it was because they were the cheapest things you could buy. You could get one for £10 or £20. Although I didn't have funds for my own motorcycle, I introduced Martin to a friend of mine who was selling a Royal Enfield Bullet for £35. I suggested that it would be a good idea for Martin to buy it, so we could share it. We would actually have loved to have had a brand-new Japanese bike, the sort we referred to as 'Jap crap', but we just couldn't afford one.

We'd meet at the Dover Patrol pub, which was an enormous 1930s roadhouse, like an empty ocean liner, along with the handful of old dossers and rockers who'd gather there. Sometimes we'd go further afield, to the other biker pubs in Plumstead and Woolwich. I went with Martin to a bikers' club just off Fleet Street one night and 'Honky-Tonk Train Blues' by Sir Hubert Pym was being played and everyone was going wild to it.

Most of the bikers were rockers left over from the late fifties, but there were hippies, skinheads and Hells Angels who had got caught up in the mix. And with my new experience of different circles, I flitted between the lot like a social butterfly.

One of my biker friends at this time was called Clive Heyward. He was quite big, about six feet tall, and full-bodied. He had rather nice teeth that hadn't been cleaned for some years and long lank hair and a beaming smile. He had a beautiful BSA 650 Lightning, lovely red and chrome tank, in combination with a bullet-shaped Steib sidecar that looked like a zeppelin with chromed edges – a really fantastic thing. In those days you could only drive a bigger motorbike without a licence if it had a sidecar, and so he and I would go and work out exactly how a bike and sidecar operated. This meant throwing ourselves very vigorously in one direction or the other as if we were in a TT race when we went round the corners of the suburban roads in south-east London.

We both proudly wore our Speed Freak originals – jeans we'd had to piss on and over which the rest of the gang had smeared unpleasantness. Clive added to this by dipping his hair in the sump tray where all the dirty motorbike oil had dripped and slicking it back with that. He didn't have a girlfriend.

But he was one of the most impeccably behaved people, as I found most bikers to be, in spite of their bad name. He came round to my mother's one evening and greeted her with the usual very polite 'Good evening, Mrs Holland, nice to see you – can I get anything for you?' This particular evening we had both drunk a lot of beer and we were sitting watching the evening news. It turned out that he'd drunk too much. With his hair dripping with sump oil, he said, 'Excuse me' quietly from his corner – and was sick. But he had pulled his cardigan out in front of himself and been sick into that, making a sagging bag. Once he'd finished, he moved out of the room and got rid of it. My mother said, 'What a nice way he said "excuse me" and he wasn't sick over any of the furniture or anything like that.' And he came back vaguely scrubbed up, apologetic, beaming and ready for more. That's what I rather liked about him – he was always beaming and ready for whatever the next thing happened to be.

Another dear friend, Graham, used to live with a whole gang of bikers and Hells Angels in the East End's Salmon Lane and, whenever a bike didn't work properly, I would take it to them and they'd get it fixed up and going again. There were some funny little pubs round there and they seemed a bit more racy than those in south-east London. One evening I went into one which was run by two retired tarts. There were just a few old dossers there, but I liked it – it had something of an extraordinary atmosphere. Just after I'd ordered my drink, this man came in, immaculately dressed, looking like a figure from a Matisse painting. A powerful man in his fifties, he had a white shirt, black tie, a homburg hat, a long black coat like an undertaker's, perfectly shined black shoes and perfectly cut greying hair like a sergeant-major's. He walked to the bar and said, 'Evening, ladies!' in a Max Miller music-hall way and then started to sing this song and do a dance, a twirl of a dance – although he looked like he'd knock you out if you said the wrong thing to him. And the few people who were in there applauded and he bought himself a drink. To this day I wonder, who was that man? I don't know where you see people like that any more.

In those days, I found it romantic going through the Blackwall Tunnel to these places. It seemed like a different world. There were the car fronts with lovely bunting outside, hopeless old bangers with brightly coloured sticky letters stuck in their wind-screens – '£32, radio, extras and guaranteed for three years' (or 30,000 feet, whichever came first). And in Limehouse there were these strange old Chinese restaurants, including one which was run by a huge Englishwoman who dressed as a Chinese woman. Really, it was a dingy Victorian world, misty and quite dark. We knew some of the bikers who lived there, modern Mayhew figures stuck in a cycle of drugs and prostitution, living in these decrepit old buildings.

And all around were these dark London brick buildings with quarter-pane windows painted in a dark green you don't see any more, and maybe the odd cream window sill which would have become completely caked in dirt. I would sometimes think, 'This is a weird little corner – how can this still be here?', and now, of course, it's not. That whole world of people, I'm not sure where they've gone, but the places they once inhabited have been replaced by a strange aluminium world, a huge corporate jungle, which I'm not so pleased to see. This isn't a criticism of the modern world, I'm just pointing out what's happened. Everyone said, 'Look at these awful places with awful people living in them', so they replaced them with more awful places with more awful people living in them. And I include myself in all those descriptions.

Back then I could feel this was the twilight moment of a dis-appearing London and, seeing that fading glint, I got something from it. I enjoyed it. We were broke, though, as noted in my diary entry of 25 September 1973, 'We went for a Chinese in Limehouse. Martin had the prawns and me and Simon had the salt and pepper.' Times were tight.

Hokey-Cokey

When he was twelve, Glenn won a talent competition at a holiday camp and now, aged fifteen, I won one too, at a traditional East End pub called the Aberfeldy Arms. It had lovely frilly curtains like in a gypsy caravan and a good Saturday-night crowd. My father was with me at the time and, when the first prize of an alarm clock was about to be handed over, he grabbed the second prize, a bottle of whisky, saying, 'We'll have that instead, thank you.' However, for me, the best part of winning was that I also got to be the main turn at the pub for a month. The week before the competition, I'd gone in and they'd had these little old ladies performing, one playing the piano, the other the drums, slightly out of time with one another. As the drummer played, her skirt would ride up to reveal her pants, so I knew I had a lot to live up to. This same drummer accompanied me one night when I was playing there and another night Glenn came with me and we did a gig together, which was fantastic. Some people danced and others got up and sang a song to our accompaniment. After it, the landlord invited us to a party upstairs, which looked like something from *The Sweeney* – big tongue salads laid out on a table with the beer and a crowd of men with very wide lapels. At one point, Glenn and I started doing rock and roll dancing and we were told quietly but firmly to stop. We were welcome to have a drink with them but the implication was: don't push your luck. And they were big blokes, so we didn't and that was that.

Glenn and I would sometimes play at the Brunswick Arms, Martin's cousin's pub in Poplar, and this would bring all our friends from the other side of London on their bikes. Glenn had a talented local drummer friend, Paul Gunn, who now joined us on these small gigs, so it became the three of us. It was a good way of earning a little money. They used to lock us in the pub afterwards in the hope that we would spend all our earnings on drinks at the bar, and we did spend some of it on bar-billiards tournaments. And that was what made up our very small income in those days – I did sometimes do bar work at the Morden Arms but soon after starting I was sacked for having dirty fingernails.

By this time, Glenn had met up with Chris Difford; he'd answered an advert Chris had put in the window of Gamberdella's. Gamberdella's was a local shop and café where we used to go. It's still open and is run by the same wonderful family. Chris and Glenn started writing songs together and very soon found it was working well. Glenn wrote the most beautiful melodies, and Chris produced some extraordinary lyrics, so it was a great combination. When Glenn introduced me to Chris, I immediately liked him – we all shared the same humour and outlook. And once we got together musically, we found that our mix of influences was stimulating – Chris was into the Velvet Underground, Glenn liked Jimi Hendrix and I liked the blues and soul. We started playing together as a group in the local pubs whenever we could.

I had a leather jacket and long greasy hair. Chris was a sort of skinhead who had vaguely become a hippy and Glenn was a hippy, at least to look at. We did one gig at the Morden Arms and, the landlord's favourite song being 'She', we played a very nice instrumental of that for him. All this was done on the pub's very jangly out-of-tune piano, with Glenn and Chris playing their guitars through Glenn's dad's borrowed hifi. My old schoolfriend, Mark Smith, the electronic wizard, adapted the lead specially – it blew the speakers before too long.

But, in order to progress, we needed to practise together and this was hard to do. We would start to play in various houses but, in no time at all, the neighbours would complain and we'd have to stop. And renting a rehearsal room cost money we didn't have. Sometimes we'd use some of the money we'd earned playing in pubs to go to a rehearsal studio. We used Underhill, which was in a cellar in Greenwich and learned that Jeff Beck had once rehearsed there, which really impressed us. We also used rehearsal rooms underneath Greenwich baths. We liked this because, after we'd finished, we'd go up and have a swim. It was my first contact with water for some years.

At the time I didn't have an electric piano and, indeed, could not have afforded one. Playing in pubs brought in some money, between us usually about fifteen quid – but buying an electric piano would have cost two hundred. Unless I'd forced the others to give me all their earnings for the next fourteen gigs and didn't play bar-billiards tournaments, there was just never going to be enough to buy one. At Underhill they had an upright piano but once you had Chris and Glenn playing their electric guitars, you couldn't hear the piano at all, it was thoroughly drowned out. So at these early rehearsals, I began to fear that we were slipping into hopeless greatcoat territory again, groupwise – except that the quality of what we were doing was improving all the time.

We were in a vicious circle: you can't do bigger gigs and earn more money unless you've got equipment, and you can't get the equipment if you've got no money. It was all very well doing small gigs in pubs but they had to have a piano, otherwise there was no point me going. Glenn and Chris were able to go and play other gigs, including a small slot at a big pop festival. Hearing about it afterwards, I felt quite left out, as they'd slept in a tent and met girls and had private moments with them. I felt that was exactly the sort of thing I would have rather enjoyed – not sleeping in the tent so much but the private moments.

Sometimes I would save up enough to rent a piano for a London show, but there was another problem: the only kind of electric piano you could get at the time was the Hohner Pianette, and even if we had suddenly raised the impossibly large sum of £200 needed to buy one, the sound would have been unsatisfactory. When they look at the world people often say that things get worse as we go along, and it's true that a lot of things do. But in the case of modern electric pianos, they're ten times cheaper than they were then and ten times better. You can now buy a digital keyboard for £200, which will give you ten times more for your money than the huge outlay of £200 would have in the 1970s.

Anyway, with all these technical and financial difficulties, I felt

I was being held back and this was worrying me. At one point I asked a group called Upp who were also rehearsing at Underhill if I could borrow their Mellotron keyboard for a gig and they agreed. But a Mellotron plays very long slow notes, which sound a bit like a choir singing – not really ideal for a fast percussive boogie-woogie style.

However, when we played in the local pubs, it always went really well and that boosted our confidence. We were good and we knew there was something about us. Glenn was writing more and more great songs with Chris, they were both helping each other discover their own abilities. The more Chris wrote, the more he found he could write, and Glenn was amazingly gifted at creating the most incredible melodies, often deliberately trying a key or instrument he wasn't familiar with so that something fresh would emerge. We knew that there were people who could play in a cleverer way than us, jazz guitarists and suchlike, but maybe they wouldn't have got the audience going as much as we did. Our rock and roll songs worked, and Glenn and I provided a boogie element too. We used to do 'Saturday Night' by Roy Brown, and the words were 'It's Saturday night, / That's what I like / I like to roam, and then going home / Might have a fight but that's all right / 'Cos it's Saturday night, that's my night.' It really used to get people going. Then we'd play our own songs, which were so sweet and pretty that people would swoon. So we had these two elements that not many other bands had.

We were like a family and, when we weren't working, we would occasionally flit off down to Kent for a family holiday at Max's parents' spare cottage. But we all shared a dream, were all completely obedient to the one master – the music we were making.

The other thing we had was a certain blind confidence; we were sure that we were going to become a big popular group. This wasn't unusual; a great many young musicians starting out have this confident belief in their future success. A great many are disappointed. We were lucky, because we did become very popular, but that was still to come.

Cum

Early in 1974 we were contacted by two potential managers, a man called Michael Cooper and his partner, John Leyton. John Leyton had once been part of the Larry Parnes early British pop music scene and had had a hit called 'Johnny Remember Me'. He then had rather a success with acting and had been in the films *Von Ryan's Express* and *The Great Escape*. He was such a charming fellow that he had become friends with the stars of those films, Frank Sinatra and John Mills, and it was hard not to like him. We thought that Mike Cooper and John Leyton would be the perfect managerial mix. We thought they could work wonders for us and, more importantly, as every teenager involved in music thinks when first meeting a persuasive manager, they seemed to be richly connected to the glamorous world of the music business. We didn't know anybody outside south-east London.

They had heard talk of our abilities but, before signing us, they wanted to hear us play as a group. We met the two of them in some strange arts club in Holland Park and played them some songs. After hearing us, they got excited and told us they were going to sign us up, which we agreed to at once. They were hoping to get us a record deal and therefore some money. They were quite optimistic and they had reason to be because, at that time, the music business signed anyone. And, as for the contracts, I'm not suggesting that they were robbers or anything but, let's put it this way, the contracts were very much in the management's favour.

After this there was another meeting, at John Leyton's recently purchased restaurant, the Sandwich Box, in Waterloo. After a meal there we all got in his brand-new Ford Cortina GXL, which impressed us no end. In those days, maybe someone's dad had a car but people you met didn't have cars, let alone new ones, and suddenly we were having meals in central London with people who did. John dropped us off at Charing Cross station, where we shook hands and said how much we were looking forward to working together, then Chris opened the car door and a Route-master bus tore it off.

What speaks volumes about John Leyton is that he didn't com-plain; all he said was, 'Don't worry about it – you just run along and get your train and I'll sort it all out.' I mean, what a lovely man. How many people would have said to Chris, 'You stupid fucking git,' and tried to throttle him? And subtract another five grand from our end of the contract. But John Leyton? Not a bit of it.

Mike Cooper was also a nice man but he wasn't so much in touch with the artist side of things as John Leyton. At our next meeting, in their Catherine Place office, he suddenly asked us what our costumes were going to be. When we looked a bit blank, he brought up the pop group Paper Lace, who wore eighteenth-century-musketeer uniforms for their hit 'Johnny Don't be a Hero'. Now, I liked pop records. Even then I knew that pop music could be as powerful as strong perfume and can have the greatest poetry. But 'Billy Don't be a Hero' by Paper Lace really didn't hit the spot for me. I wouldn't want to knock Paper Lace, because I'm sure they're very talented and out there somewhere and I wish them good luck, but we didn't particularly want to dress like them or, in fact, to wear any kind of costume. However, we agreed with Mike's next suggestion, which was that we needed a name.

Our first idea, and a name we had already been using, was Cum. This fitted brilliantly inside the white bit of a no entry sign and, although I will never admit that we had anything to do with it, there had already appeared a great many of these Cum logos on no-entry signs across south-east London. But neither of our new managers was as enthusiastic as we were about this name, and Mike Cooper especially disliked it. It was becoming clear that his taste lay more towards musical theatre and our sensibilities were those of early punks. The actual punk movement hadn't happened yet and the music in the charts was largely grandiose and overblown or long-haired and earnest. We didn't want to emulate this chart music either but wanted to play the music we liked or had written in our own style and tempo. I don't think Mike ever got this, but he was right to think that we would have inspired prejudice from certain quarters of the general public with the name Cum.

Tapit and the Rocker Boxes was one idea of mine, and probably the worst suggestion of all. (You needed to know that a tapit is a component of an engine's rocker box.) Hub Caps was another and, again, I'm pleased we didn't go with that. The name we came up with in the end, and the one that everyone liked, was Squeeze.

Riff

Having the name and this management team behind us made us all feel upbeat. But apart from the occasional Squeeze gig in the local pubs, there still was no immediate work and, while we were waiting for the management to get things going, I was still bouncing around trying to play as much as I could. In the mornings I would play at home and in the evenings, whenever possible, get up at the local pubs myself. In Greenwich at that time there were quite a few that had a piano. There was one called the Mitre just by the Blackwall Tunnel whose landlord often used to book New Orleans jazz musicians to play there. I saw Neville Dickie, the great stride pianist, and Chris Barber on another very special night. There would also be British dance bands from the 1930s, such as Harry Gold and His Pieces of Eight, who were lovely old men. There was a man called Wally Butcher who worked in the docks and was also a singer in these groups, and he was one of the few people I've come across whose name suited their look. He was a giant of a man in his late sixties with close-cropped hair and a huge face like Arthur Mullard's. And he would sing songs like 'Georgia on My Mind', which would make everyone cry. He was like an English Big Joe Turner – a great working man who would do his song at the end of the evening. I must have had something because he would often say, 'Git 'im up on the piana, he's a goodun.' At that age I was keen to prove myself. There were other people who could play the piano well, but I felt that I could always just cut them, as they say in that world.

One night I played at this pub called the Tolly, and there were some female teachers there. They were only in their twenties but seemed a lot older to me, and I ended up snogging one of them after having played. That really was exciting. I thought, copping off with a geography teacher – this piano stuff is really good . . .

Another time, Simon Ellis and I were walking along the old river in east Greenwich, in the very romantic old docklands on a hot summer's evening. As we passed the Royal Standard pub we could hear them inside singing the song that goes 'Fa da lee, fa de la, fa da lee' and, just as Simon and I got to the open door, the whole pub in synchronization went 'Haha ha ha ha ha . . .' It was the most beautiful thing we'd ever heard, mind-blowing, the whole pub, laughing in unison together, in an orderly and good-humoured fashion.

So we went in, in our bus greasers get-up, looking like we'd been fired out of a human cannon ball, and they were dressed in suits and ties for their Saturday night out, but they were all very welcoming. I liked the days when people wore a suit and tie to go out on a Friday and Saturday night. It was a proper London custom you don't see so much of any more.

The pianist was this man in his sixties with big bushy whiskers, and a big moustache almost like a sergeant major's, greased-back hair, slightly long at the back. He wore quite a shiny waistcoat and had a lot of cushions on the piano stool propping him up in front of the old upright piano. And the customers all shouted, 'Sing your song, Vic – sing your song!' And he said, 'OK,' and started off just playing a few little chords on the piano and, then, with a half-spoken, half-sung music-hall-style introduction, he began, 'There are a lot of wonderful fish in the sea but there is only one lovely fish for me/ I've had salmon and I've had cod, but my favourite fish is – aw, my gawd/ I'll tell you . . .', and the whole pub together sang, 'AHH SOLE, AHH SOLE, ARSEHOLES ARSEHOLES,' etc., and then everyone howled with laughter. After a few more verses, he then went, 'OK, I'm going to play another,' and he hit the thing and started playing this Fats Waller piece called 'A Handful of Keys'. A lot of pianists attempt this but it's almost impossible to do right. Vic not only managed it but the syncopation was so great it made me float. And the whole place was swinging with this old song, almost as if all the people drinking their drinks were swaying from side to side in perfect time with the piano.

At the end of it, somebody pushed me forward and said, 'You

play something.' So I played one piece and they all cheered and
Vic said, 'Come on, I'll do a duet with you.' And he shouted out
the chords – A, D minor, D, and he said, 'You just play slow and
then we'll get faster and faster.' It was this piece called 'Black Eyes',
an old Jewish tune, and we played it faster and faster until the
whole pub was bouncing up and down. It was like that scene in
the *Aristocats* of a wild party getting madder and madder with a
load of cats crashing from floor to ceiling. He finished by saying,
'Thank you – and if you're driving, don't forget your car . . .' He
was just lovely.

Before the modern world of rock and roll, for Count Basie and
his contemporaries, for example, the worlds of music hall and great
music were very close. Vic was from that tradition, old-fashioned
in the nicest way. He was another person who helped lead me to
where I am now, by giving me a chance when I was young.

The man who ran the Royal Standard, Teddy Garrett, had been
in the war, and the pub had been decorated just after the war –
and never been redecorated. It had dark-cream tobacco-stained
gloss paint, and a giant 1950s photo of Windsor Castle. All sorts of
Greenwich characters and cousins of mine would be in there of a
Friday night, spending their money. The pub was never shut, you
had to move the cigarette machine in order to open the side door
to get out after hours. Teddy used to say, 'Oh, tell the police
you've come from here if you're stopped.' He used to sit and drink
with us, and every time anyone bought a round of drinks, they
bought him a whisky. Needless to say, he's not with us any more.

They were marvellous big-hearted people in that pub and in
that world – that's what I liked. They weren't ninny people but
full-on characters. Simon and I were spotty herberts in leather
jackets but we were welcomed. And Vic was really charming, not
only a good stride piano player – he was great. Like Willie the
Lion Smith, Jelly Roll Morton or the Brute, James P. Johnson, he
made the whole place sway to a certain rhythm and have a certain
vibration just because of the way he played.

I used to see him and his wife quite a lot and, when they

finished, they'd sing a Victorian duet called 'At the End of the Day', which was very moving. He was very accepting of other people's ways so, later on, when Squeeze were having jazz cigarettes in front of him, it didn't bother him. I think he even tried them a couple of times – wheezing, he said, 'This is a laugh, innit, eh?'

I ran into him in Greenwich many years later, just after I'd got together with Christabel. There'd been a lot of stress over breaking up with my previous girlfriend, Mary. He was arm in arm with Eve, and he said, 'I hear it's all been going off a bit with you . . . Well, I tell you what – I've been with the same woman now for thirty years and we've been very happy, so . . .' He gave a huge broad smile and added, 'Whatever you do, don't tell the wife.' Patted Eve's hand and off they went. He was fantastic but, of course, he's gone now too.

Raff

At this point I was starting to meet more girls. I hope it's not caddish to write about this, but after all these years I do look back with great affection on the girlfriends I had then. Of course, there were girls I had crushes on who didn't even know who I was, and probably girls who had crushes on me I didn't really want to have anything to do with – except perhaps to have sex with them.

That is the way things were then, always have been and probably always will be. There was one girl that I liked called Torly Drake. She wasn't really interested in me but I would go round and throw stones at her window in the evening. She'd tell me to go away but I would work my way back into her favour and grudgingly she would sometimes come out with me, but then she'd always go off with other friends and leave me. I kept wondering how to win her over, of course; it was an impossible task. If there's someone you have feelings for and the feelings aren't reciprocated, the worst thing you can do is make a fuss of them. And if you ignore them they just forget they ever knew you in the first place. I thought about going round one night and taking her out for a drink but, when I did, I drank too much and ended up being sick on her bed so that ploy didn't work so well. Martin had to take me away in a black cab. I think the other thing that probably didn't help was the fact that Martin was there too.

My first proper girlfriend was Alex Seth Smith. She was very beautiful and a friend of Kaethe's, the girl who'd introduced me to Glenn. Alex came from a very good family and lived in a Georgian house overlooking Greenwich Park. At the time, I was infatuated with motorcycles and wanted to lead the bikers' wild lifestyle, which was not something Alex was so keen on. In the end, she felt I was paying too much attention to motorcycles and not enough to her. Things were brought to a head when one evening, after taking her to an East End drinking club, my trusty Velocette Venom conked out on the journey home. Alex suggested using a more reliable form of transport like a bus or a taxi and, in the heat of the moment, I said, 'If it's a choice between you and my motorbike, I'll take the motorbike, even if it's not working.' This was a rather regrettable remark. The end came not long after.

Other girlfriends came and went. My parents were very liberal and didn't mind me bringing them home to stay over. My room was specially prepared for this purpose. I had dark-blue bedlinen and some old painted motorcycle petrol tanks on the window sill. I had cut out the letter Z ten times, each time slightly larger, and stuck them in a cartoon line on the wall behind where I slept. I had a large valve radiogram with sliding doors which had belonged to my Auntie Daisy and Uncle Stan. On this, I'd play hifi recordings of Ray Charles and Stevie Wonder. What with the dimmed light and valve sound of the vinyl playing, I have happy memories of romantic evenings in there.

In the daytime, Chris, Glenn and I would work out new songs. It was a very creative period, Chris was writing great words and Glenn started setting the words to his songs brilliantly. I would also write with Chris and, because he knew I liked boogieist music, he would find words to suit those sorts of songs. Our concerts were getting increasingly popular, and now Harry Kakoulli had joined us as bass player. All the girls liked him because of his good looks and thick flowing hair.

There was a definite sort of vibration that had started happening. From the very beginning we had drawn a local crowd and by now had a small gang consisting of all manner of friends, hangers-on and incredibly attractive girls, some of whom were our girlfriends. There was Nicky Perry with her raven curly hair, who has since opened a hugely successful tea shop in New York called Tea and Sympathy selling English goods to New Yorkers, Hatty Wilson, who looked like a Renaissance Madonna, and Mary Leahy, whom everyone would fall in love with.

We would all pile into Harry's Ford Anglia, which he had repainted himself with aerosol cans of paint. It must have taken him hundreds of cans to change the car from green to blue and, going fast around corners, the passenger door would often fly open and we'd have to hold on so as not to be flung out. Dangerous — but these were very happy days. When we arrived somewhere we'd announce, 'It's us, we're here!' and people would go, 'Yeh!' Although, on paper, an old Ford Anglia painted with aerosols doesn't sound so glamorous, I think we must have seemed like a tip-top hip crowd. Everywhere we went, we attracted more people. And this was how we built up a following. We'd quite often have a wild time of it: let's put it this way — there was no suppressed sexuality in those early days.

We probably weren't quite so popular with people's parents, though, since we would usually end up staying at somebody's house, helping ourselves to everything in sight before leaving. We were like a south-east London version of a medieval royal family, travelling as a court from house to house, consuming everything and then moving along, leaving the hosts bankrupt. But we were popular with our contemporaries and they shared our sense of anticipation: we felt that success was just around the corner.

Pirates and Priests

In reality, no record company was yet biting and, without the great advance they had been hoping for, Mike and John had rather lost interest in us, and we felt that we'd had enough of them too. Every other herbert in south-east London was keen to manage us but by then we had realized we needed somebody who actually understood the music business. We were even prepared to get a rotten deal from the right person at this early stage, knowing that we'd make up for it later on if we were successful.

In the meantime, enter Miles Copeland. He came in a round-about way. Harry Kakoulli's sister Zena was married to Pete Perrett who had a band called The Only Ones. Pete had asked us to back him on some demos he wanted to make. Glenn thought it was a good idea and so we did some session work with him and even played with him at a couple of shows, including one at the Marquee. As a band, The Only Ones had quite a cult following and rather good Bob Dylanesque songs, one of which, 'Another Girl Another Planet', has recently been used in an advert broadcast worldwide.

Pete Perrett had a manager called Lawrence Impey, the son of a very successful lawyer from Bournemouth. Lawrence had gone to school with Stewart Copeland, Miles Copeland's brother. He took Pete on as his first venture into the rock and roll world but by the time we met him Lawrence was finding him a bit demanding. It wasn't that Pete wasn't talented but − how shall I put it? − you would go round to his house in the day and there would be a lot of people lounging around in a very sleepy state, too sleepy to talk. One afternoon he opened the door wearing dark sunglasses and with a rock star's mullet haircut. Upstairs, there were three scantily clad girls lounging around on his bed, which of course impressed me. There are people who have the whole affectation of being a great rock star and, although they haven't actually had a rock star's success, they are still very successful at getting girls. Pete had a Dr John record I was interested in hearing but he insisted on playing the new one by Lou Reed instead. I've always loved Lou Reed, but this particular album had just been done as a reluctant contractual obligation to the record company. And what it consisted of was feedback. As a protest statement, it was a good idea and for a minute we all went, 'Yeah – right! Fuck the suits!', but after another minute, I rather wanted it off and the Dr John record on. Instead, we had to have another half an hour of this feedback.

When it finished, I held up the Dr John record again and started to say how much I'd love to hear it but I was interrupted by Pete saying, 'Yeah. Jools, the van we used for the gig needs to go back. Do you want to take that back now?'

'Oh all right . . .' (Mug!)

Chris was very much alienated by our involvement with The Only Ones. He could play the guitar perfectly well but his interest didn't lie in session work; his forte was writing and singing his own songs. As we didn't want to go forward as a group without Chris and seeing he was unhappy with this set-up, we ended up sticking with Chris, leaving Pete Perrett and taking Lawrence Impey with us.

At first, like us, Lawrence had thought, 'Oh, Pete's got an audience, he's got a vibe, he's got a load of girls lying on his bed – it's looking good.' But the appeal didn't quite come to anything, and Pete began to suggest it was because Lawrence wasn't doing enough for him. Lawrence may have thought he'd be better off with this load of blokes from south-east London, who were incredibly impressed even with the fact he had a bright-red Mark 1 Ford 3 litre.

And we were. Went like a rocket. Nobody of our generation had a car as grand as that. How he got it I don't know. Well, I do – his dad had bought it for him.

Lawrence was a nice fellow, completely honest and trustworthy, and he loved music. In other words, he didn't have any of the credentials required to be a manager. His schoolfriend Stewart

Copeland was now playing drums with the band Curved Air, one of the successful alternative rock bands playing the college circuit. For us, this was the big time: not even knowing them but knowing that Lawrence knew them – that was enough.

Stewart's brother, Miles, was the manager not only of Curved Air but also of Wishbone Ash, the Climax Blues Band and other successful working bands of that time. Lawrence's father, doubtful of his son's new venture into the unknown of the rock and roll world, suggested he team up with Miles so as to benefit from his greater experience. Miles agreed with this arrangement and he and Lawrence formed a partnership. Miles advised Lawrence from the wings and sorted out the paperwork, Lawrence ran the band day to day. Both Miles and Lawrence thought we might be able to get a record deal; they could see that we had built up our own following and were sought after when it came to playing smaller gigs.

For our first meeting with him in his Euston office Miles employed the classic tactic of having lots of people there, to lend the meeting an air of great importance. This worked; one of those present may have been the window cleaner but they were all listening to us and we felt important. Miles told us that the most constructive thing he could do at this stage was to get us more gigs, and he was right. We had played to our own crowd at the acoustic pub gigs but getting out and playing to a bigger, unknown crowd would be an important step forward. So, using his contacts, we now played one or two slightly bigger venues, one of which he drove us to in his fawn-coloured Series 1 Jaguar XJ-6, which impressed us no end. Typical Miles not to have the 4.2, which was actually the better car, but the 2.8, which was a bit cheaper but looked the same.

We would start off with numbers such as 'Sweet Little Sixteen', 'Shake, Rattle and Roll' and 'Help Me Take My Blues Away'. We had realized by then that we had to get the crowd whipped up before hitting them with our own songs, such as 'Raymond' and 'Monkey On You', which were really great commercial-sounding numbers. There was one called 'Annie Oakley', which Chris and

I had written, 'Love Potion No. 9', which Glenn loved to sing and sang very well, and 'Fancy Nancy' and 'West Indian Princess' – these were all the different songs we were doing. I remember singing 'Down the Road a Piece' too.

Sometimes we would support bands at these slightly bigger venues and, after we finished our set, there would be a round of applause and we'd go off. For the first time, we discovered the disconcerting moment of having to return to the stage after the applause had stopped in order to take all our equipment off before the next set, hearing the loud echoing sound of our footsteps and feeling that our equipment had suddenly got particularly heavy.

A few months earlier, my friend Martin had taken a temporary job at the BBC. Being such a huge corporation, even after his departure, they still continued to send him pay cheques – this is the sort of thing our licence fee was going on. However, having retained some connections there, Martin now told me that he had got us both tickets for the Oscar Peterson piano party that was due to be filmed there on 8 September 1974.

I loved Oscar Peterson; here was the man who could play in any piano style he wished. He was technically gifted and could also hit it – he was a master. So Martin and I, long-haired greasers in our leather jackets, went to this TV recording. Alan Price was one of the guests, as was a schoolboy reputed to have perfect pitch. Oscar would play something for him and the lad would say in this little voice, 'I think that's B flat . . .' And it wasn't. They'd try another and then another; he got every note wrong until eventually he managed to get one right. And that was a take.

When you see people playing live, its quite different to listening to a record. It was the first time I'd seen Oscar, but I had listened to the live record of his show in Moscow which my father had given me. And, of course, he was fantastic.

Afterwards, Martin urged me to go and meet him, as he was just at the side, mopping his brow. He would have been in his late forties then, around about my age now. I went up to him, rather nervously. He's a big man, not just as a talent, but physically too.

And so I said, 'Hello, I'm a piano player. I really like your work. Really great. Er, any tips or advice you could give me?' And he took the question seriously, didn't just say, 'Why don't you get lost, sonny?' No, he considered the question and looked at me. I must have looked like a drowned rat to him in my bus greaser's gear, because he was quite elegant in a shiny suit, tie and cufflinks. He then took and shook my hand with his huge one, like me cuddling the hand of an Action Man doll, and said, 'Well, son, good luck with it, and the only advice I can really give you is – practise.' That was it. Although I was really pleased with that advice, I didn't like to say, 'Well, I've been doing that, so – what else?'

Thinking about it afterwards, if I'd pushed him what he might well have said (and this would be tip number two for my own music-biz-advice section) was 'OK, if you've been practising and you're playing good, what you need is a good agent.' He would have known that artists aren't the best in the world at promoting themselves and so need a good agent or manager. And this is what we had now with Miles and Lawrence. At this stage, we still hadn't been signed but, because Miles had got us so many more gigs, various record companies started to sniff around. Inevitably, once this happened, John Leyton and Michael Cooper took an interest again and were suddenly back on the phone. Michael Cooper at first threatened a bit of legal trouble over our having switched managers but John Leyton soon took the upper hand and told us that he would tear up their contract and wished us good luck. I always thought our initial instincts about him were correct.

George Harrison told me once that the Beatles had formed a theory that everybody they met in the world of music was either a pirate or a priest. And half of the people were priests dressed as pirates and the other half pirates dressed as priests. Rather complicated but, in other words, some people appear to be nice and it turns out they really are and other people appear to be horrible and it turns out they are actually nice. Some people appear to be nice and it turns out they're horrible. It's really a matter of working out who are the pirates and who are the priests and who are the priests dressed as pirates and who are the pirates dressed as priests. John Leyton was a priest dressed as a priest. Michael Cooper, I think was a pirate. No, he was probably a priest dressed as a pirate. Well, the readers will have to decide for themselves.

In Transit

A big part of our lives was now spent sitting in the back of a hired Transit van on our way to and from the shows Miles was starting to get us outside London. In one form or another, that's something every band does; there's no way around it.

By now my very dear friend Mark Smith had become our roadie, in between going out and doing deejaying stints on Radio Caroline under the name of Mark Lawrence. Our routine was to meet at my house, collect the gear stored in the little garage my parents had and load it into the van we'd rented from the cheapest hire company there was. If ever you want to find the cheapest place to hire a Transit, look for a band – they'll tell you. One we hired didn't even have a light in the back, so we had to travel down to the West Country and up to London again sitting in the pitch-black. Lawrence was quite proprietorial about driving, for several good reasons: it was one thing he thought he could do very well, none of us had a driving licence and, most importantly, it guaranteed him a comfortable seat in the front of the vehicle with whoever else was lucky enough to join him. The equipment would go in the middle of the van and there would be a metal screen between it and the driver. On some occasions we would hire vans of the sort that fill the back with fumes, so it was rather lucky we weren't all dead from carbon-monoxide poisoning. At first, we didn't even think of putting armchairs in the backs of the van but would just sit on the floor or wheel arches, which was quite wearing. But when you're young that sort of discomfort is character-forming; it is why I have absolutely no feelings of guilt about travelling to shows as comfortably as possible nowadays. I feel as though I've paid my dues.

Now I seem like an awful 'worked to get where I am' know-it-all fat bloke, but I wouldn't have changed any of this van travelling;

in fact, I've got a Mark I Transit now to remind me of how enjoyable those times were. However, there was one instance when I decided that going on a motorbike would be even better. And, at first, it was; following behind the Transit van on the way to our show in St Albans, I could hear wafts of the Beach Boys' lovely waltz song 'Tears in the Morning', which Glenn was playing inside it.

We were on at quarter past one though, the graveyard slot, and by the time we were ready to set off for home, it was pouring with rain. I asked Lawrence if I couldn't just lift the motorbike into the van, but he decided it wasn't convenient. So I arrived back drenched, and the next morning, Lawrence came round to unload the van, already rather smug and amused by my soaking journey, and accidentally ran the van into the back of my motorbike, knocking it over. There was some resentment on my part for the next few days, but that's life, and on the whole we were a happy family.

So, we'd make these journeys, get there, hang around, do the show, go and have a drink in a pub, taking it in turns to oil up to Lawrence to buy a round, since he was the only one with any money. We'd then try to meet a girl, have some horrid takeaway food, get back into the van and drive all the way back to London. It would take us so long – we'd usually have to stop because one of us would have to be sick, having drunk too much – and it would often be quite an arduous drive, not like modern motorway journeys. But the bit that really took a long time would be dropping everybody off at their different homes at half-past six in the morning – a very boring final hour.

In those days back in London late at night we didn't know any nightclubs to go to when we arrived. I'm sure there were places, but they were all probably too expensive for us and we certainly didn't know anybody in the West End. Sometimes, being hungry, we'd go on to places like the tea stand at Aldgate, along with the down and outs, Hogarthian grotesques and prostitutes, with whom we blended in well. There was another great tea stand in Leytonstone where all the bikers went, and there would be a hundred bikes at two o'clock in the morning, Triumph BSAs and Vincents, which was very exciting. And there was a club called the Jailhouse where all the Hells Angels used to go. There you could get gin in your cup of coffee, which was rather good. And we knew one or two pubs that did late drinks, but you had to go in there before they shut and then get locked in. There was a pub in the East End, on Commercial Street, called the Golden Heart, with a great landlady called Sandra. This was open early in the morning for the fruit and veg lorries, so if we were coming back that way we'd sometimes go there for a drink or for food. We often arrived while it was still dark and, surrounded by the shells of the bombed-out houses on Club Row, we'd make our way round the people selling clothes, pets and jewellery. And nearby Brick Lane was as it had been for centuries, Hassidic Jews selling second-hand pairs of gloves off the pavement, and vegetable markets with their lovely smells. Brick Lane is still pretty extraordinary, and Sandra and the Golden Heart are still there – but the fruit and veg sellers and Dickensian villains of Spitalfields and Whitechapel have all gone now, replaced by a much tougher crowd, that of London's new contemporary art scene.

When we started to go to the north of England, we found it quite an adventure suddenly to be in places we'd only ever seen in sixties films. It was still industrial, with mines, docks and shipyards. We did a show at the Hard Rock Club in Manchester and a show at Leeds Polytechnic supporting two bands, Moon and Roger Chapman and the Streetwalkers. Roger Chapman has a great singing voice and we were very impressed with his band because they had had records out. And they had these Marshall amps, painted white with carefully added snakes painted all over them, which we thought very glamorous. The truth is, they wouldn't have lasted five minutes on the road with us – they'd be scuffed up and ruined – but we didn't know that then. I found it worthy of noting in my diary that myself and Chris went into Leeds and were able to have two pieces of fish and chips wrapped in news-paper for twenty-six pence. That was the seventies for you.

Although I never actually attended college in pursuit of a higher education, we were now playing a great many of them all round the country, using them to better our act and stagecraft. They were useful to us and, without them, I don't think there would have been a lot of places we could have played then. When we went to a teacher's training college in Chichester they gave us tea and biscuits, which was a fantastic luxury. Then, at Warwick University, there were lights round the dressing-room mirrors, which we hadn't seen before, and the unusual treat of soft arse–wiping paper. It was at the Middlesex Poly gig, supporting the Sutherland Brothers and Quiver, that we first worked out how to do stage announcements. We'd watched some of the bands we'd been supporting and had taken in that they didn't all shout together as we had been doing, that a bit of thought had gone into it.

Although only supporting, we had to change our attitudes in all sorts of ways now we were playing in these bigger places. We soon realized that when playing music the audience hadn't heard before, we had to win them over first. There's a whole way of dealing with it, learning to keep their interest up. Keeping your audience engaged is the first duty of any artist – if you're boring, you're not doing your job properly. Sometimes people had come to see the main act and, when they saw us, they were disappointed or bored. But, generally, as we picked up these first parts of stage technique, we found that we were starting to go down really well, that the bigger audiences liked us and that the applause was going on longer.

Even in those days there were *X Factor*-type talent shows such as *Opportunity Knocks*, but we wouldn't have lasted five minutes on any of them because, if the judges had tried to make a critique, we would have told them to get stuffed. We were young, aggressive and sure of ourselves, and often went a bit nutty on stage. On the whole the audience appreciated this. However, the Fiesta club in Plymouth was a cabaret club of the sort we'd never played at before, bouncers with dinner jackets and five people in the audience eating chicken in a basket and waiting for a singalong tune. Performance frenzy having taken hold, we started kicking the equipment around, but our pre-punk anarchy went down badly with this particular audience. In fact, half-way through the set, the bouncers appeared at the side of the stage saying, 'Come on, stop now, just get off.' And then, to round the evening off, since we didn't have money for a hotel, we spent the night at Lawrence's parents' house, where I had to share a bed with Glenn (in a Laurel and Hardy sort of a way).

Lawrence's parents had this grand home in Bournemouth; his dad was rather well off, with business connections in Africa, and they had a white-jacketed butler called Thompson who had tribal scars on his face. Obviously, we'd never met anyone with a butler before; we were impressed enough if somebody had a car.

In the morning Thompson brought Glenn and me tea to our shared bed. I didn't really get to know Thompson very well, but I appreciated the fact that he didn't seem to make value judgements about us. I don't think there was anything wrong with his life with the Impeys but we did worry a little that he wasn't being treated correctly. When it became clear that Thompson was being paid well and certainly having a more comfortable life than we were, we lost that idea. But had we ever discovered that Thompson was being abused or not being given a proper deal, we would have got him to join the band. Then he would have seen how bad things could really get.

Incidental Notes

In July 1975, we had a show booked at Brunel University in Uxbridge, not too far down the old A40. This time we were in a blue Transit van, which again had the metal division between the back space and the front seats. Mark Smith, Glenn, Chris and myself were stuck behind with all the equipment, and Paul Gunn and Harry Kakoulli were in the front with Lawrence, having a nice comfy time of it. It was a very warm day and, as we got to the A40, just past Shepherd's Bush, the traffic slowed to a crawl and everyone was hot and bothered and sticky in the back of the van. To pass the time, we started writing and holding up signs we thought would amuse the other motorists. The first one said, 'We've got a gorilla hidden in here,' and the next, 'Would you like to see him?' We grinned as we held them up. A few of the motorists smiled half-heartedly, but the woman in the car immediately behind us looked bored; it didn't make her laugh at all. We thought, if that didn't make her laugh, how about, 'And he's got an enormous penis.' We thought that was ever so funny. Then we moved to the next one, 'Would you like to see my gorilla's penis?' And then, after some thought, 'We've got an elephant in here . . .' and, of course, knowing what was coming next, we were all howling with laughter. And most of the people in the other cars were laughing as well by now. We couldn't catch our breath we were laughing so much – it was all about what was coming next . . . 'He has an enormous penis.' And to the laughter of the other drivers and the growing irritation of the woman behind, we held up a new sign, 'Would you like to see my elephant unfurl his enormous penis?' On reflection, I can see that this barrage of vulgar signs might have been offensive – but it was the anticipation that amused us. And, of course, the penultimate one was 'I've got an enormous penis,' then, finally, 'Would you like me to unfurl my enormous penis?' Now, standing alone, as a remark to someone, this would be incredibly rude and foul-mouthed. But, taken in conjunction with the signs that had come before, it was all part of what seemed to us like a traditional comedy routine.

The traffic then started to move. We, of course, being at the early stages of our performing careers, had by then given up trying to amuse the woman and were playing to the appreciative drivers either side of her. But now I noticed another man, in a grey Morris 1100, with balding hair, a tie and a green tweedy jacket and a rather brown complexion now going deep red. I thought that he looked a bit cross. Then I saw him driving in a very mad and erratic way to the curb, where there was a motorbike policeman with his Triumph Saint, goggles, gauntlets, the lot.

Meanwhile, in the front of the vehicle, in great comfort, Lawrence, Paul and Harry were sitting on their springy seats, listening to the wireless, completely unaware of what was going on behind them. Out of our rear window, we saw the police motorbike come up behind and overtake; the van stopped. This didn't look good and, to get rid of the evidence, we rolled up all notes and pushed them up into the little air vents. As far as we were concerned, that was that. The furious witness had driven off to have a rage-induced heart attack and we could smoothly respond to any enquiries with, 'Can't imagine what you mean, Officer! What a ghastly business – so sorry your time has been wasted!' We heard the van doors shutting in the front and, preparing ourselves, the rear door opened and the policeman said, 'Out you come then, lads. Anything you want to tell me about?' We managed to mumble a denial and he said, 'Nothing at all, is it, lads?', and then, just like in an episode of *Gideon's Way*, he reached over our shoulders and there, hanging out of the vents of the van, was all the evidence. My mind momentarily turned to when I was a small lad again, wanting to be a policeman. I realized admiringly that this was the perfect arrest: all the culprits together, all the evidence and a convenient van with which to take the miscreants off to the police station.

In the meantime, Lawrence was pacing around almost in tears, mouthing at us with a furious, impassioned face, 'What are my parents going to say?' The policeman then ordered us to follow him to Acton police station, and we set off. Had it been a more serious offence, they might have thought to separate us culprits in the back but, instead of perfecting our excuses, we spent this time worrying about Lawrence's reaction. He seemed as irate as the motorist who had made the initial complaint.

At Acton police station they put us in a room with the evidence, but the notes they had laid out were the ones about unfurling enormous penises – none of the lead-up ones. Fair enough, the others weren't obscene, so they hadn't gone for them, but it did lose the point of the humour. The policemen didn't seem to take it too seriously, but Lawrence remained furious. Harry and Paul were equally disappointed because some people they knew had gone from Blackheath to see us play and this incident had made us miss the gig. Having decided to put on those big reproachful faces, they then let it be known that a major record producer would have been there too and we would probably have been signed. All in all, it had almost certainly made us miss the most important gig of our career. In fact, it would almost certainly have been just another gig supporting Curved Air.

A couple of days later, we were summoned to appear in Acton magistrates' court. Sitting in the corridor, we could hear the case before us being presented: a huge joint of lamb had been stolen from a butcher, so that was carried in as evidence, with a label on it. Then the arresting officer had been attacked with a hose, so that was brought in. And then this same criminal had stolen a car and driven it through a shop window. We waited to see who this brute could be, this – animal! Finally, two policemen led out this tiny little ginger-haired lad of about ten years old.

Inside the courtroom was a big public gallery full of the same sort of people who, in the sixteenth century, would have gone to public executions but in 1975 clothing. One of them did this big noisy hawk and spat on the floor and the judge said, 'Remove that man from the court!' The whole thing had a Dickensian feel to it.

We were all squashed into the dock together and we had to say who we were and what our job was. I said, 'Julian Miles Holland – musician,' but all the others said their name and announced that they were unemployed. They had obviously been given a tip that being unemployed would lead to a lesser fine and hadn't passed it on to me.

The policeman said, 'Well, they've been good lads and owned up, but they were caught displaying obscene material on the A40, on the 24 July at five o'clock in the afternoon.' And the judge said, 'Well, what did this material say?', and the policeman said, 'I think I'd better pass it to you, m'lud.' He tried to pass over the bits of paper, but the judge said, 'No – no! Just read them out!' And the policeman, 'No, I think it would be better to pass them –'

There was already an air of hilarity in the public gallery because of the ginger lad being so tiny. The judge said, 'No, read them out, man! Read them out!' The policeman only had the punchlines, which he now read directly to the judge: 'Would you like to see my gorilla's penis?' And, of course, incredible laughter from the public gallery, people falling off their chairs as the judge was banging, 'Silence! Silence!' And then the next one: 'Would you like to see my elephant unfurl his enormous penis?' The judge, looking stern, asked, 'Anything else, Officer?' The policeman replied, 'Would you like me to unfurl my enormous penis?', at which point even the clerk of the court was laughing. Really, the joke had improved again, thanks to the judge having ordered that the material be read directly to him. And the judge said, 'Oh, you think it's funny, do you?', and we were trying to keep straight faces and he went on, 'Well, see how funny this is – £10 fine each and one week to pay.' Which was, at the time, a lot.

We saw Miles Copeland and Lawrence a few days later, and Lawrence started to say, 'I've hushed it up so that my parents don't find out –' and Miles interrupted with, 'Hushed it up? This is the best chance for publicity the group has ever had – let's get it in the paper. These guys are geniuses.' And Lawrence said, 'If you do, I'm having nothing more to do with you.' And so, to stop

Lawrence being upset, the idea was dropped and soon we were back on the road, a happy family again.

The first trip after this incident was to far-off Wales. The excitement of crossing the Severn Bridge stays with me today: it's like going somewhere special – because Wales is like the land of fairytales for me. Then, it was the furthest west any of us had ever been and we picked up driving-licence application forms in Welsh and sent them to people back home as souvenirs. We did shows in Cardiff and Bridgend, which went really well and, after the Bridgend show, we were asked for our autographs for the first time, which was great.

When we got to Haverfordwest, Lawrence took our very first publicity photograph on the beach there and, when I look at it now, I understand why people used to ask me how I achieved my complexion, that of a beautiful gypsy prince. In fact, it was by not washing – either my hair or my flesh. It didn't seem to deter attractive girls from wanting to be with me, though. I thought it added to my charms until one girlfriend, Nicky, managed to persuade me that it was a good idea to wash my hair as it was getting very long. I was so startled by the result that I subsequently had it all cropped into the length it is now – I had no idea it would turn into a vast mullet once shampooed.

After our gig at the Haverfordwest air force base that night, we set off for London and arrived back at eleven o'clock the next morning. I'm sure the M40 had been built by then, but perhaps Lawrence thought it was cheaper to go on the B roads. This is how long journeys on B roads took then; going north or west took as long as a transcontinental flight nowadays. On another gig in York a month later we just managed to catch a glimpse of the cathedral and walled medieval city before getting back in the van and driving through the night only to hit the London rush hour traffic at 6 a.m.

Shortly after this, we started to do the first of our few shows at London's Marquee. Initially, this involved endless running around, borrowing equipment and sorting things out. By now more people were coming to see us and it was clear that we had gained a certain broader popularity. The shows were always pretty lively. We would knock over bits of equipment and run around on stage barging into one another, which heightened the tension. My father came to a few of these early gigs, as the Marquee was around the corner from his office in Berners Street. Luckily for him, he missed out on the gobbing that was just starting to catch on. However, this meant he also missed out on my driving a motorbike on to the Marquee stage a few months later, a piece of stagecraft that would now be completely forbidden by health and safety regulations. This was a good ploy at the time, though, as the gobbers weren't sure whether me or Martin's Triumph Bonneville should be the target of their adulatory phlegm.

The Drum King Enters

By Christmas 1975 the balance on our set list had changed and, instead of starting off playing other people's music, we'd play our own. By now we had learned to deliver our own songs with as much conviction as the well-known ones. We would do an early version of 'Take Me, I'm Yours', 'Monkey On You' and 'Night Ride', which was a pre-punk-sounding song. We would also do a fast version of 'White Christmas', although we didn't know the middle bit.

When we were with Mike Cooper and John Leyton the sort of bands who were getting signed either fell into the category of light entertainment or had members with huge mullets, and we didn't quite fit in. We were closer to the ethos of the newly emerging punk scene, although we weren't really pierced-hooter type of people. By now there were other groups playing this sort of music and getting people going – it wasn't all the Sutherland Brothers and Quiver, although that was still the sort of rock played on the radio and the kind of rock acts we were supporting.

We used to go and see the Clash sometimes, and we played with U2 in the Hope and Anchor in Islington. On that occasion, there were literally three men and a dog in the audience. Then the men left, and then the dog, so our only audience was U2 and theirs was us. They were in the same predicament as us in that they had something to say and something to play but they weren't quite sure where they fitted in.

Miles understood that punk was a convenient label – it's actually very difficult and unwise to put labels on music. Miles had all sorts of people involved with him, such as Generation X, Cherry Vanilla and Wayne County, who were on the same circuits as us and in the same pre-punk mode. Miles viewed us as dirty and unkempt and foul-mouthed already and, once punk took hold, he was keen for us to move more officially into that category by getting our hair spiky or other such stamps of authenticity. But we said that getting your hair 'done' was what ponces did. That's how the chats would go at our management conferences.

The punk movement was very exciting, the music itself exhilarating, and the energy it created opened up possibilities of getting a record deal. It was thrilling to witness the beginnings of something new, but some of the punks seemed to us to be rather well-off people, dressing in panto clothes to look tough. We were genuinely unclean and frequented a world where the men really did have rows and were hard. In fact, some of these men wanted to manage us. However, although they were well qualified to take care of stolen property, little old ladies crossing the street and acts of violence, we didn't feel they had the right qualifications to manage us.

We continued to play at some of the pubs on our doorstep. The Bricklayers Arms was run by our friend Harry Rogers, whose father had been in dance bands in the 1930s. The main pub was empty and vast and it had a stage in the corner, very brightly lit with strip neon lights. It was mostly old Greenwich crooks and policemen who would go and drink in there, but there was another smaller, separate bar to one side through some doors, which Harry had opened. It was long and low-ceilinged and as dark as a Dutch brown bar. To go to the lav, you'd have to go back out through the strange Victorian ghost pub of policemen and crooks having a drink, hearing your footsteps echoing in the decrepit space before returning to the groovy world of this lively, dark Dutch bar.

Our routine was to rehearse at Greenwich swimming baths and then wheel our equipment along the street to the Bricklayers Arms. We would play there once a week and get the crowd going with both old and new songs. You've got to try new music out all the time, and it's good to do so when you're relaxed so as to be able to play it to a harder crowd later on.

The side bar at the Bricklayers Arms stayed open very late and was always getting raided as people smoked jazz cigarettes openly and drank after closing time. The police would suddenly come in;

many of them would have been drinking in the main pub the week before. The local station commander had brown leather gloves and a hat and cane. He would look around, asking, 'Has anybody been served drinks here?', and everyone would just look away at the wall and up at the rather gloomy lights. The doors would have been flung open to get rid of the smell of marijuana and the tills would have been removed but, other than that, nothing would have been hidden. Then the commander would have stern words with the publican and everyone would be herded into the bright lights of the main bar. It was like being a creature taken from its natural dark habitat and placed in a horrible, overlit observation centre to be peered at. Eventually, the pub was closed down for good.

At this point Miles had generated some interest in us from Island Records, and arranged for us to do some demos for them in the professional Basing Street studio. Muff Winwood, Steve Winwood's brother, was our producer for this, and he wasn't really happy with the sound. Because of this, we did the complete opposite of our present system of recording in one or two takes – we kept doing the songs again and again.

We also recorded at the much smaller Pathway Studios in Islington, which had a great atmosphere but a control room the size of a paperback book and a tiny live room with an upright piano. We recorded two sets of songs, and some of them were so incredible that, looking back, it makes me realize again the extent of Chris's genius as a lyricist and Glenn's gift for amazingly beautiful melodies. We all wrote some songs about a strange nightclub called Trixies, one of which was called 'Lonesome Joe'. I later recorded it myself with my orchestra on my *Sex and Jazz and Rock and Roll* record. These songs didn't fit into 'punk' music or what the mullet-haired people on *Top of the Pops* were playing, but they were extraordinary, sometimes complex, sometimes dark and often very catchy.

One of the difficulties with the music industry is that they want to know where you fit in. If you're genuinely original, they get very confused. Better for them to have things which fit into criteria they understand. That was Squeeze's problem at this point and, since neither of these sessions worked out for Island Records, we remained unsigned.

Here's another tip: I would say to anyone about to attempt to enter on a path of music that you must understand just how cruel it is and what hard decisions you will have to make. The music comes before your friends and your family, and you've got to be prepared to cut off your best friend, brother or sister if their playing doesn't suit the music. They might be people you've grown up with and who are fun to play with but, if they don't cut it, you can't have them in the band. So, music comes first – very beautiful, but often very cruel. Everyone involved in music has had to learn to make those types of decision early on, whether you're in an eighteenth-century chamber orchestra, the Louis Armstrong band, the Rolling Stones or Squeeze.

Paul Gunn was a really good friend of mine, and a good drummer. However, because there was a feeling that his style of drumming didn't quite suit the direction in which we were going, especially after these unsatisfactory sessions with Muff Winwood, he was kicked out just at this point, before we became very successful. I haven't really seen him since.

We advertised in the *Melody Maker*, preparing to audition potential drummers. Various people came in, but nobody seemed quite right. It's very frustrating auditioning people: you start off feeling sorry for them as they are trying their best to get the job but they just don't fit. However, by about the sixth applicant, you start not to be so sympathetic, you're just impatient to get on with it all.

But, the seventh applicant, Gilson Lavis, swept all weariness away because he was so big, aggressive and bossy. He started by saying to us, 'Oy, you – *boy*. Come and help me carry my drums in!' Not only did we do that without protest but in doing so we saw that he had a car, which was very impressive. It turned out it was actually his mum's car, but we didn't know that at the time. He also had an Octoplus, which consisted of eight tom-tom drums that went around the drum kit, on which he did drum fills, starting off with the little one and moving right round to the big one – and he was brilliant.

It has to be said that drummers are the most important part of any group, the final piece of the equation. There's no group that's had any success without a good drummer. The Beatles couldn't have been the Beatles until Ringo came along, because the way he cut it made all the difference. The same with the Rolling Stones and Charlie Watts – the group was sounding good, but there was one thing that was going to make it really work. And good drummers are hard to find – so you have to be a good group to get a good drummer, because they're in demand. You can't always put your finger on what it is, but they bring everything to life. You can bluff or get away with being a poor guitarist but you can't get away with being a poor drummer, because you're the core. Anyway, this great hairy bloke Gilson had excitement and drive, and he blew all the other auditioning drummers out of the water.

It turned out he had already played with all sorts of amazing people – country singers of the kind we loved – and he'd toured with Chuck Berry. He had nearly married Chuck's daughter, then fallen out with Chuck and offered to fight him. He'd actually been part of a world that was just a distant imagining to us, so we were quite happy to give him a few drinks and listen to his great boasts of dealing with Chuck and his daughter.

He was a bit older than the rest of us and seemed, in many ways, a bit wilder. At one of the first shows after his having joined Squeeze, there was this audience member sitting throughout the whole of our set with both arms raised in the air and two fingers raised on each hand, waving relentlessly, from side to side which was a bit annoying. In the bar afterwards, Gilson suddenly flew across to him, knocked him to the ground and stood above him holding his fist above his head saying, 'Is there something you want to say??'

'No no . . .'

'Do you want to say sorry??'

'Yeah.'

'Are you going to do that again?'

'No, I'm not!'

'Right. Don't. See you later then.'

We really warmed to Gilson after that.

The Valour of the Drum King

Miles is an extraordinary manager, and he is responsible for a lot of my success because he got so many different things going for me. His father, Miles Copeland Snr., had been head of the CIA in the Middle East when it started in the 1940s. His mother was an archaeologist and at one point she actually discovered a missing Dead Sea scroll, a most important religious document, which could possibly have changed the meaning of the Bible. She told her husband about it and he suggested he photograph it for the American government. She said 'never mind about that, I'm taking it back to the British Museum'. But when she wasn't looking, he took the document up on to the roof of their building and unfurled it so he could get a shot in proper sunlight and, of course, it completely disintegrated. That was Miles's family's first claim to fame. Then his brother Stewart became the drummer in the Police and his other brother, Ian, having served in Vietnam, famously asked to be sent back because he'd enjoyed it so much. That's the kind of family they were. Miles rubbed some people up the wrong way and he got knocked down a lot. When we first met him in 1975, the huge Star Trucking Tour he had just organized had left him practically bankrupt. But he has always had the ability to pick himself up again after any disaster.

In 1976 Miles got us a deal with RCA, who put up the money for us to go and record at Rockfield Studios in Monmouth. This seemed like a real step up, as Rockfield was a place at which big records had been made. It was one of those studios that had accommodation, in a terrace of cottages near the studio barn. There would be two of you in a cottage, with a bedroom each, a kitchen downstairs and someone to make and provide the food each evening. I felt this was a nice chance to get to know Gilson better, since we were sharing a cottage.

Monmouth seemed a very beautiful place which hadn't changed with the years, and the pubs looked good so, on our first night, Gilson and I decided to try visiting them all. In one of them, the locals said, 'Oh, look, it's Laurel and Hardy.' Gilson wanted to avenge this great insult to the death, but I managed to get him out of there before he did any damage.

Later that night, I decided to wash my pants in the sink before going up to bed. After I'd gone, Gilson thought he'd help me by putting them on to the cooker to dry. Of course they just caught fire and the whole place was soon filled with smoke. I was woken from a peaceful sleep by this maniac shaking me and sobbing, 'I'm sorry about your pants!! I'm sorry about your pants!' I thought, 'What's he talking about? Is this suddenly an unwelcome and ugly side of him coming out . . . ?' Then I said, 'Never mind about the pants – the building seems to be on fire.' And then he said, 'Oohh – fucking hell, yeah, the building's on fire too . . . quick – I've got to save you, get you out! It's all my fault.' He then dragged me out of bed and carried me (I didn't really want to be carried) out of the building. There had been so much shouting that everyone else had come out by then to ask what the problem was.

Gilson said, 'I've saved him. It's all right – it's all right!', and I said, 'Yes, he's just burned my pants in there, that's all. Go to bed – there's nothing to see.' The charred pants were taken off the cooker and the smoke dispelled, but it was my first inkling that sharing lodgings with Gilson could be fraught. On another occasion, some years later, in an American hotel room, I woke to find his face inches from mine, a clenched fist raised above me aimed at my face. He said in a big and frightening way, 'Don't move, *don't move*.' And I wondered what the matter was, what I'd done. I just couldn't imagine what had gone wrong. And he continued, 'Don't move, there's a spider next to you – but I'll save you,' and on the pillow was a spider, just minding its own business. I couldn't have cared less and neither could the spider, but Gilson punched it and smeared it all over my clean pillow. I told him I would have been perfectly all right if he had just ignored it, but he said, 'No – it could have gone in your ear, laid eggs and killed you.' Once informed of this, I felt grateful to have had my life saved for the second time, grateful, too, that I could sleep easy with Gilson in the room on tour, keeping one eye open for me throughout the night.

Touring in a band can be a bit like national service – except you have long hair, go to bed really late and do lots of snogging. And there's no running around and marching. So it isn't really like national service at all, except that you're obliged to share a room with somebody you wouldn't normally have shared a room with.

George Harrison told me that, even when the Beatles were playing Shea Stadium, they were still sharing hotel rooms. When they questioned this, they were told that it saved them money. They protested and, from then on, got the luxury of their own rooms. I take this opportunity to give music-biz tip number three – and the reason managers will be so keen for you to share a room. When a young band signs to a manager, the manager will take a commission of anything between 10 and 99 per cent of your earnings (if latter, seek legal advice). You need to check whether the percentage is to be from your net or gross earnings. For instance, if it's gross earnings, the manager takes his percentage from that and then you pay all the expenses and keep the tuppence that's left. If it's net, however, all the expenses are paid and then you split what's left with the manager. In this instance, the manager will be very keen on keeping expenses to a minimum, which is why they may suggest sharing occupancy of a shoe box. So my tip would be to go for the net earnings option and stand your ground. If you're going to be poor, you may as well be comfortable.

At Rockfield studios we met Del Newman for the first time – he was a great arranger. Fritz Fryer was our producer on this recording and he too was a dear fellow. He had been in a group called the Four Pennies, who'd had a hit with a song called 'Juliette'. We did a great version of 'Take Me I'm Yours', for which he set up this fantastic sound effect of a bell being rung as it was being lowered into a bucket of water. Gilson, being the drummer, was given the task of hitting and lowering the bell, which he did with great care and precision. But it took us all night to get this effect and, rather typically, the final version was never released or used.

That's what recording is like – you just have to enjoy the process of getting something down. But I started to realize then that the idea of going over something again and again wasn't so stimulating for me. Later, when I recorded with George Harrison, he told me that when John Lennon was in the studio in the days before instantaneous digital equipment, he used to urge the man winding back the tape recorder at the end of a take to wind it faster as he was so impatient to re-hear that first moment of excitement they'd just recorded. But, of course, the tape machine could only go as fast as it could go. In the recording process, apart from the accuracy of the notes, you are also trying to capture the excitement of the moment. Lightning in a bottle – that's what recording is about, and it's hard to achieve.

Having done these recordings, RCA rejected them; it just wasn't quite for them. They also worked out that we owed them £14,000 – not that we seemed to have got any money from them. This is the other thing that happens: you seem to get through money on recording or packaging costs and never seem to trouser any of it yourself. So music-biz tip number four: if you are going to get into debt with a record company, at least have someone make sure that some of the money has gone into your pocket in the first place.

At this point, the very dedicated Lawrence Impey decided to leave us as manager to pursue his great talent as a photographer. His naturally kindly nature and generous spirit were at odds with the cut and thrust of the music business. And so we were left with Miles as manager and, for some reason, although we had absolutely no money, two roadies. John Lay was one and a man called Jerry was the other. Miles always had to cadge equipment for us, and he had managed to get hold of an RMI electric piano for me so I could be heard on tour. Dr John had just such a one but his used to seize up because all the glitter from his gris-gris make-up fell into the keys and jammed them. Mine didn't have that particular problem but it did have one equally inconvenient, which was that its legs used to break and we couldn't afford to get them repaired. Soon we took them off altogether and perched the piano on a flight case balanced on top of bricks. The first time one of its legs broke on stage, John Lay rushed on heroically and placed himself under the piano, resting its entire weight on his shoulders for the rest of the show like an architectural caryatid. We knew we had another dependable chap on our team.

Folk Dance

In December 1976 we went to Holland – the prospect of it was so exhilarating. Before we went, I kept wondering what the people would look like, how they would differ from us and what their customs might be – I couldn't imagine.

We set off in a box Transit van, which basically meant no windows. John Lay, Jerry, whose van it was, and Harry had agreed to take it in turns to drive, so they were in the warm snug of the cab, with a heater and de-mister, while we were in the freezing cold back. In those days, to have four or five blokes cooped up in a Transit van was perfectly acceptable to the immigration authorities and we were waved through. So, suddenly, we were in Europe and driving across Belgium towards Amsterdam. Crouching on top of the cab, it was possible to see out of this tiny hole in the roof of the van, but the icy wind blew in my eye and rather hurt as I strained to get a glimpse of a native in traditional costume. And, even if I did manage to put up with the pain of the wind in my eye, it looked to me very much like a normal motorway. But even the signs with kilometres on them were a novelty. We were playing it cool like we'd seen it all before, but we hadn't. And we certainly hadn't seen anything like Amsterdam before – the bars staying open all night, the little streets and canals, the tarts in the windows, marijuana in coffee shops and people behaving reasonably. The only thing that got on our nerves a bit were the old English hippies who had moved there twenty years ago and had smoked so much dope they'd gone daft. Other than that, we thought it was the best place we'd ever been to.

Our first show was in a place called Boddy's Inn, run by this big, cordial Oklahoman and his Dutch wife. They gave us two rooms to share in the hotel they also ran but, whatever late hour we got back, the Dutch wife would come out and glare at us as we stumbled up the stairs. Then, at seven in the morning, her bellowing voice would boom through the loudspeakers in our rooms, 'De breakfast is now being served! You will have eggs! You will have eggs!!' So we'd have to drag ourselves up and have breakfast because, having no money, it would often be all we'd eat that day. My father had given me $50 in traveller's cheques in case of emergencies, but Gilson and I had decided that having no food wasn't an emergency and that having no beer was, so that's what we spent it on.

Our next show was at the Milky Way Club and, on this occasion, a girl in the audience wearing a beret on the side of her head took me back to her flat in the gables of one of the romantic buildings alongside the canals. She seemed like a fantasy figure from a sophis-ticated continental film, someone you'd watch making love to some European character. But, in this instance, she spent the night with me – an enjoyable, golden evening.

This is more than can be said for my next night, in a hotel which resembled a prisoner-of-war camp. All of us boys shared the one room, which had a small double bed and some really uncomfortable bunks. This isn't the beginning of some racy story, but it was so cold we all got into bed together. It was as desolate as a Gestapo interview room but slightly colder, and less comfortable.

We were hungry too. And this moment of hardship once again showed John Lay in his true heroic light. He told us that he only had a bit of money left but that he was going to go out and buy some bread and cheese with it so that we could eat. This was in contrast to Jerry, who had used his money to buy himself a huge pair of furry boots. Before the trip, Jerry had seemed useful, not least because he owned the van, and Miles had entered into a percentage arrangement with him. But, after this boot incident, we all thought that John would be a good manager and, on our return, he became partners with Miles, and our official manager and roadie.

Our last stop on this trip was a little Dutch town where we played in a community centre run by these very welcoming Dutch hippies, who invited us to stay in their houses. At the end of the evening, they urged us to join them in a ritual dance around a marijuana plant. And so, to be polite, we got up and started dancing around it, holding hands, which was not something we'd ever done – and certainly not with one another, as we cringed away from any physical contact. We caught each others' eye and couldn't suppress our laughter at this singsong and holding-hands ritual, but it was a lovely end to our first Dutch trip.

Back in London, we still owed RCA £14,000 and hadn't yet been signed by anyone else. But, now that we were used to slightly bigger venues, playing the piano in a small pub for a tenner didn't seem an option any more. And so, after Christmas, we did a string of shows, starting with the Red Deer at Croydon, which was like a huge Mecca ballroom but, on this occasion, more or less empty. In those days, Gilson used to climb up on top of his drums at the end of our set, throw the sticks at the audience and behave like a wild animal caged by his kit. We'd kick it all over when we went off – a good way to finish. Many years later, Stewart Copeland once did the same and his drumstick hit someone in the eye. They sued the Police for a fortune – not something we had to worry about in those days.

At this particular gig, Gilson ended up at the front of the drums, and Harry thought he'd try climbing on them too. This made Gilson completely furious, and he flew round and knocked Harry off. He was about to strangle him on stage until we managed to pull him off. Afterwards in the dressing room we suggested to Gilson that he was being a bit unreasonable – but he told us that Harry didn't know how to climb on drums in the correct fashion.

Soon after, one of the owners of a local Greenwich pub called the Bell had a wedding, and they asked us to play at it. They had always been very supportive of Squeeze and we were glad to be able to do it. But then, when the dancing had started, suddenly the drums and the bass stopped. Glenn and Chris and I played on, but I looked back to see Gilson once again on top of Harry, pummelling him. I think it must have been over what are termed 'musical differences', although a lot of feelings come to the fore when people are tired and emotional. Everyone dancing looked a bit confused but the two of them seemed to sort it out eventually, and we all carried on. They say, 'Where there's a wedding, you'll find tears, laughter and a bit of a fight' – although it's not usually the band. But we were like brothers and, as with all family life, you do have rows from time to time, however much you love each other.

Some time after that we went to Liverpool, where my great-grandfather was born. I felt that the old red-brick buildings, the docks, the heavy industry and the fact that the Beatles came from there made it a very romantic place, but our lodgings made this visit memorably horrible. We always had to stay at the very cheapest places we could find, if we had anywhere at all – sometimes we just had to ask the audience if any of them had a spare room. But this time we managed to find a hotel for migrant workers, one of the few still in existence, where they told us that there would be three of us in one room, two in another and the roadie would have to sleep in the van. Breakfast finished at seven thirty and you had to be out of the room by eight. We asked whether we could have a drink when we got back from the show that night. No. Also, they announced that there were fines for any misdemeanours. Upstairs, on the wall, was the list. It cost so much if you wet the bed, so much if you had a crap in the bed, and so much if you were sick in the room. And on the beds were these really horrible nylon sheets. In themselves, I wouldn't have minded these – they can be quite sexy when you're tucked up with the right person – but the rubber sheets underneath made us realize that the misdemeanours happened on a regular basis. We managed not to incur any fines, but it was pretty gloomy.

In the early part of 1977, soon after this trip, Richard Jones left the Climax Blues Band and the rest of the band asked me if I would consider stepping in and replacing him on the piano. We had supported them at shows in impressively big halls (so it seemed to us), so this offer seemed quite an honour. I didn't want to stop being part of Squeeze so had to refuse, but being recognized as a pianist in my own right was heartening. That same year, I also got some session work. One was for the London R&B group the

Count Bishops, for which I got paid £19 in cash by the boss of Chiswick Records, Ted Caroll, which came in very handy. Another was for Alternative TV, the seminal punk group lead by Mark Perry, the proprietor of *Sniffin' Glue* magazine. The next was for Wayne County and his group, the Electric Chairs. I arrived at the Marquee Studio to find that the lyrics weren't yet on the song; they just had a backing track. Wayne came out and I asked him what he wanted. He said in a very camp New York way, 'Make it really burlesque. Can you make it really burlesque?' I said, 'Yup, righto.' I played and, after I'd finished, I explained that what I wanted more than anything was to get a copy of the finished record, pressed up and printed. This was an important first for me, a professional record with my playing on it, something I had yet to achieve. They promised to send a white label, a test pressing, as soon as it was finished.

The moment it arrived, I rushed home and said to my family, 'Oh, here's the record I've played on!' My mother and little brothers were there, as well as my aunt and uncle, and they all said, 'Oh, how wonderful! A record you've played on!'

I took it out – it didn't have a label yet – and put it on. It started off with a long piano introduction, and then came the lyrics: 'If you don't want to fuck me, baby baby baby fuck off.' The song was, in fact, called 'Fuck Off'. And it got faster towards the end, until it was just a chant: FUCK OFF. FUCK OFF. FUCK OFF.

After it had finished, there was a pause, then, 'Oh, well done, isn't that clever, isn't that lovely, he's managed to play on a record. Well *done*.'

I said, 'Oh, I wasn't expecting the words to be like that. I just did the piano.'

'Well, that was by far the best bit – very nice piano, wasn't it, Auntie?' Their response was as if to a five-year-old who had successfully eaten a bun.

But it's now considered a seminal record, one of the highlights of punk. If you manage to get hold of a copy, it would now cost you $100. And I'm pleased that that was the first piece of vinyl I got to play on. When I took my mother to see Wayne at one of his later shows, she was a bit worried because, when he came on, the entire crowd started shouting 'Fuck off' at him, but I assured her that they were asking for their favourite song – our song. My wife's ex-husband, Ned, is now a great friend of mine, but one of the first things he said to me after Christabel and I had started living together was 'I wasn't sure about you, but I've always thought that "Fuck Off" was one the greatest records I've ever heard, and because of that I've got respect for your musical credibility.' I appreciated that and squeezed his hand earnestly.

Colourize

In February 1977 I managed to pass my driving test and so the road suddenly opened up for me. Sales Force, the company my father worked for, was going from strength to strength. By now it was working on a lot of contracts and needed hundreds of operatives to launch chocolate bars, sweets, soaps and other household items. Since my father was short of operatives for one particular product, he suggested that Gilson and I step in. It happened to be a month in which we were doing very few shows and, more importantly, had no money. The job was four days a week, with a car and salary. Both very welcome, because I had neither.

So, in our Ford Escort Estate, Series 1, white with contrasting black plastic interior, Gilson and I set off for the first job. Johnston Wax were launching some new beeswax spray. It was my task to check the supermarket shelves, see if they were running a bit short of the beeswax, then to go the manager's office and point this out. I'd tell them about the improved version just coming out, give them a free sample and ask if they'd like to order more. It was yes or no and off you'd go and that would be that.

We'd been given a map and had to cover the south of England so we were going to all these odd places. We did this for two weeks, and it was quite fun – we'd do six of these shops and then go to Southend and have a day out. Afterwards, I managed to hang on to the car for a bit, which was useful because we used it to go to some shows.

Then, all of a sudden, my father got a contract from Berger Paints. They had given these paint mixers called colourizers to every paint shop in the country. The colourizer was a machine which would squirt tiny splashes of coloured paint into a big pot of white emulsion, mix it up and so match any colour the customer wanted. But, shortly after they had sent the machines out, Berger found that the nozzles were too small and everything was getting clogged up in the mixing process. So, urgently, within a two-week period, they had to send out hundreds of people to drill holes and mend these paint machines, and I was one of those who stepped into the breach.

We were taught to do everything in a particular order. After having apologized on behalf of Berger (a bad way to start, I felt), you had to employ a very exact technique to repair the machine: open the valve, drill a little, close it again; then open the valve a bit more, and then drill a bit more. You had to do this five times to each of the nozzles. And you had to fill in quite a complicated form and, finally, hand over a free paint token. And that was that.

This was another dead time; no money, nothing going on. Gilson was staying with me at the time rather than out in Bedford with his mother, and I said to him, 'Look, I've been offered this new job – it means some money again and I can keep the car. But it takes so long to drill the holes and then to fill the form out – if you came with me we could do it in half the time. I'll give you some of the money and we can be back in time for lunch.' He agreed, and we set off to the first shop, where I showed him exactly how to follow the careful valve procedure, doing it myself so that he could watch.

Then, at the second place, I said, 'Well, you saw what I did, so you drill the holes in the machine, I'll fill in the forms and we can get it done really quickly.' I started to do the form, and I could hear behind me, 'Oh, how do you do this then . . . ?' I looked round and there was paint oozing out of the machine on to the floor. I realized he'd missed out one important thing and not closed the valve first. A bloke came up and started to say, 'What's this?' I said, 'I'm really sorry – but if you send off this token, you can claim your free can of paint – here.' So we left and went on to the next one.

We went to about four more and, at each one, Gilson just seemed to drill four holes and leave a complete mess of paint and a leaking, dripping machine. Even the car got covered in paint.

And I think after a few days, complaints got back and we were asked not to do that job any more.

I realized then that if I hadn't been able to play the piano, I would have been in a hopeless situation – there wasn't any job I would have been good at. Apart, perhaps, from Divisional Commander of the Metropolitan Police, Ambassador to Venice, or secret-service operative. And I think it's the same for Gilson – we just didn't have any other career choices. So when people say to me, 'My little Johnny plays the guitar well, should he do it professionally?', the truth of it is: if you have to ask or think about it the answer's no.

Deptford Fun City

For Squeeze, the early part of 1977 was a difficult period. We knew we had something going for us but we couldn't reach the next stage and get a record deal. There would be a few shows and then a gap; it was frustrating. When the Bricklayers Arms closed down for good, we had to find somewhere else to perform, somewhere we and our friends could use as a centre. The Bell took over for a while, then that went too. It was sad, but we must take the word of the Buddha on this matter: all things must pass – even good pubs.

On 1 April we did our first BBC session. Unfortunately, it was only to help train BBC engineers but we were given a tape of it, which featured a particularly good song called 'Black Jack', which Chris used to sing. It just shows what a generous organization the BBC is, going to all that trouble to provide us with a free demo. However, we still couldn't get a record deal.

But, full credit to Miles – if nothing was happening, he always made it happen – he decided to pay for and put out a Squeeze record himself. He formed a label and called it Deptford Fun City because he had been so amused by Deptford High Street, never having seen or heard anything like it before. This great big posh American – this was where my grandmother had been born.

Anyway, one of the things he did was to bring John Cale on board as producer. We had idolized John Cale for a long time because we all loved the Velvet Underground. We knew him to be a rebel, forefather of the whole punk spirit. Famously, at music college, he'd sawn the leg off a piano to give the authorities what for. To us, he was a fantastic teacher on the one hand and a great cult legend on the other, but he was also quite a wild and frightening figure. From the start he took us to a more abstract place and made us think of music in an artistic way. He was very clear about it: there was nothing wrong with pop music, but we could learn to touch other parts of the psyche too. He was aware of elements of music that we hadn't previously been aware of, for example, modern classical music and sound effects; up until then we had only been thinking about songs. He emphasized that there was more to music than just a pretty tune: there was the intention behind the work.

The EP we produced was called *Packet of Three* and contained the tracks 'Cat on a Wall', 'Night Ride' and 'Backtrack'. It was recorded at Pathway Studios in May 1977. On it, John mashed our different styles together; he was very clever and got really electric and exciting sounds out of this tiny little studio. And I was very pleased that a journalist described one of the big piano bits I did on 'Cat on a Wall' as 'punk piano invented'. In fact, I'd nicked one of the riffs off Vic's playing in the pub and had just played it a bit harder. In music that's what happens all the time, and it was great to be able to mix it all up on this EP.

More recently, just before I did my first Friends record of collaborations, I bumped into John in Belgium, where I was doing a show, and he was one of the first people I asked to do a track. He agreed immediately and I was really pleased. He's always got a different take to other people and is obsessed with music. He's forever listening to something, whether music or his inner voice. A great singer and songwriter himself, really he's one of the geniuses of our time.

In October 1977 we had some shows booked in Europe, which was good news, since the prospect of being poor in a foreign land seemed a bit more glamorous to us. So off we drove to the port and then on to Paris. Gilson had a bottle of whisky, which we drank in the car – a bad idea. We stopped for a pee, someone fell down the bank, we went to rescue him and dropped our passports. We did find them and, eventually we arrived at our cheap hotel in Paris, which was linked to the Gibuse Club we were due to play at for three nights.

After the first show, the undermanager of the Gibuse, Christian, took Gilson and me to a jazz club, then to his rather dubious office. He was talking all the while and we were going along with everything he said as he was giving us free drinks and hospitality. Judging by his talk, I think he was some kind of revolutionary or anarchist and hoped we were too, but we were just musicians. Anyway, we ended up sleeping in this very cold office, waking up a long way from the hotel, freezing, with no money and no idea how to get back – it was all a bit difficult, although we managed in the end. In fact, walking back first thing in the morning and seeing the attractive prostitutes still plying their trade, Paris seemed rather an exciting place to be. The following night Christian took us out to a couple of similarly sleazy bars, paying for everything and giving us his views. And, again, we ended up back in his office. Gilson, perhaps thinking he hadn't been making enough of an effort at conversation, asked in his friendly London accent, 'What you been up to today then, Christian? Wanking and sleeping?'

Christian replied, 'I do not understand what you are saying,' so again Gilson said, 'What you been doing – wanking and sleeping?'

Again Christian didn't understand so Gilson raised his eyebrows and in a rather impatient manner pointed at Christian and acted out sleeping and wanking. Poor Christian looked so insulted and hurt. I tried to explain that it was just the way we were, but I think he ended up not thinking much of us.

After Paris, we drove up to Amsterdam, to play again at the Milky Way. Unfortunately, Rod, our roadie, managed to block the police station with our van and, for the first time in its history, the police had to enter the Milky Way club. A disaster. And because El Stupido had left the lights on, the battery went flat so we all had to help push the van away from the police station, just before we were due to go on stage. Now, my advice concerning Amsterdam would be that there's no need to go mad, cramming everything in and consuming all that's on offer; there's plenty to see and do and plenty of time to see and do it all. However, we, unfortunately, did go mad, because we were young and foolish and, by the end of the night, I was dancing and laughing uncontrollably with a dustbin on my head.

After this experience, I would add this traveller's tip: don't have any Amsterdam space cake. If you do, just have a quarter. And, most importantly of all, never ever, if you do have a bit of space cake, think, 'This hasn't had any effect, I'll have some more.'

Silly-Billy

At that time punk rock was the most exciting phenomenon emerging and there were a lot of bands which took advantage of it. Bands like Paper Lace might have found it hard to assimilate into that world but, for a lot of the others, including ourselves, it was an attractive scene. Boogie-woogie fitted in with the punk ethos, rock and roll and rhythm and blues were allowed too, but we now kept quiet about our fantastic credentials of making songs that were as sweet as Burt Bacharach's.

After *Packet of Three* was released, various record companies did start sniffing round. One record producer came to see us play and suggested we get rid of the pianist, without him we'd be very successful. I was delighted that nobody wanted anything to do with him after that remark.

Conveniently for us, Derek Green, the head of A&M Records, had recently dropped the Sex Pistols. Being a sharp fellow, he had spotted their talent and had initially signed them in a famously photographed ceremony in front of Buckingham Palace. However, there had been a bit too much bother with them subsequently and they had been dropped. He needed another band, and this is where we came in. We were signed to A&M but, in our case, there were no iconic photographs taken of the signing ceremony, taking place as it did in the lawyer's drab office in St Martin's Lane.

It was then decided, in agreement with A&M, that we would make a whole LP with John Cale, since he had done so well with *Packet of Three*. It was further decided that our lovely songs would need somehow to be subverted for this record. It was entrusted to John to put us right if we were in danger of sounding too sweet – he was a good man for the job since, just by looking at it, he could remove the saccharine from a diet Coke.

One evening he turned up for rehearsals after his supper. He lay on a sofa and bellowed instructions and orders at us until suddenly there was silence – he had fallen asleep. He remained asleep for the next few songs, exhausted, I assume, and snoring quite loudly. We moved the microphone round on to his chest, then pushed the loudspeakers of the PA either side of the sofa, turning the volume up as loud as it would go. The din of his own snores should have deafened him, but even this didn't wake him.

We then got some lipstick off Harry, who wore it on stage, and gently wrote the word 'cunt' on John's forehead. Now, I'd like to stress that, at that time, this was a friendly south-east London term for a 'bit of a silly-billy'. Nowadays, in some quarters, the term is taken to be highly offensive, but we used it in the most affectionate way to suggest, 'Oh, I'm such a daft one' or something of that sort. We then left him snoring and, presumably, he woke at some much later point and went home. The next day he told us that the taxi driver had kept asking if he was all right while looking at his forehead in a concerned way. It was only when he got home that he knew what the driver had been on about. But if there was any anger from John towards us it soon passed, and I'm very glad to say that it didn't put him off producing us, and we went on to make our first LP, *Squeeze*, together.

John toughened up our music, as if injecting us with steroids. He encouraged Gilson to do this great drumbeat on one song, 'The Call'. Then we did an instrumental which, at John's suggestion, included the screams of the poor girl from the cafe, who had been told to try and sound as if she were being manhandled by medieval torturers. For the title of this strange instrumental, he suggested that all four of us put a word in a hat and draw them out randomly. It came out as 'Wild Sewage Tickles Brazil'.

John had to go back to America while we were putting the record together but we still felt we needed a few more tracks so we went into the studio and recorded a couple of songs, one of which was 'Take Me I'm Yours'. We basically built this song up track by track, starting with a cheap drum box that Glenn had bought – proving again that there are no rules in music, as this was the opposite of our previous method, which had been capturing a spontaneous live performance. But this song was just as enjoyable to make and very effective. That's the great thing about music – you don't know how it's going to hit you. Anyway, this did hit people, because it was a hit. A&M were pleased because it got to number nineteen, and we were pleased because, with our first record in the charts, we were launched fully into the thrilling world of television, including a first appearance on the legendary *Top of the Pops*.

When I was fourteen I had been to watch *Top of the Pops* being recorded with my friend Steve Springham. A neighbour of my mother's, Mrs Bevan, had got tickets for it but we were only told about her gift to us on the night, so myself and Steve had to dash over there on the Tube and then take a taxi in order to get there on time. When we arrived, we didn't have enough to pay the driver but he felt sorry for us, realizing we were kids, and let us off. We swaggered in like Marlon Brando and Lee Marvin in *The Wild Ones*, only to be told that the main act was to be Tony Orlando and Dawn with their 'Tie a Yellow Ribbon round the Old Oak Tree'. Yellow ribbons would be handed out to everyone and the audience would have to skip around doing English country dancing, because the band weren't going to be there. We were mortified – this was unthinkable. But we had to comply or be kicked out, so, in our tough leather jackets, we found ourselves skipping about waving these yellow ribbons. But there was a bonus: they announced at the end that if anyone wanted to stay on they were filming something for the following week's programme – Roxy Music doing 'Virginia Plain'. Much later, Bryan Ferry would introduce me to the love of my life and now wife, Christabel, but at that time he was just a glamorous icon up on the stage. And now I was going to play on the very stage where I'd watched him play and be able finally to overcome the humiliating memories of those yellow ribbons.

On the day of the recording, an absurdly vast Austin Princess limousine was sent to pick us all up, the sort the Mayor of London used to have. It pulled up outside my house and the chauffeur, fully uniformed, with boots and hat, knocked at my door, and all the neighbours were peering round their curtains. He was the most horrible grumpy bloke, greeting me with, 'This is your one big day, so get in!' He continued with this dismissive tone when we picked up the others, saying testily, 'It's your one-off chance so you might as well enjoy it while you can, tomorrow you'll be back at your day jobs.' Throughout the journey he kept shouting at pedestrians and putting two fingers up at other motorists. At a roundabout in Bermondsey, he carved a car up and yelled, 'Wanker' – but what he hadn't realized was that it was a plain-clothes Flying Squad car. The light started flashing, he was pulled over, told to get out and was then shouted at by the policemen. We made no pretence of hiding our amusement – 'Yeah, well, given that this is our one special day, we're allowed to have a laugh 'eh?'

The other TV show we did was *Magpie*, out in the studios in Teddington. For the uninitiated, *Magpie* was a children's programme like *Blue Peter*, with one friendly presenter with curly hair, another serious one who made things out of bits of wood and a rather nice blonde woman who was the love interest. It was a very popular programme at the time, and we all liked it.

When we got to the Teddington canteen, the first person we saw was the glamorous film star Diana Dors, now, sadly, dead. I'd loved Diana Dors films for years and I went over and got her autograph because I thought she was just fantastic. And she gave me a big kiss and a cuddle and said, 'Well, you're just starting up, luv, but good luck, Jools – you'll have a nice time and it'll be all right! See you in a few years!' It was such a shame that I could be her friend only for those few minutes, but ships in the night – so often the way in show business.

Before we went in to tape the TV show, we thought it would be hilarious and confuse everybody if we all swapped instruments, but what we had forgotten was that nobody knew which instruments we played anyway. The promotions man for A&M, this bluff old London geezer called Tony Burfield, came storming in half-way through the recording shouting, 'Do you want to end up with egg all over your boat! What's the matter with you? Get established – then you can lark about!' So we shuffled around apologetically. And I think the people in *Magpie* were also disappointed we hadn't taken it seriously, but we just put this down to a bit of over-earnestness on their part. We were quick to dismiss this trait in others and whenever we met fellow musicians who took a determined and serious approach to the whole business (which is only sensible, in fact), we found it a bit pathetic. We thought of it as a big joke really – perhaps a mistake, looking back. But at that time we were feeling pretty cocky, what with our single being a success. There's always a possibility that, if your first record doesn't get anywhere on release, your record company will drop you, but A&M were pleased with us because of our hit and because we were building our name as live musicians within the whole popular atmosphere of punk. Also, they were aware we had all these great songs of our own, which lots of other punk bands didn't have. They put up quite a few posters for the album in Deptford, which pleased us. The front of the LP *Squeeze* featured a muscle man and we appeared as muscle men on the back in a photograph taken by Miles's girlfriend, Jill Fermanovsky. A lot of people asked me if I had put anything down my pants for the picture and it's still a question I refuse to answer.

This time was a milestone for me in that Miles now suggested I do a solo five-track EP. For this, we went into Surrey Sound Studios, which were in an old dairy in Leatherhead, a place picked by Miles, since it was cheaper even than any other cheap places around. It was run by a young well-spoken chap called Nigel who had initially studied to be a doctor, and he did indeed have the manner of an old-fashioned GP or of an army officer. Nigel was the engineer on this record and Glenn came along to play bass, because I didn't think it was really Harry Kakoulli's bag to play on a record like this one. We recorded two songs I'd written with Chris, one called 'Buick 48' and one about the toilets on Deptford Broadway, 'Broadway Boogie'. There was one song I'd written alone, 'Should Have Known Better', a cover of 'Mess Around' by

Ray Charles and a song called 'Boogie Woogie Country Girl'. Glenn had done a guitar solo on 'Should Have Known Better' in which he sounded nothing like a twenty-year-old, more like a guitar genius who'd had a whole life of experience playing. The title of the EP was *Boogie Woogie 78* and it was all done live and finished in a weekend. Miles was pleased – he kept boasting that it had cost nothing to make, nothing. (And he hadn't paid any of us anything either.) It was put out on Miles's record label and, unbelievably, not only did I hear 'Broadway Boogie' being played by Alexis Korner on Radio 1 but the EP was Record of the Week in *NME*, the *Melody Maker* and *Sounds*, all of which delighted me. I didn't mind that I didn't see any money for it and, when Miles informed me that it had sold only 25,000 copies, I thought that sounded quite good too.

A year later, I went to record again at Surrey Sound and Nigel's manner had changed; he seemed less like a military chap – his hair had got a bit longer and his shirt a bit more open. This had something to do with the Police's first big UK hits having been recorded there, which Nigel had produced. Then I didn't see him for quite a few years, the next occasion being after our show in New York in the 1980s, when the Police had turned from a top British group into one of the biggest groups in the world. The door of a limousine opened and a massive cloud of smoke poured out, followed by Nigel, with two glamorous women on his arms, hugely long hair, a fur coat and sunglasses. And he said, 'Hey, Jools – hey, man! – nice to see you . . .' Completely unrecognizable from the well-spoken GP from Leatherhead I'd met all those years ago. You've got to be careful – that's what rock and roll can do to you.

CBGB's

The next big step up for us was when Miles announced that we were going to go to America. In 1978 the English papers were doing a great job of drumming up the new punk movement and word had got to the States. It seemed about time for another 'British Invasion'; nothing like that had hit there since the first one in the sixties, fourteen years earlier. Fourteen years seemed an age to us then but now seems no time at all. But this is what everyone starts to say – the days get shorter and then you're dead – so I won't bother going down that particular avenue.

America hadn't heard of us particularly, or our LP *Squeeze*, but they were hearing more and more about this punk movement, which they renamed New Wave, since the word 'punk' for them had different connotations. They wanted English bands to tour but no one had got round to it, partly because of the expense. But Miles was brilliant at seeing opportunities and, as there was a new airline, Laker Airways, which could fly you to America for £100, we could afford to go.

This trip was probably the most exciting thing that had ever happened to any of us. I'd seen America on the telly but could never have imagined going there. One friend of mine, Eddie Gittings, had managed to travel to the United States and, on his return, we all sat at his feet and listened spellbound to his stories, like inhabitants of medieval England welcoming back an explorer, astounded that somebody had been to distant lands, returned and could tell us all about it.

One thing we did know was that New York was extremely dangerous. One person had known of fifty British SAS soldiers who had gone on a night out in New York; all were gang-raped and stuffed into a sewer. And they were the elite fighting force so what chance did we have? That's what we were expecting –

extreme peril as soon as we got off the plane. But, actually, Miles had arranged for a limousine to pick us up, and it was exhilarating to drive through to Manhattan and to see all the classic sights: steam coming out of drains, hookers on the corners and big yellow checker cabs rattling around.

The first place we went to was the Chelsea Hotel which, in spite of its legendary rock and roll reputation, was absolutely revolting. There was a dish of rat poison in my room, with RAT spelled out in case the rat could read. After one night we insisted on moving to another hotel, but that turned out to be just as disgusting, if not worse, which taught us not to complain.

Before venturing out for the first time, we all agreed to meet in the lobby so that we could go out and get something to eat in the relative safety of numbers. We set out into the sweltering summer's evening, so hot that all the drains smelled. We all stuck together in a huddle, turning our heads as one at the slightest movement. We even viewed an old woman walking her poodle with suspicion, waiting for her to whip off her disguise and rob us, or worse. But after dinner and a few drinks we relaxed, realizing that New York probably wasn't quite as dangerous as we'd feared. In fact, the only one of us to suffer any injuries during his time in America was Harry. At one early gig, he got so carried away he threw himself off the stage and broke one of his legs. He had to do the whole of the first part of the tour with his leg in plaster. Then, later, when some of us were having a jumping competition, higher and higher, one by one, up and off some steps (I wouldn't recommend this to any readers, young or old: it wasn't big, it wasn't clever – it was just a jumping game), Harry insisted he join in. He climbed up to the step we had reached in the game, jumped off and broke the other leg. He had to be wheeled around for the remainder of the tour.

Miles's brother Ian was an agent for live work in America, and he had managed to get us a few gigs throughout the country, including some in New Jersey, but one of our first shows was to be at the iconic CBGB's punk club. CBGB's was situated in a seedy area of New York, but it was a great place, very lively, and before playing there ourselves, we went to see the Ramones, who did a wild set. The Ramones treated CBGB's as their club; there were pinball machines they used to play on for hours at a time. They told us they were going on to a nearby club called Kayzee's, which opened at five in the morning and closed at nine. They asked if we wanted to join them and Gilson and I decided to give it a go; we were used to everything in London shutting at eleven, unless you were lucky and got locked into a pub – but then you couldn't get out.

In those days, the area all round Kayzee's club was particularly grotty and derelict. The club was being run by the same Hells Angels who were doing the security at the door of CBGB's. American Hells Angels seemed a bit more businesslike and interested in organized crime than our British ones who really only like messing with motorbikes and having a nice time. These knew us from CBGB's, so they let us in. Before or since, I've never seen anything like it – it was Rome before it fell. People were openly taking hard drugs, and in one room there was a load of people having sex together. Pretending all the while that this was absolutely nothing out of the ordinary for us Londoners, I got talking to one of the Ramones, who said, 'Yes, I like to come here for a drink after work sometimes' – much as our fathers might have popped to the Plume and Feather on their way home from work of a teatime. Ten minutes later, I went and joined him in another room and continued our conversation as a girl administered oral sex upon his person. He smoked his cigarette and continued discussing the catering arrangements at the gigs we were going to do, or whatever other subject I'd picked. Meanwhile, the girl was trying to get his attention, thinking I was being rather tiresome and, eventually, I said, 'Well, I can see you're busy, so I'd better be off.' In retrospect, I probably seemed a bit boring compared to the girl, but I didn't want something like that to get in the way of a good old chat.

For this tour, Miles had bought a blue Chevy van and he did all the driving himself, so now we continued on to Boston and did some shows there. Afterwards we drove down to the South, playing at these strange bars, making friends and enjoying the look of the places we passed through. The intense heat made the journey seem even more foreign and fantastic. Because of our earlier experience of freezing weather in Holland, I'd made the big mistake of buying the biggest, heaviest synthetic-fur coat I could find for the trip, and snow boots. And on our second day in New York, I'd been to F.A.O. Schwarz, the famous toy store, and bought a piano-sized model hot-rod kit for one of my brothers and a huge great tin lorry for the other. I now had to transport these enormous packages round with me for the whole tour in the already quite crammed van, along with my suitcases already filled with fur coats and boots. Music-biz tip number five: travel light, especially in the early days.

Eventually, we reached New Orleans, which was like a dream for all of us. Although, as a band, we had varying musical tastes, we all loved its particular music and were thrilled to think that Louis Armstrong had walked these streets, as had Fats Domino and Dr John. We'd hoped that the city would resemble *King Creole*, the Elvis film, and it really seemed that it did.

The French Quarter was made up of wooden buildings chucked together as in an eighteenth-century European city, but had a fifties feel about it. Much as we might have liked to, we couldn't afford to stay there, so instead we stayed in an out-of-town motel with a swimming pool Miles had found. We got to this industrial estate and there was indeed a great big swimming pool next to our motel, but it was empty of water.

Because it had such legendary connotations for each of us we gave ourselves a couple of days off in New Orleans. The first evening, we went to this club on the edge of the French Quarter where James Booker, a New Orleans piano legend, was playing. As he played, the whole place seemed to swing in time with him – the doors, windows, drinks, everything – the sign of a great pianist. It was beautiful to hear and be part of. There weren't that many people in the bar and, when he'd finished, very much encouraged by Miles, I approached him and asked if he would mind if I got up and played something. In New Orleans there are a lot of musicians, and they have to learn to be quite protective of their patch – if they have a job they don't want somebody barging in and taking it. But he generously said, 'No, son, go right ahead, go right ahead . . .'

Afterwards I joined him at the bar and we had a chat. I was able to tell him what a big admirer of his I was. He was a very thin man, with a diamond-encrusted black patch over one eye and a gold tooth like a pirate would have, and there was no doubt about it, he certainly had lived a life. He looked at me and said, 'Well, son, I liked what you played, and I'm leaving this job to go to Europe on tour. I know the people here – why don't you do the gig for me while I'm gone and, when I get back in two weeks, maybe I can find you other gigs in New Orleans.' I was thrilled at this compliment from my hero and momentarily imagined my new life in New Orleans. On the one hand I thought, 'Yeah, I'll move to New Orleans, play in this club. I'll make new friends, start my life anew!', but in the next room, through the tassels over the door of the bar, I could see the rest of Squeeze laughing and enjoying a joke. Then I realized that I loved this load of loud-mouthed London johns and that my destiny for the time being lay with them. With regret, I told James Booker that I was on tour in a band and would have to stick with them. Had I stayed there then, I wonder if I would be there still, instead of in London writing this.

And so we got in the van to head for the next show, somewhere in Texas. It was very hot and there were clouds of dust everywhere as we drove. One of the high points of our car journeys was that America, like England at that time, still had these individually run small cafes at which we would stop for our breaks. At one point we pulled over to one, which was just a wooden shed by a railway track. Inside, this one really looked as if it hadn't changed since 1947. In one corner, they had a huge old jukebox with original 78 records on it and, choosing an old western swing record and watching the 78 being lowered, I felt as if I were in *The Last Picture Show*. As his family sat and ate, this old guy with dungarees served

us, in a nice if rather melancholic way. Above the counter was a
big black-and-white photograph of a young man in the army.
Seeing me looking at it, the owner said, 'That was my son, killed
in Korea. We haven't changed a thing here since.' And in the
corner the lively western swing record was playing – I felt I didn't
know whether to burst into tears, shake the father by the hand or
write a play about it. Ten minutes later, we were back in the van
and on our way.

Having made it all the way to Los Angeles and played our gigs
there, we flew back to New York. Since our first time there a bit
of word-of-mouth had built up, and some press – and, now, when
we went back to CBGB's it was packed and there was a queue to
get in. Miles was one of the few people connected with English
punk who also had connections in America and, for that year
anyway, there were no other English bands touring the States. And
so, whether you liked us as a band or not, it didn't matter – if you
wanted to see an English New Wave band you had to come and
see us.

On 1 July we played a particular show at Rochelle, New Jersey,
in a club called, appropriately, the Hole in the Wall. New Jersey
was quite a tough place and this club was run by bouncer types –
crooks, really.

Our roadies, Mike Hedge and Russ, were what might be
described as Jack the lads. As Mike was trying to carry some guitars
through a door, this old bearded guy had let the door go on him
and Mike had got so cross, he stupidly and unforgivably whacked
this old bloke – I don't know what he thought he was doing. Mike
was also unaware that this bloke happened to be the father of four
of the biggest and heaviest blokes in the club – the owners.

We had no idea of any of this – we'd just come off stage, and
the crowd had gone mad, so we were feeling quite pleased. Packed
together in the dressing room, we were drenched in sweat. All
Glenn had on was a towel, Chris was dressed and I was half-dressed.
John Lay and Miles and Gilson were all just sitting there, and we
were listening to the exciting plans for all the great new shows

coming up. Suddenly, Mike Hedge ran into the room, 'Don't let 'em in. Don't let 'em in.' He ran over to the toilet in the corner of the dressing room and locked himself in. The next thing we knew, there was a kerfuffle at the door, and Miles was saying, 'No, the guys are just getting changed . . .' Then he was banged out of the way and, into the room of these semi-nude young smelly London blokes, burst this gang of gorillas – gorillas with such expressions of revenge-seeking hatred on their faces, it was quite fearful to see. Miles started saying, 'Get out of here. Get out.' But, like a pack of hounds, they sniffed Mike out, kicked down the door of the toilet and dragged him on to the floor of the dressing room. It looked as if they were going to kill him. We started shouting – 'Leave him alone. Leave him alone' – and Chris threw a tin of beer, which hit one of them on the back of the head. This gorilla then very slowly turned round, at which point Chris moved out of the way and John Lay was left standing there. And the gorilla looked at John Lay, and John looked at him as if to say, 'How can I explain that wasn't me . . . ?', but before he had a chance to say anything, the gorilla had punched him and knocked him out. He then turned back to Mike. We realized that this was now looking really bad.

Thinking that they were going to kill Mike and working on the assumption that they couldn't kill all of us, we started shouting, 'Get off him,' and chucking stuff. Mike was well trained and well used to being knocked to the ground and beaten by lots of people so he had rolled into a ball. This meant that quite often their kicks were finding one another instead of him. Throughout, the old guy whose club it was and who had been insulted, had been talking to Miles over the din. Suddenly, Miles, in a moment of brilliance, waded into the middle of all these gorillas, put his hands up and said, 'STOP IT, EVERYBODY. LISTEN – I'VE GOT AN IDEA.' And, unbelievably, they stopped. One of the reasons Miles was a good manager was that he was was able to think quickly in difficult situations. He immediately lowered his voice, making respectful eye contact with the biggest, nastiest-looking one, and started to say, 'I can't apologize enough for what has happened here tonight.

This guy' – he pointed down at Mike, who was looking up between his fingers – 'this guy will never work in show business again. He's getting on a plane, paying for his own ticket. Then I'll see that when he gets back to England, he never works anywhere, not for us nor for anyone else in show business. It's an outrage and myself and the band will personally do anything we can to make up for this great insult. And, after the marvellous time we had tonight, when you managed to get the band who are about to be one of the most successful groups (and who played for nothing tonight), what a shame that everything should be marred by this man's appalling behaviour . . .' And he carried on with this whole spiel.

As he was talking Mike got up, ran and jumped out of the window of the dressing room and into a car that Russ must have had waiting for him. We heard them driving off. This made us feel a bit uneasy. And the old guy, who was probably in shock, kept repeating in this New Jersey accent, 'By the time this thing is over you guys will be working for me.' I don't know quite what he meant by that, but Miles continued to calm the situation down and, finally, we left, went back to the hotel, wiping the sweat from our brows, and asked Mike why he'd been such a tosser.

But there is a side story here. Miles had been very clever in identifying who was vaguely in charge and playing to him. He was the biggest of the lot and, as we were to learn, was called Larry. At one point Miles told him that, if ever he wanted a job, he would have it. Some time later, Larry got bored being at the Hole in the Wall and did get a job, as promised, becoming the personal security man for Sting on one of his world tours. I'd like to point out that Sting is so well loved by the people that he doesn't really need any security at all, much like Her Majesty the Queen.

But, on this tour, it was lucky for Sting that he did have security in the shape of Larry. The band was flying above the South American jungle in a tiny plane and the door suddenly flew open, banging against the fuselage. The pilot said, 'I can't hold the plane. Without the door being shut, the plane is going to go down!' In the chaos of nobody knowing what to do, Larry climbed out on to the wing of the plane like the mad hero of a Hollywood blockbuster, closed the door and saved all of their lives. It's strange how little incidents lead to others. In a bizarre way, Mike's own strange and reprehensible action would save Sting's life. Maybe we have our own guardian angels watching over us – certainly Sting and Mike did that day.

Upward Modulation

Back in England, we did two long tours with Eddie and the Hot Rods and Dr Feelgood, and a group called the Radio Stars who had just had a hit. Now that punk had started to take off, it would just be a shower of gob wherever you played, whoever you were. We played one gig with Blondie on their first visit to England, at a veterinary college in Bournemouth. As well as gobbing on us, the students started lobbing body parts of dead animals they had been practising on, and the promoter John Curd, who was rather a tough figure, got hold of them afterwards and gave them a bit of a slapping behind the scenes. Blondie had been watching with trepidation – they had had no idea that punk was like this, the opening group showered with dead animals and people duffed up outside the dressing room. They'd thought they were in nice, polite old England.

Because a muscle man featured on the front of our LP sleeve, we had a muscle man, Ron, who used to come and do odd performances with us, especially for 'Strong in Reason', which, we decided, was a muscle man sort of song. During one performance at the Astoria, the audience started to gob and, since Ron only had his pants on, he was really upset at being showered by it all. It was rather a revolting custom, and I'm pleased it didn't last.

On these tours, because I was thought to be a bit of a bigmouth, I would be persuaded to go forward and start ranting at the audience, which would usually go down quite well and amuse them. I also wanted to entertain the other people in the group, so everything would be improvised and different each evening. I would wear big suits and do dances on stage. One of my distant ancestors was a clog dancer, and I think that informed my stage presence and dancing style. Still, if the mood takes me, I will burst into a dance

– people have to be careful what they do, what songs they play, as I become unstoppable.

With our advance from A&M Records, we decided to buy a keyboard so that I could be heard properly. We went to Rod Argent's in Denmark Street to look at the latest ones. Moogs had been used on *Songs in the Key of Life*, then Stevie Wonder's most recent record, which we'd loved, so we were quite interested in seeing them. Most Moogs were monophonic, which meant that you could only play one note at a time, but there was a Polymoog in the shop so we bought that. It had various sounds on it, harpsichord and bells, for example. Looking back, this wasn't as convincing a sound as even the cheapest keyboard you can buy now but, back then, it sounded good.

Everyone bought a new guitar and Gilson was probably allowed to buy a tambourine. But, gearwise, the Polymoog keyboard, and its flight case, was the thing that cost the most money – it was £3,500. We were all still living on twenty quid a week and, in those days, for that sort of money you could probably have bought a house – in retrospect, we would have been better off had we done just that.

We also bought a Mercedes van, diesel, with aircraft seats, quite swish, but of little use to us because we were in America so much at that time. Miles allowed all the other groups he was involved with to use it instead and it got wrecked.

The Polymoog keyboard was good but, the thing was, I was a pianist, and pianos are not the same as keyboards. Pianos are a percussion instrument, they can be soft (*piano*) and loud (*forte*), unlike, in general, keyboards. So when Yamaha brought out the CP80 touring electric piano, which folded together, we were one of the first groups to buy one. It had a bit of a clonky sound to it but I thought that was charming and it was a piano. I still have it to this day.

With these new instruments, we started recording the next album in a studio over in Islington owned by Pink Floyd. However, when someone from the record company visited they said we'd have to start again, because they didn't like what they'd heard. It was a bit of shock, because we all thought it was going so well. In the end, they were right: we were on the way to something good – but hadn't quite got there.

We then moved to a studio in Old Church Street, and that's where we ended up recording 'Cool for Cats'. Glenn's lovely girlfriend, Jo Davidson, and Ba Hopewell and Eve MacSweeney did the backing vocals for it.

Another song, 'The Knack', had a good few keyboard parts and on it we managed to use the Polymoog. I wrote a song called 'Hop, Skip and Jump' with Chris, which was more in the rhythm and blues mode. Glenn played us 'Up the Junction' on an acoustic guitar. I thought it was one of the most amazing songs I had ever heard. The lyrics and the melody were just fantastic and it was about a London we knew and lived in. Gilson and I helped come up with an intro, and I was convinced it would be a hit. And, during the recording of that song, the Polymoog came into its own.

The recording completed, it was time for the photo session. The record company told us that we'd never really got the right end of the stick as far as our image was concerned. They'd hired this very good art director, who agreed with them, telling us that, in our day-to-day clothes, we really didn't look up to much. Butting in, Miles said, 'But look, Jools has got a leather jacket, long greasy hair and dirty fingernails, and that's because he's real punk. And Glenn's a hippy and Chris is – well, I don't know what, but they're just great!' We all felt a little hurt by these comments, but then the art director suggested that instead of looking like all these different everyday characters we'd go to Berman's and Nathan's and rent costumes.

Looking back, we missed the whole point of the exercise. Glenn came out as Henry VIII, I got a giant Humpty Dumpty egg outfit with just my legs coming out the bottom of it, Gilson was Robin Hood and Chris was a guardsman or something. We hadn't added to our mystique at all, the whole idea had been a waste of time.

Dressed normally again we went to one of our regular pub

venues, where a very drunken woman was doing a striptease. She attacked the director of our photo shoot because he wasn't interested in taking a picture of her. Finally he'd had enough, and left.

We went and had a cup of tea at a cafe called Popular Prices, each one of us disappointed it hadn't worked out. Someone took a picture of of us there and that's the photograph they put on the back of *Cool for Cats*. They ended up having to put a logo on the front.

We then made videos for 'Cool for Cats' and 'Up the Junction' at Titenhurst Park, the house that once belonged to John Lennon, and afterwards Ringo. On arriving we noticed that there was a huge dinosaur in the garden, which we thought was very Beatles-y. Then we found ourselves in the room where John Lennon had filmed the video for 'Imagine', and for us that was amazing. We were suddenly inside the world of the people we really admired. As a band we had varied musical tastes but all of us felt as one about the Beatles: we loved them. Recently, Ricky from the Kaiser Chiefs said to me, 'If you don't love the Beatles, you're a liar or you don't know about music.' I agree. They represent an essential part of the history of twentieth-century music; they changed it for ever.

The single 'Cool for Cats' went to number two in the charts, which was fantastic. We were delighted and, although we were touring in America and didn't really have time to take it in, there was much back-slapping and firm handshaking all round. I don't know what kept us from the number-one spot, but the single went gold, selling half a million copies. Nowadays, to have a gold single you only have to sell about ten thousand copies, because nobody buys them any more, but then – half a million people going out to buy a bit of plastic, that was one in a hundred of the population in Britain.

The song became an anthem for a lot of people in London, especially in the south-east, because of all the words it used and the rhyming slang. It was a bit like a rap record and a few of the lines were perceived to be sexist by some, but the song was really more a reflection on the life and the people around us. We didn't intend to be sexist, we were just telling the truth as we saw it, and not unaffectionately.

The fact was, Chris was a brilliant writer and his lyrics were like nobody else's. Having such a perfect understanding of the metre of the lyric of a song, he would hand the words over to Glenn or me and it would be a joy to work with them.

We returned from America just at the moment 'Cool for Cats' was dropping out of the charts, thus missing out on all the euphoria and adulation. But then 'Up the Junction' was released and that got to number two as well, so now we could headline venues and enjoy some of the glamour of fame. When we appeared on *Top of the Pops* for 'Up the Junction' they asked if I would like make-up. I'd just seen David Bowie's make-up for *Aladdin Sane* – the lightning flash across his face – so I requested that. They had actually just meant did I want a bit of powder and my hair combed but, patiently, they spent ages painting this lightning on my cheek. Then, filming our performance, they didn't show me once – there was only a close-up of my hands. For our next *Top of the Pops* I had lightning make-up put on my hands. Then, of course, they just showed my face.

Really, being young and big-headed and confident, success came as no surprise to us. But success in music keeps you very busy and now we didn't have a spare moment: interviews, TV shows, radio and tours, there was always something to be done. The Beatles each said to me individually that the reason they split up in the end was that they just couldn't do it any more – they were tired. With that level of success, the pressure to do more is overwhelming.

For us, success, and all the chaos surrounding it, was a novelty and we loved every aspect of it. Unfortunately, the necessary ruthlessness of musical creativity now reared its head again. Harry was a friend of ours and a talented bass player. He had played on our first record, toured England and America with us and had even broken both his legs in the course of duty. But now, it was felt that his grooving dance-funk bass playing wasn't quite so suited to our new material. We had to be hard about the music and Harry had to go.

We auditioned various bass players and ended up with this fellow called John Bentley, from Hull, who had played in such groups as the Fabulous Poodles. He was very funny and an accomplished player but I think Gilson rather missed having someone to have fights with once his playmate had gone.

I didn't see much of Harry after this. That's the funny thing about groups. It's like I imagine boarding school to be: you're cooped up with the same people but when term or school ends you don't really see them. Then again, I have just written a song with Dr John, and I probably see him only once a year, but when I do, it's as if no time has passed at all. That's the other thing with musicians: we tend to enjoy the time we have and don't waste it on big goodbyes.

'White Punks on Dope'

There was another group, the Tubes, famous for their record 'White Punks on Dope', with A&M Records at the time. They were booked into a world tour and A&M suggested killing two birds with one stone by asking us to join up with them for this tour. It was quite a commitment – we would be away for half the year – but we decided to do it.

This was our first experience of a big, expensive tour – the Tubes had a luxurious Silver Eagle American tour bus with a huge sitting room in the middle and TVs to watch. We became very friendly with them, and Gilson got on particularly well with their percussionist, Mingo Lewis. Mingo, like Gilson, was a bit of a wild card and the pair of them were like long-lost twins reunited, going off together and having a good time in their own particular way.

The Tubes' stage show was very elaborate and Fee Waybill was an amazingly energetic man – the whole thing was like theatrical punk. They would have girls sashay on holding twenty-foot-long cigarettes, for example. Our shows weren't so much theatrical as rowdy. At one point, we did bring on a blow-up doll and gave it a cigarette while Chris did an obscene-phone-call song, but this particular piece of stagecraft never really caught on, so we stopped it.

By now the more successful punk bands had been whittled down to those who could break into the mainstream; we were one and the Police were another. Miles managed both groups and a host of other bands besides; he could never stick to just one. During the course of our tour with the Tubes, Fee Waybill kept telling us how good and attentive their manager, Ricky Farr, was. And so, rightly or wrongly, there began to be a feeling among the group that Miles was spreading himself a bit thin and not paying us enough attention. We'd replaced the drummer, the bass player and now it looked as if the manager might not be up to the mark. This is the sort of thing that happens with groups: dissatisfaction tends to spread. And Ricky Farr, sensing these rumblings of dissatisfaction, started telling us how good he was himself whenever he got the chance.

When we arrived in Detroit, Miles stepped in to help us, which turned out to be a bit of a mistake. The American audiences had heard of the Tubes and we were a strong support – it was a good package for the promoters. But, for Detroit, the promoter had mistakenly double-booked us with a local band called April Wine. He suggested that Squeeze open for half an hour, April Wine would follow and then the Tubes would finish the show. However, Miles protested strongly that we were far better known than April Wine and, due to his insistence, it was agreed we should go on in the middle.

Being a local group, April Wine went down well with their followers, a tough crowd, in this big theatre in Detroit. When the curtain rose again, the crowd was expecting the Tubes and there was a huge roar of applause but once they saw it was us, a group they had neither expected nor heard of, the cheers turned to really nasty boos. Then they started chucking missiles at us. The missiles turned into a shower, and Chris and Glenn at the front were really getting it. A couple of bouncers came on stage at one point and looked menacing, which quietened the audience down for a minute, but then the anger surged up again, to shouts of 'Get off – You're shit.' Finally, a bouncer edged on stage again, having to duck missiles himself, and said over the angry cries, 'I really think you'd better get off now, because we can no longer guarantee your safety.' Glenn did something then that was one of the most brilliant pieces of stagecraft I've ever encountered. We finished the song and he said to this ugly mob, 'Right. Do you really hate us?' And there was a great roar of hate from the crowd, who looked as if they would attend an execution with pleasure. 'And do you want us to go?'

'*Yeah.*'

'And do you want the Tubes to come on?'

'*YEAH.*'

So he said, 'OK, if you really want us to go, cheer – no, louder than that.' So they were cheering and he said, 'Now, if you really want us off, stand up.' So we left the stage to a standing ovation, though Glenn perhaps let the side down after his magnificent speech by showing them his bottom.

When we got back to the dressing room we were all rather tense – we had never experienced this sort of reception before. The dressing room was very small, and a tray of sandwiches had been left on the floor for us. As we were discussing the crowd's reaction, somebody accidentally stood back and put his foot on the sandwiches – it was such a tiny room, it was difficult to avoid them. But, instead of expressing regret, whoever it was said, 'I was sandwich-dancing,' and the cry went up, 'Sandwich-dancing!' Because we were so nervy, we started dancing on these sandwiches in a manic way. Then there was a knock at the door, and one of the huge bouncers came in. He said, 'I was really sorry the way you guys were treated on stage, I just wanted to make sure you were OK. Do you want any more sandwiches? My mother does all the catering here, she made them for you.' So we shuffled round into a semicircle to cover up the nasty mess and thanked him and, as soon as he'd shut the door, we hid the mangled sandwiches as best we could and left, tail between legs.

After this we headed towards Canada. Canada is so huge. It's a very picturesque country with great big hills and so forth but 'big' is the operative word for it. Between the cities there just seemed to be miles and miles of nothing. On this leg of the tour, I began to find that Gilson's snoring was a bit loud for me and really wanted a room to myself. But even with all the drawbacks of touring, your enthusiasm for the music is never numbed. At one point, after we'd driven 800 miles to Edmonton, we saw that Fats Domino was on and went to see him. Just hearing Fats sing 'Be My Guest' and 'Ain't That a Shame' – it was as if we hadn't travelled any distance at all; our exhaustion was forgotten and everything seemed all right again.

In Vancouver our show went quite well and, afterwards, the

promoter took us out to a nightclub. We weren't really used to people in bars trying to scam us because we hadn't ever looked like we were worth scamming before. But in this bar some girls came up, all smily-smily, saying, 'Gee, you're great, you're great . . . You're from England?' Just as a friendly souvenir at the end of the evening, I wrote one of them a cheque for £1,000,000.

When I got back to England a few weeks later I had a stern letter from the bank manager of Barclays of Westcombe Park informing me that a cheque for £1,000,000 had been presented and summoning me to a meeting. Looking exactly like Arthur Lowe, the bank manager told me that he was very disappointed in my behaviour. He hoped that this incident would teach me not to be so irresponsible. Had the funds been in my account, he would have had to honour the cheque without clearing it with me first. Fortunately, in this instance, he had been unable to honour it, since I only had £38 in my account. This incident did teach me not to be so irresponsible with money but I still regret not having kept the original letter, just to keep me on the straight and narrow.

La Formidable

By now we were touring constantly. In 1979 we travelled to Denmark, Germany, Amsterdam again, and then back to America. And because of all the time we spent on the road, Squeeze was evolving into what I can only describe as a blob. People would kindly ask us to parties in all the places we stopped at and at once there would be ten arms helping themselves to drinks or anything that was handy and loose – the blob had arrived. Throughout the evening, one mouth would be helping itself to food, another's hands would be groping some sexy person, another would be making boasts from his corner, and another would be making a phone call at somebody else's expense. And then the blob would leave, having sexed the girls and helped itself to all the peanuts. It was not something you would have wanted in your home, but it was a benignish sort of entity. Having been used to having no money, the blob had trained itself so that when there was free food or anything like that it would overly help itself.

Whenever I returned to England, I was still just about living at home but I was beginning to realize I needed a space of my own, as people do when they're no longer teenagers. My parents had given in to my brothers' demands for a pair of collie dogs and I arrived home after one tour to find the dogs fighting in one room, my brothers fighting in another and my despairing mother threatening to leave in a third. I said, 'I'll create some more space for you, I'll go first.' I loved them but it was time to move on.

There was a couple I knew called Maureen and Dickie Dobson. What a lovely man Dickie was. How to put it? There are some people who have had brushes with the law but who remain naturally pure of heart and thoroughly decent. Dickie had a lot of large and menacing-looking friends, let's say, but he himself was the friendly face of villainy. He was a man of his word, and in his own way a spotless character. Anyway, I'm not here to give value judgements, I'm just here to give you the facts.

Dickie and Maureen lived in a maisonette with a three-room flat above it. It was empty and could only be accessed by going through their downstairs flat. So I offered to rent it off them, as the arrangement seemed to suit us all – particularly since I wasn't going to be there very much.

They agreed and I moved into those three rooms. There was no bathroom, so I had to share theirs, and no kitchen, which didn't matter, as there was a Chinese takeaway next door. I've never cooked a meal in my life. I've always been fortunate enough to be with people who *can* cook – some people can, some people can't. I'm one of the latter so sensibly allow somebody else to do it for me.

The one concern I had about the flat was soundproofing; neighbours complaining was one thing but also I didn't want to feel self-conscious about people hearing me play. As the flat was on the top floor of a detached house, and if Dickie and Maureen were out, which they were every night, I could play the piano without disturbing anyone. The only neighbour was a lady called Mrs Webster who was very old and, more importantly, very deaf. However, I did want to be able to play without disturbing Dickie when he was in the house, but the way I went about it was rather naïve. Somebody had told me that putting newspaper under the carpet made a very good job of sound insulation. So I got some friends round to help and we laid the newspaper down and then put this ex-military carpet I'd bought from somewhere in Catford on top. This, of course, did absolutely nothing whatsoever towards soundproofing the room. I suggested that we'd better test it, so we jumped around violently and, within two seconds, Dickie had flung the door open and said, 'What's going on? The ceiling's going to come down.' I explained that we were conducting sound-proofing tests but Dickie left, still looking a little bemused. I have since improved my knowledge in this area.

At one point Dickie and I thought about going into the car business together. We bought the first car at auction for £20, a

Triumph Toledo, what in the motor trade is known as 'an Old Turd'. We polished it and sold it to someone for £200. This made me think we were on to a bit of a money-spinner, but when I said, 'Great – what shall we do now?', Dickie's answer was 'Go to the pub.' We spent the afternoon there, and spent the lot. Dickie Dobson was a man of utter integrity, you could trust him to the end of your days, but he did like a drink. He would drink ten pints in an afternoon and still remained as thin as a rake. Each to their own but, in the daytime, drinking just knocks me out – I can't do it.

By now, I had started a relationship with Mary Leahy, my first really big love. I'd known her for a while, as she had been a great friend of the Squeeze gang, but what singled her out was her extraordinary beauty and gentle manner. Many of the people in our circle had either openly or secretly fallen in love with her, so it was doubly rewarding when she fell for me. We had some good times together in the flat and would also go to the old local singalong pubs and have very jolly nights out. We both liked a lot of the same music. Her father had been a musician in a dance band and had introduced her to a lot of the good old music of that time. And we sometimes had visitors. Dickie had one big prize-fighter friend who used to come round and listen to my Dinah Washington records and, in spite of his tough appearance, he would always end up bursting into tears because he loved them so much.

I was happy in my new flat, and I felt it was a relatively safe and peaceful place to be where I could write music without interruption. After a while it was back to touring, during which I hoped I would sample the food of some of the grandest foreign restaurants in the world, including those of Paris, our first destination, as I was getting a bit bored of the Chinese takeaway next door.

When we arrived in Paris we met up with a man called Marcus, who ran A&M in Europe. Although we used to complain about it, it was actually rather pleasant to be met by hospitable record-company representatives when travelling to a foreign city, as they would take us out to dinner and fill us in on local lore. In this instance, Marcus presented us with a lovely gift of penknives with our initials engraved on them. I'm afraid to say that the other band members scoffed at this gift, but I've still got mine. It's extremely useful and if Marcus is reading this, I'd like him to know that.

The first night, after our show, Marcus very kindly took us out for dinner at the grand Parisian restaurant La Coupole. It's a famous place – everyone goes there. It was big and buzzing with high ceilings, globe lights and elegant white tablecloths. We were all at one long table with Miles and John Lay and several representatives from A&M. I was sitting next to one of them, a chic and glamorous woman. She was talking to me in her fabulous French accent and it was like being in a suave Juliette Gréco film, drinking armagnac with our coffee and being served some dainty cakes. Then I heard Gilson ask from the other end of the table, 'Hey – shall I do my trick?' Now, Gilson's trick, which in harder times had won us the occasional free round of drinks, was to bet anyone that, by the time a handkerchief dropped from their raised hand touched the floor, he could down a pint of beer. He had learned it during his time with the greats and was now being egged on by Marcus. I suggested to him that this wasn't the time or place, but unwilling to disappoint Marcus, he kept insisting, 'No, come on – why don't I show them my trick?' Finally I said, 'If you must.' John Lay had his head in his hands, but the French people from the record company were politely responsive – '*Ah oui*, a trick. *Très bien*. Bravo' – and clapped their hands together in gentle encouragement.

Gilson explained that they would need a hankie and a pint of beer, but the word 'hankie' seemed to create some confusion and, being metric, the only equivalent measurement they had for a pint of beer was *la formidable* – a litre. So, with some ceremony, *la formidable* arrived – ice-cold, sugary and half as much again as a pint, not much like our enjoyable English beers. The next step was the dropping of the hankie but, again, a misunderstanding – the person from A&M didn't stand up but dropped it from where he was sitting. Gilson, seeing this, had to up his game – he was always the champ – but in this instance, the hankie reached the floor just before he'd poured the whole of *la formidable* down his

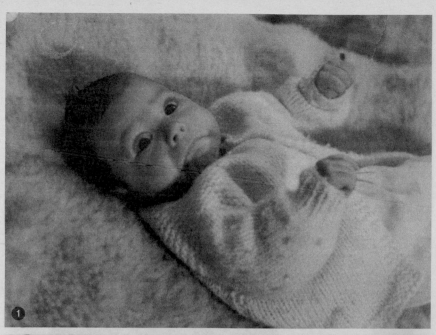

1. 1958: optimistic view of Britain

2. Mother and Father – they were
married at Caxton Hall, opposite
Westminster Abbey, a glamorous venue
used by film stars and celebrities

3. Mother, self and quiff

4. Nan (*centre*), Aunt Lil (*left*), Aunt
Daisy (*right*), English tomatoes
(*foreground*)

5. My great-grandmother Brittania,
grandmother Rosie, and my mother,
June.

6. My father, Derek (*foreground*)
with (*left to right*) Brian, Ena and
Percy (owner of a Wolesey)

7. Uncle David, the piano guru, and self (*foreground*) in Nan's front garden

8. Christmas 1966 ... prior to the stilt experiment

9. Self – armed – with grandfather and shed

10. 1972: self with brothers, big handlebars and big hair

11. My father, Derek in the first photograph taken by self

12. Early 1970s: from bus greaser to ton-up boy

13. Cum

14. The drum king enters – self and Gilson

15. Squeeze's first publicity
photograph, taken by the multi-talented
Lawrence Impey

16. Dancing in Deptford

17. Squeeze at the Old Albany Empire

18. Self, Polymoog and Glenn

19. (*Left to right*) Christopher, Harry, John Cale (with fringe), Glenn, Miles Copeland, Gilson, self, Derek Green

20. A Squeeze rehearsal

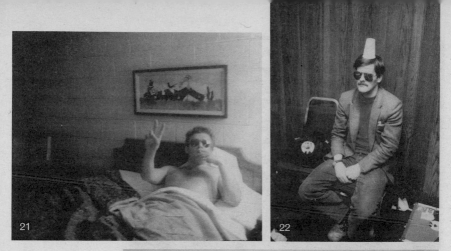

CLOTHING BARGAINS
FOR MILLIONAIRES

21. The drum king would keep a watchful eye on me as I slept

22. John Lay, wearing his management hat, at Madison Square Garden, New York

23. Chris Difford and my father, sharing a joke at Christmas in London

24. On tour in the USA (Mike Paice horizontal)

25. Millionaires in Caracas

26. Self, Martin Deegan and musical giant Pino

27. Self in the custom-made piano suit (now missing, presumed stolen)

28. Chequered history and chequered floor

throat. He slumped, beaten. At this point, Chris looked away and John Lay remained head in hands because all of us knew what was going to happen next. Looking as if he was going to die, Gilson threw his head back and then vomited over the table in a violent movement which propelled his face into the cake, which had written on it, 'A&M Paris welcomes Squeeze.' Then he clutched his chest and threw himself backwards again in another violent spasm, hitting the cake trolley behind him and shouting, 'Get an ambulance – I'm having a heart attack.' (As if his condition had nothing to do with having just downed an ice-cold *formidable* in one.) All the waiters were flustered and the record-company representatives were looking rather embarrassed but, by the time the ambulance had arrived, of course Gilson was much better. We just said 'thank you so much' to the nice Marcus and 'sorry about that, see you later.' That was the thanks he got for the dinner and the penknives. After this, we didn't go back to France so much as a band, since we found the promotional team were not quite so strongly behind us.

Some years later Mick Jagger took me to La Coupole and I told him this story. He seemed to be rather disappointed by Squeeze's behaviour in this instance, which was strange, as his group must have witnessed the odd bit of rock and roll behaviour themselves in their time.

'Dr Jazz'

In March 1979 we all went back to America for another tour, once again living out of suitcases. We all loved being there but did find that we hardly had any time to enjoy a place before we had to hit the road again. On long journeys there was a song Glenn used to sing by Wild Man Fisher, that went 'My name is Larry, my name is Larry, my name is Larry, my name is Larry'; it used to go on and on and on. And we sang other songs and made up the verses. It was great fun actually. It was half like being in the Boy Scouts and half like being in the SS, arriving in a town and raiding it. There was one babyish trick we discovered that didn't require any money and only a bit of time. In those days, they didn't charge international callers until the person being called was on the line. So, from San Francisco, say, we would get on the phone at three in the morning and say, 'Could you get me a person-to-person call to Martin Pugh in London at Greenwich 6304.' Then, huddled round the phone, we would hear the lovely English ring tone and then the voice of Martin's dad saying, 'Hello.'

'Is this London, Greenwich 6304?'

'Yes, that is our number. Who is this?' (A lovely *Passport to Pimlico* voice and then cut back to the Space Mission voice.)

'Am I speaking with Mr Martin Pugh?'

'No, he's still in bed.'

'Is Mr Martin Pugh there? This is the United States calling.'

'Oh, hang on a second. Mother, it's America calling for Martin.'

And we could hear Mother going upstairs, banging on the door, and her distant voice saying, 'Martin, quick – get up, get up.'

'What, what?'

'Quick, get up. It's America on the phone. He won't be a minute, love.'

'Is this the correct number?'

'Yes. He's just coming.'

And so on. Anyway, finally we hear this sleepy voice: 'Oh, what, what?'

'Is that Mr Martin Pugh?'

'Yes, it is.'

'OK, caller, go ahead. You're connected.'

And then we'd shout '*Tosser*' and put the phone down. It hadn't cost us a penny and had given us a million dollars' worth of laughs.

On 18 April we went down to Atlanta, which by then was getting warm. I was very pleased to be there as I love Georgia and the South. We were playing in the Agora Ballroom and, over the road from it, Smokey Robinson was playing. I remembered sitting in my grandparents' front room listening to his songs on *Motown Chartbusters* aged about nine and loving them more than anything. So I went along to hear him and was surprised to find that I was the only white member of the audience. I didn't feel uncomfortable or out of place, I just wondered why it was – surely I couldn't have been the only white person in Atlanta to love Smokey Robinson. But I was beginning to notice the cultural differences in America, especially in the South. Music just didn't cross over. People knocked British radio at the time but you would hear a wide variety of music, from British pop records one minute to Motown hits the next. In America music was pigeonholed; each radio station stuck to its own sound. Squeeze was being championed on the New Wave stations but often I would turn over and listen to the mad amusing religious stations or the R&B ones, but there was never that mix you get in England on any one station.

After the Smokey Robinson gig I went backstage and met him, and he was the most gracious bloke in the world. He didn't know who I was but, when I said I was from Squeeze, he said he'd heard of our group and would like to come and see us play. I shook his hand, never dreaming that, years later, I would make a record with him myself.

The following day, during the soundcheck, I made two other

new friends whose names were Big Filthy and Tramp. Certainly Big Filthy's name very much suited him. I recognized that they were members of a bike gang as they had the colours of the gang Dealer's Choice emblazoned on their backs, so I had got talking to them about bikes, although I could see security casting anxious looks in our direction. At one point, one guy took me aside and suggested I shouldn't be talking to them, but I didn't see the need for worry. Big Filthy then offered to take me out and, stepping outside, there was this old beaten-up Ford panel van, the sort that serial killers in films use for kidnapping their victims. They told me to get in the back, and I did have a moment's twinge of concern but, of course, it was fine. We went and had drinks at a couple of bikers' bars, then stopped at a lap-dancing place. Big Filthy started commenting on the various naked women dancing on the platform behind us, discussing who was better and so on. Then he said, 'That one's good, but that one there is even better, doncha think?' And I turned to realize that I had a viewpoint perhaps only an examining gynaecologist would ever have, and I was certainly getting a gynaecological performance. Really, I was more interested in discussing bikes, but I showed a polite interest. Anyway, the woman finished, pulled on her pants and came and joined us, and Big Filthy introduced her as his wife. What a gent he was not to have mentioned that before. I said, 'Oh, my pleasure, delighted to meet you. Enjoyed your dancing so much.'

After that, they took me back to their house for a drink and then on to a couple more bars, and then they accompanied me back to the hotel, just to make sure I got back safely – they couldn't have been more hospitable. Big Filthy had a pickaxe down his trouser leg which, as he was so big, I hadn't noticed. He showed it to me as we were walking along the warm Atlanta streets to reassure me he could protect me. He was the most charming man you could ever wish to meet. All of the Dealer's Choice gang were gracious hosts. They obviously fell into the category of priests dressed as pirates. When I arrived back there were a lot of con-cerned faces – people had been worried that I'd been abducted – but I'd had a lovely time. What with the spring weather, the music coming out of the jukeboxes as I wandered around the city and having met Smokey Robinson, Big Filthy, Tramp and Big Filthy's wife, I felt that Atlanta had treated me well.

On we went, and there was a lot more sitting in vans, playing long-drawn-out games, reading, refreshing ourselves with sleep and looking out of the window at America. We went to Florida and had a drink in a clipjoint with some scantily clad girls then, in Tampa, we had a pool party during which all the band were hurled in fully clothed. Then back to New Orleans, where we saw the Neville Brothers playing. In each town the record company would take us to the record stores so we could be photographed with the people there. We didn't mind this, as we were always offered lots of free records, and we always returned loaded down, having helped ourselves just a little bit too much – Blob greediness always crept in . . .

A huge thunderstorm swept through New Orleans while we were there, the rain was hitting the streets and everyone was hiding inside. It was a magical atmosphere – those wrought-iron balustrades on the buildings and the hanging plant pots outside, music everywhere. It seemed so romantic. This is when I wrote 'Dr Jazz', my love song to the city.

We went to Houston too, which was where Lightnin' Hopkins came from, one of my great heroes and a genius of boogie-woogie. I regret not having tried to look him up but I didn't know he still lived there. When the Beatles first visited America Ringo said in an interview that he'd quite like to move to the States because it was Lightnin Hopkins' homeland, but none of the interviewers knew who he was talking about.

In April we went to Oklahoma and played in Tulsa's legendary Cain's Ballroom, where so many of the greats of country music had played, the very place that Bob Wills and His Texas Playboys had used as a base. As a band we loved country music, not only for the melodies, but for the reason that Charlie Parker gave when asked why he liked this redneck shit: for the stories. The rock and roll music we have now is a mashing together of the blues, hillbilly music, a bit of jazz – all those things thrown in together. We were now in the heart of western swing. Although we liked the music in New York, here lay the roots of the music that touches the soul, the deepest part of the human spirit.

As we were playing the audience got blind drunk and danced madly to us – we could have been Bob Wills, they were so enthusiastic – and, the dance floor being sprung, they were up and down and all falling over. It was the best night we could have had.

Afterwards we had a drink with the owner, a larger-than-life cowboy figure in a big hat. His office had signed pictures of Hank Williams, Moon Mulligan and Bob Wills all over the walls, and he gave me a publicity shot of Bob Wills, which I've still got. He then offered us a drink of tequila, which was of hallucinogenic strength and out of a bottle in which a snake was crawling around – happy memories . . .

We then went up to Kansas City, where we played at an amusement park and were given free rides; this, again, made us feel the benefit of being in a group. American amusement parks with their high-tech intergalactic space rides were so much better than English fairgrounds, where you're lucky if you get a laughing policeman and duffed up by the local herberts.

Then, back in New York we were picked up by limousines and a baggage truck, which we'd never had before. Now, instead of doing shows at tiny clubs like CBGB's or small venues which just came up and disappeared again, we actually sold out reasonably sized shows. The *Squeeze* LP was starting to have a buzz about it, and it was becoming apparent that success really was coming our way. We were playing in the Ritz, which was packed out and sold out; all the promoters – in fact, everyone – were being our friends. Suddenly, people wanted to know us: the phone was ringing, people wanted to feature us in magazines, have us on their radio shows. We used to go to the Blarney Stone bar, which was a great, proper New York place that hadn't changed in years. One evening we went in and saw all these people turning to look at us – I remember that moment of realization, thinking we were really getting somewhere. Often, in groups, because you're in the middle of it, you don't understand what it is that's going on all around you. But here we felt a tornado of success coming our way. We saw a giant boxing glove in Macy's, and we bought it to show that we could now take on the world single-handed.

Rock Stars in Their Underpants

In a roundabout way, this American tour led to the beginning of my friendship with Paula Yates. In New York I met and became friends with a glamorous model called Bebe Buell, who had been married to Todd Rundgren and later went out with Elvis Costello. She was just a friend, as I was going out with Mary and certainly wouldn't have wanted to upset that apple cart. But, in her column in the *Record Mirror*, Paula Yates wrote a piece about my friendship with her friend Bebe in such a way that it got me into a bit of trouble at home.

On our return to England, we did *Top of the Pops*. It was when 'I Don't Like Mondays' was a hit, and Paula and Bob Geldof were there. I went up to Paula and told her what had happened as a result of her article. She hit her head with her hand and said, 'Oh, sorry. Didn't want to get you into trouble. It was all just meant to be a bit of a laugh. But don't worry – leave it with me.' And the following week she wrote something along the lines of 'Jools Holland – saint and genius.'

At the recording of *Top of the Pops*, she was clinging on to Bob, and they made a very glamorous couple. We got chatting, and he was much like he is now, larger than life, funny and confident. She looked great and really fresh. She had been modelling, didn't drink a drop or do any drugs and was incredibly fast-witted and funny. In some ways, it was as if the two of them were in their own little gang and we too were like a gang, so this was two gangs meeting up together. It was great to meet her, we made each other laugh – there was no suggestion of saucy business. After all, Bob was there and he was quite a bit bigger than me.

A year later Paula rang me to say that she was doing a book called *Rock Stars in Their Underpants* and to ask if I would be in it. I thought about it carefully for half a second and said yes. My thinking was: she was going to come round, we would be alone and I'd be in my pants. Good start. Better if it was the other way round, but a start. Perhaps if I were in mine, it was only fair that she be in hers? That was the sort of thing that was going through my mind.

Paula went round to my mother's house first because she couldn't work out where I was, but she'd eaten something bad the night before and was being sick over my mother's sofa. She was very apologetic, my mother gave her a cup of tea and an aspirin and they got on famously. I joined them there, and then we went round to my flat. She had a Polaroid camera and another big camera with her and she did a quick so-called test with the Polaroid. I suggested she use this Polaroid picture instead of one from the posh camera in order to achieve more of a 'Readers' Wives' look. This had been her intention all along, so we were thinking along the same lines.

In 1976, my paternal grandfather, Percy, had died, one of the sweetest and most agreeable men you could ever meet. At the time, my dear grandmother Ena was afraid I might feel slightly left out, as he hadn't bequeathed anything to me. I was happy and content that I had inherited his good humour and looks, but Ena insisted on giving me a pair of his old pants, which she said were his lucky ones. She told me they would be lucky for me too. And in this my grandmother was once again proved right, as I was wearing these pants at the *Rock Stars in Their Underpants* photo session, and it was then that Paula and I cemented our friendship.

By now it was clear to everyone that Squeeze was on the verge of becoming very successful, but it was equally clear that Miles's time was largely taken up with the Police. He had had this unbelievably good piece of luck where he had two groups that were very successful – most people only get one successful group, if they get any. People can always sense when something is about to take off, and the world and his wife appear on the scene, trying to get involved or take over. Now people sensed there was a window of opportunity; Miles couldn't take care of both groups, and they could smell the growing whiff of dissatisfaction from Squeeze.

We started to become friendly with Elvis Costello at about this time and, the grass always being greener, his manager, Jake Riviera, began to seem as if he was doing a better job than Miles. I never took the view that Miles was doing such a bad job, as he was the person who had got us where we were, i.e. being quite famous. None of us had made a lot of money yet but I felt that if we kept going it would probably even itself out. Hardly any successful musicians do well financially in the beginning, they have to figure the business side out too, but they usually manage to do all right in the end. First you need to get where you are going. Miles did have a certain sense of loyalty and strength and going behind his back didn't seem quite right somehow. It might have been better to confront him with our various dissatisfactions but he was very busy; we were successful but the Police were becoming a mega world phenomenon.

One night Jake Riviera came down to meet us in a pub in Greenwich, and explained to us all why we should sack Miles, trying to convince us, of course, that he would be the better manager. He kept buying us pints but I noticed he was only having halves. He kept laughing really loudly at everyone's jokes, including his own, and behaving rather like an archetype of a devilish cinema character – I found I didn't really like this approach. Miles had been straight with us, and this seemed a bit of a betrayal to me. I wasn't so keen on Jake.

The next step we took was to go and see a lawyer in Mayfair, who worked out how we could get out of our contract with Miles. We were all drinking quite a lot and it was clouding our decisions a bit, so none of us was thinking that clearly. My view was that we should just talk to Miles, let him know we weren't happy. After all, you can't continue working with somebody you're not happy with; most people would agree with that. Although Miles had his faults, he had been very good; apart from anything else he'd saved our lives in the Hole in the Wall. The Police might have deflected some attention from us but, on the other hand, we seemed to be doing quite well in spite of this.

At the same time I was starting to wrestle with a monumental decision of my own. It was all very well becoming a bit famous and having a bit of success but the thing that meant more to me than anything was playing music. I loved the music we played with Squeeze but I felt that there was more that I wanted to do, things I couldn't necessarily do with them. My dilemma now was whether I should stay with Squeeze in the safety and excitement of their growing success or try branching out on my own, with no guarantees but with the chance to develop my own music.

I felt a responsibility towards the others; we were like brothers, and were very close friends. Apart from anything else, I felt that if I did leave I would be letting them down. I decided to talk about it to Glenn and, when I did so, he urged me to stay on. He knew I was unhappy with all the talk of leaving Miles but I told him that wasn't the point, I just wanted to make my own music. That's what it's about, ultimately. The joy of music, for me, is the joy of making it, whether it's at home or in front of an audience. When I play music, I'm plugged into it all the time, on stage or at home, it's all part of the same thing. Squeeze gave me some of that joy but I was instinctively feeling that it wasn't enough for me. We had a certain thing we were doing, which I loved – but I wanted to go off more in my own individual direction too. It was intensely difficult to make the decision and I wasn't sure where it was going to go at this stage.

During this period I had a phone call from Elvis Costello saying that he had to do a TV show in Italy and his piano player, Steve Nieve, couldn't make it. He asked if I wanted to stand in for him, to become, as he put it, 'an added Attraction'. They were good fun to be with, so I was glad to be able to do it.

The TV show itself was mimed so, in fact, I didn't actually have to play anything at all. There were some hardcore Italian Elvis Costello fans pointing at me, saying, 'Fraud. Fraud,' possibly because I was miming or possibly because I wasn't Steve Nieve. But we couldn't really have cared less, and we all went back to the bar afterwards and sang some Hank Williams songs round the very ropy piano they had there. Elvis sings those songs very beautifully.

One thing I did notice was that it was a bit more comfortable travelling with Elvis and the Attractions than with Squeeze, which was probably one of the reasons Glenn and Chris quite liked Jake Riviera. Everybody had their own room and we got taken out to dinner, which was paid for out of a central fund. We were just looked after a little better than on the tours I was used to. Sometimes managers provide you with all these fantastic things but actually it's the group that ends up paying for them in the end.

We had the next day off, an unheard-of luxury, and somebody took the time to show us Rome. We started out at the Colosseum, where I suggested I hire a lion's suit and have a boxing match with Elvis dressed as a Christian, but he didn't go for that. We then went to the Trevi Fountain where, as was customary, we threw in money and made a wish. Just for a joke really, I shouted out, 'I'd like a Bentley Continental.' Now, some years later, I got a Bentley Continental, and I was rather pleased. But when I thought back to the fact that my wish had come true I felt a twinge of guilt: how shallow and selfish of me to have wished for that – why hadn't I shouted, 'World peace' or 'Salvation for all mankind,' something that might have benefited all humanity. Still, I enjoyed the Bentley while I had it.

The whole day was very relaxing, like a little holiday. I wondered if that's what it was like in Elvis's world all the time – I even found myself wondering why it wasn't like that with Squeeze.

Shortly after my visit to Italy, Squeeze went back to Los Angeles again, and the contrast was clear. Instead of staying at the legendary Tropicana Motel, as we'd requested, we'd been put in Copper Penny motel, which had drug dealers and prostitutes milling about and stinking horrible food. I had to borrow a motorbike and drive all around Los Angeles just to get away.

While we were in LA Chris and I went and saw Dr John playing in a small club. Afterwards, I met up with him and really got to know him for the first time. Chris suggested we play him a song that he and I had written, 'Foolish I Know'. We thought he might like it, and he did. He then answered a question about one of my favourite of his songs, 'Louisiana Lullaby'. Although he'd grown up in New Orleans and I'd grown up in London, we had an immediate connection.

During this time in Los Angeles I found it so frustrating not to be able to have a piano and write songs I asked to use the piano and writing room at A&M Records. Once the Charlie Chaplin film lot, the building was an amazing place to visit. Its car park still had designated parking spaces for the Carpenters, because they had been such a big-selling group for them. Jerry Moss, who owned the company with Herb Albert, was such a thoughtful man that he had placed a huge crystal in the central hall to improve the vibrations of the building. Unfortunately, since none of the employees could resist nicking bits off it to take home, it ended up a quarter of the size it once was. But he was a lovely man who genuinely loved music, Herb Albert too, and we were lucky to be with them, although we didn't appreciate that at the time. We often used to go in, since Miles had his own record label in the building and there was always something going on.

On this occasion, I noticed some sheet music lying around and, having listened to a bit of the tape from the previous demo, I realized that it must be Dr John's writing room. So after I'd finished writing, I left him a friendly note on the piano. I didn't see him for another two years after that, but when I did he immediately said, 'Yeah – you've been in my room.' From that day on we were great friends. He told me that he kept the note and he keeps mentioning it still, every time I see him. I wish I could remember what it said, why it was so memorable. Perhaps it said, 'I'll give you fifty quid when I next see you.' Who knows?

Whinging Poms

'Cool for Cats' was, surprisingly, a hit in Australia, so the record company arranged for us to do some shows there and pick up our gold record at the same time. We were told that it would be lovely and warm in Australia in January but, of course, being so contrary, we ended up grumbling about the trip. For a start, the journey to Sydney took so long, and none of the tricks we employed to be moved to first class worked – not even our favourite, pretending to be dead. I ended up sitting in the middle of a row, a lively Gilson on one side and a poor woman with very bad Parkinson's disease on the other, dribbling on me. It was one of the most unpleasant journeys I can remember. Then, when it finally came to the end and all I wanted to do was to fall out on to the runway, men with big Australian hats boarded the plane and showered insecticide all over us.

Once we were actually there, I loved Australia; all the people were very friendly, and we found the girls especially friendly. From Sydney, we travelled on to Adelaide, which seemed to have a unique atmosphere and was where I celebrated my twenty-second birthday. We worked out that if we started my birthday in English time and finished it in Australian time (or perhaps the other way round), my birthday would last three days, more or less. So the celebrations were endless; like a happier version of the journey there, they went on and on. I noted in my diary that the band had clubbed together and bought me a little Australian train set. I've still got the locomotive, which has a light on the front of it, and it works rather well to this day. We went out for dinner, and I had such quantities of oysters and champagne I was nearly sick. After dinner we went back to the hotel and Gilson pushed me in the cupboard of our shared room as a joke, but then wouldn't let me out for slightly too long a time.

Our next destination was Broken Hill, which we reached by light aircraft from Adelaide. This was a mining town in the middle of the desert, and our show was for the mining community; we were the Saturday-night group in the local dance-hall. It went just about all right, but it was a bit touch and go. Then we had to fly back afterwards on the same little plane. Taking off, the pilot couldn't get through to flight control on the radio. He was saying, 'Adelaide, Adelaide, Adelaide, Adelaide,' and then there would be a gap, no noise but a sort of crackling sound, and then, 'Adelaide, Adelaide, Adelaide, Adelaide.' His voice was calm at first but after what seemed like the sixty-fifth time of 'Adelaide, Adelaide,' it became rather panicky. We asked whether everything was all right and he said, 'I'm gonna have to go back and land and ring them again on the landline.' So we flew back and it was dark and he couldn't really see how to land. Gilson asked if he had been doing this long and he replied, 'Oh yeah, don't worry. I've flown intercontinental jumbos for years.' Gilson asked why he wasn't doing that any more, and the pilot said, 'Oh, the old ticker. It's not quite up to it, you know.' And the plane was bumping around, and we all looked at one another, and he started again: 'Adelaide. Adelaide.'

Having landed safely back in Adelaide in the end, the following night we drove out into the desert, because we had been told that, if we parked the car there and left our headlights on, we would see some kangaroos. We turned our engine off, waited and eventually heard something crashing a path through the undergrowth towards us. However, when it came on to the road in front of us, it wasn't a kangaroo but a spider, as big as the biggest man's hand you have ever seen. First it looked up at the headlights; then it looked at us, menacingly. I decided we had to get a picture to show people back home so we very gingerly opened the door and took a photograph over the top of the closed window. And I said, 'That's no good. It could be half an inch wide. Somebody go and stand near it to give some scale.' They all said, 'Why don't you do it?' and I said, 'Well, no. I'm busy composing the photograph, but somebody should do it.' Spiders don't usually bother me but this one was so big I thought he would crush me if he sat on me. We weren't really desert wallahs, or whatever the term is. Being in charge of the situation, I said, 'Look, give me a cigarette packet.' We had a packet of Benson & Hedges, which we threw next to the spider for scale. Finally the spider went crashing off – you could see the undergrowth parting as it made its way through.

We showed people the photo when we got back to London but all they could see was a blurry shape next to a little blobby gold thing so it never got the reaction we'd hoped. I think in many ways it was probably a mistake to use this story as our main Australian boast.

A rather nice man from the *Melody Maker* came over to do a feature on us while were still in Australia but, unfortunately, he caught us on a bad night, and we all started complaining about our time there. The subsequent cover of the *Melody Maker* was a picture of us on the beach in Australia, in our suits with our trousers rolled up, with the caption, 'Whinging Poms Go To Australia'. It appeared on the news stands in Australia while we were there, and the article inside described how miserable and horrid the trip was for us, which left us feeling guilty and meant some hurt looks were thrown in our direction. It was very unjust, too, because we couldn't have been treated better – we were given lovely food, friendliness from womenfolk, the lot.

Our next destination was Brisbane, Queensland, which was apparently run by a sort of despotic dictator, with rules and regulations for everything. We were playing at a hotel on the beach and, after the concert, we all decided to go swimming in the hotel pool. Suddenly, the manager came storming out, asking us what we were doing, there were clear notices stating that the pool closed at ten. When we started protesting that it wasn't that late, she said she was going to call the police. We said, 'What are you going to say to them? That some guests at your hotel are using the swimming pool – arrest them?', and she said, 'That's exactly the sort of attitude they don't like, and neither do I.'

The following day we marched to the beach in our swimsuits. On arriving we noticed there was a fence cutting across the beach down into the sea and on one side of it were thousands of mugs, all squashed together on the sand. The other side was luxuriously empty. So, naturally, we laid our towels on the empty beach and ran into the water. Within seconds a coastguard speedboat arrived and told us we were on the wrong side of the shark net and to get out of the water immediately. As he did so, Gilson mimed being dragged under by a shark, which the lifeguards didn't find at all clever or funny. We thought it was both. I regret this now, because somebody could be reading this and know somebody who was killed or maimed by a shark. I'm really sorry, because it's not funny; it just was at the time. Before the coastguards left they passed on one tip, which was to carry a pencil when you swam so that you could stab the shark in the only sensitive spot it has, its eye. One of us asked if that wouldn't make it even crosser, but no, we were assured that this would get rid of it. So maybe this book will end up saving the life of a reader who will sensibly carry a pencil with them the next time they go into the Australian seas.

'Foolish I Know'

The point had now arrived where I was going to have to make up my mind whether or not to leave the group in order to commit to my own music. Some of my friends were suggesting this wasn't the time to leave, in fact it would be madness, as Squeeze was clearly about to go through the roof. Our American tours were becoming more and more successful and everyone was trying to book us for the next one; the album was starting to happen; every time we did a show, there'd be a radio or TV interview. But I really felt that if I didn't break away now I'd never get round to it. I felt that, as time went on and Squeeze's success grew, it would be harder for me to leave. I would get complacent and become accustomed to a certain sort of lifestyle. Thus far I hadn't really had much of a lifestyle to get used to.

I loved the people in the band and they loved me; it was going to be a very hard thing to do, like leaving family. But you have to do your own thing in the end, artistically – that's what it's all about.

In some ways, it was probably too soon: I had a lot of music I was trying to develop on my own but I hadn't really yet discovered what my own sound was. On the other hand, if I were looking back and advising my 22-year-old self, I would still say, 'Good luck – if you're going to do something, put your hand up and have a go.' And although it wasn't to work out as I envisioned, the feeling that I just wanted to commit to my music was an authentic and valid one. And so, in 1980, I left Squeeze. I explained to each of them what I was doing and why. They were all very understanding and knew I had no wish to harm Squeeze but it was difficult, because we all felt that, together, we had that elusive thing that makes a group work. We had a divvy-up of everything, and I somehow ended up with the Mercedes van. I suppose everyone thinks they've ended up with the rotten deal after a break-up of any sort, so maybe the others were thinking, 'Lucky bastard – he got the van.' Squeeze then left Miles for Jake Riviera but Miles and I decided to stick together. Miles appreciated the fact that I'd stood by him and said he would see if he could make things happen for me. John Lay also stayed with me because he didn't really want to team up with Jake Riviera either. We decided he would be my manager, in partnership with Miles.

The first thing Miles suggested was that I play some shows. He told me he liked the songs I was doing but I needed to work on them a bit more. There were 'Lonesome Joe', 'Foolish I Know' and 'Pineapple Chunk', which I had written and liked, and another called 'Bumble Boogie', which got people excited. I could play them on the piano but I didn't have arrangements for them, partly because I was playing them on my own. This being the time of punk, the prospect of going out and playing solo shows with just a piano was quite daunting. Without a drummer or being able to pogo around the stage, I knew I would feel quite exposed.

Stewart Copeland was then living in Shepherd's Bush and had a little studio in his basement. He suggested I come along and do a couple of demos. All of them sounded pretty good, but I did feel I needed a group to go forward. I decided that, instead of having guitars like all other groups, I'd just have piano, bass, drums and sax. I didn't realize you could get people to do gigs here and there with you, which is what usually happens. I assumed, as with Squeeze, that you had to be in it together from the start, create your own world as a group. So I went out and formed this group, which I decided to call the Millionaires.

The first member of the Millionaires I recruited was this brilliant sax player called Mike Paice. I went to see him play with a band called Red Beans and Rice in the East End one night, told him I was starting a band and got his phone number. He is one of the most fantastic players; he'd play by ear alone, somewhat in the style of Junior Walker, and was always perfectly in tune with this very happy blues way of playing.

Mike was connected to the London rhythm and blues world,

and he told me about this extraordinary bass player he knew in Cardiff called Pino Palladino. He suggested we bring him to London for the day, which I then did. My songs were quite complicated, funny keys flitting about, but Pino was very enthusiastic when I played them to him and that made me like him straight away. And when he played he was absolutely unbelievable. We were all good musicians in Squeeze but Pino was in a different league. He must have been about twenty-two and he could play anything and add something to it. He had this style which I'd never heard before, a fretless bass style which later became incredibly famous and copied by many people. Nowadays, Pino is a top session player, sought after by everyone and currently playing with the Who. However, back then he was just a lad.

Having secured Pino for the Millionaires we drove to Wales to collect him and his belongings. He came from the most wonderful Welsh Italian family in Cardiff. They had a lovely restaurant and were part of what's known in Cardiff as the Taffia. After a delicious dinner at his family's restaurant, Pino took us to some clubs on the docks. These have all gone now but then it was like another world, the East End of London looked modern in comparison.

Back in London I had two property-developer friends, Paul and Helena, who had an empty property they kindly let us set up as a rehearsal room. By now there were four of us – myself, Mike, Martin Deegan on drums and, of course, Pino.

Being six foot six, Pino needed regular feeding. He was used to these beautiful Italian family feasts and we found that if he didn't have food at the appropriate time he would start getting twitchy. He is an angelic man, but he could have a row if he wanted to, and that wasn't pleasant to see. And, after all, having captured this rare and incredibly talented creature, it was our duty to take care of him properly. In the end, my mother used to make big dinners for us, and these kept Pino happy. I would make sure my mother had the meals ready for us by six thirty so that, after rehearsing all day, we could then break for dinner. It was quite a nice routine for that short period.

The record company came to see us at our rehearsal room and

we played them some songs. They took back some demos and, after Derek Green, who ran A&M, had heard some of them, he gave me a record deal and an advance. In spite of this very promising start, I found the money didn't last long after paying everyone in the band every week. At that time I used to see Chris and Glenn in the local pubs and hear tales of their next big tour of America, with Paul Carrack, my replacement. They were going from strength to strength and I was beginning to find it a struggle. There began to be the odd twinge of doubt in my mind: had I done the right thing?

Piano Solo

The Police were planning a show in a big top on Clapham Common at Christmas in 1980, and Miles suggested that I come on for twenty minutes in the middle and play the piano. When I arrived, since I was known as a bit of a bigmouth from my days ranting on stage with Squeeze, I was asked if I would introduce the first band, that of Rico Rodriguez, the legendary Jamaican trombonist – I did so with pleasure, little knowing that, years later, he would join my big band, which he has now been a part of for more than a decade.

Then I was told that there was another artist performing at the show who wanted me to do some backing for him. I agreed but wondered who it was. Walking in, I couldn't believe it – standing there, in a dinner jacket, with a fez, was Tommy Cooper. He said, 'Oh, hello, mate, you the pianist?', then, 'Do you know "The Sheik of Araby"?' I did, because I was a Fats Waller fan and Vic used to play it in the pub and had taught it to me. Tommy said, 'What I want you to do is to go out, play "Sheik of Araby", I come on, I look at you, I look at the crowd, and I get out a gun and I shoot you.' He added, 'You all right at dying?' I said that I was and the whole thing was agreed. I just couldn't believe what a fantastic way I was ending that year – shot on stage by Tommy Cooper. You meet some people who are really famous and it's quite exciting, but you meet someone like Tommy Cooper and you bathe in it. I just wanted to hang around him and bask in every moment of his conversation. He was incredibly funny – he had one of the funniest faces I've ever seen, that could express confusion and concern simultaneously, and he would use it all the time, in a charming way.

There was a huge crowd in this big top. The trouble was, Tommy Cooper was used to working in smaller clubs where everyone could see what he was doing. Here, the first four rows could see but, beyond that, everything was lost. Tommy looked at the audience, shrugged his shoulders and shot me. Everyone saw me fall down, but not his brilliant moves and expressions. He said, 'Oh, well,' produced a frying pan, threw a match into it and, as it caught light, lobbed it into the audience saying, 'That was just a flash in the pan . . .'

When the gig was over, I couldn't wait to rush home and tell Mary: 'You'll never guess what I've done – played with the Police, yeah, introduced Rico Rodriguez, yeah, but the really exciting part is, I have actually backed Tommy Cooper!'

It was a wonderful start to Christmas and, after having been away so much that year touring with Squeeze and rehearsing with the Millionaires, it was great to be home, and Mary and I were really pleased to be able to spend some time together. By this point, we were living together, sometimes staying in my flat above Dickie's, sometimes at her house, and that Christmas was particularly good. To paint a family picture for you, we invited some friends over to my parents' house and, after a few drinks, my dad suggested playing Pass the Matchbox on the Nose and, simultaneously, Pass the Orange under the Chin, in the opposite direction. Now this is a super game. To this day, playing Orange under the Chin is guaranteed to raise a laugh. So it was a very jolly Christmas, but then we all had to get back to work.

The Police were doing these big shows around the world, and Miles suggested that I go along and open at some of them. The first was in Fréjus in France, and this concert featured in a punk-rock documentary produced by Miles and Michael White called *Urgh – A Music War*.

A rather good moment is captured in this film: I go on stage at this big Roman amphitheatre, and it's clear nobody is sure what I'm going to do. I probably don't know either. Somebody chucks a bottle of beer at the stage and it hits the top of the piano and, without thinking, I say, 'Thanks very much – a drink for the pianist!' The French audience seemed to understand and warmed to me. U2 also did the show and, at the end of it, Bono, Sting and

I all performed together, which was also immortalized in the film. Both Bono and Sting were very encouraging about my decision to go out on my own. And, thankfully, A&M Records, France, seemed to have forgotten entirely about Gilson's sick-up experiment in La Coupole or hadn't quite associated me with it, as they were all very friendly.

Miles then arranged for me to open the Police's concert at Madison Square Gardens. For their show, the Police had a huge dressing room, literally packed with palm trees and a cornucopia of fruit, veg and champagne, great platters of food, iced beer – the lot. And my dressing room was exactly the same size as theirs but it had one tin of Coke and a beer. This amused John Lay and me; in fact, we took a picture of it.

But sitting in the empty dressing room, I began to feel quite nervous about going out into this vast stadium. If you're going out on stage with your mates, that's all right, it's a laugh, but the prospect of going out on your own is quite nerve-wracking. Trying to calm my nerves, John said, 'All you've got to do if it goes really badly wrong is faint, and I'll take you off. Just close your eyes and it will all be over.' That seemed a good idea to me, although I haven't actually ever seen anyone in the piano world resorting to this device.

Going out there, it was even harder than I'd imagined to keep my nerve because they'd left all the house lights on and I could see all the people in the audience. Usually it's dark and you can't see anyone. I opened with a joke John had suggested – 'Good evening, ladies and gentlemen, I'd like to thank Mr Madison for lending us his square gardens.' Surprisingly, this went down well and I started playing 'Mess with a Rich Man', still aware of all these people I could see. At one point I wondered what they were all looking at and then I remembered: it was me.

By the end the crowd was going wild for me and my piano. Encouraged that my support act had gone so well, I then did a few more. There was one on the West Coast at which A&M's representative, Bob Garcia, got a girl to come on just before my entrance with a big sign saying 'Ladies and gentlemen – Jools

Holland.' This didn't seem to help much but, then again, the show went all right and I think doing these big concerts toughened me up.

Millionaires in Caracas

After a few more shows with the Police I returned to London and the Millionaires went into action, doing gigs and trying to get some press coverage. We did shows with bands like Nine Below Zero, another at Dingwalls, which Sting came to see, and we played another with the Q-Tips, Paul Young's group.

John Lay had found two girl singers, Kim Lesley and Maz Roberts, to do backing vocals for the Millionaires, which added a whole other dimension again. Because we had no guitars, just piano, bass, drums and sax, we were producing an original sound, and Kim and Maz contributed to that with their wonderful backing vocals. Maz had an enchanting voice with which she ultimately beguiled Pino – they now have grown-up children together. Kim sounded like Aretha Franklin, and she still has an amazing voice. She is now a reverend in the Unitarian Church in New York. Looking back, I should have just got her to sing all the songs. Also, with the benefit of hindsight, it may have been a mistake to call them 'the Wealthy Tarts'. We thought it went well with the Millionaires, and it was supposed to imply their wealth of talent. But times were politically correct even then and, when we played our first gig with them at the Albany Empire in Deptford, the name made people uneasy. But the Wealthy Tarts boosted the whole thing and made it more fun. The musicians were already great, but the two girls really perked up the energy. Also, they had worked as backing singers for other people before so they seemed very experienced, more so than the rest of us, in a way. Pino was young, so he had just played in the tough clubs of Cardiff, and I'd only played with Squeeze, whereas Kim and Maz, although they were the same age as us or younger, were more like professional musicians. With them on board, things seemed to be looking up, and even more so when, in March, the Millionaires made the cover of *Melody Maker*.

Soon after this we went in to record some songs with a talented man called Pete Wingfield, who'd written 'Eighteen with a Bullet'. He did a great job with the tracks and we thought they sounded bang on. A couple of journalists heard them and loved them and suggested we release them as they were, but the record company wasn't happy with them and we decided to try Glynn Johns as producer instead. Glynn Johns was a very gifted man, he had engineered and produced some of the Beatles and Rolling Stones songs but, looking back, I don't think he was the right producer for us at that time. It's hard to figure out whether a recording process is working or not until you reach the end of it. In my view, the first Pete Wingfield recordings had captured some of the excitement generated at our live shows. The record that Glynn Johns produced was sonically perfect but didn't have the same immediacy as the songs we'd cut first with Pete Wingfield. This is quite a common phenomenon in music, known as demo-itis: the first demo tape has a spark about it you can't seem to recapture when you go in to make a 'proper record'.

At one point during the recording Glynn suggested using Ted Astley for the string arrangements, which had really pleased me. He had written the music for *The Saint* and many other classic British film scores and I loved his work. However, it was then decided that there wasn't enough money left in the budget for this. Soon after this Ted Astley died, so I lost this one chance to work with him – another regret.

At around this time I found this to be true – lots of things were not working out. Just before I left Squeeze, everything was beginning to fall into place and, to a certain extent, it had been like that from the beginning, but with the Millionaires it was rather the reverse.

The record, *Jools Holland and His Millionaires*, was released to all-right reviews, and it sold OK, but things weren't really happening for it or for us yet. Miles and John were both telling me that the record advance was going to run out soon and I wouldn't be able to pay the band much longer. So, as well as shows with the band, I would also go off and do odd shows on my own in order to earn extra money. Once you've got people on the payroll in a band, it's quite hard to keep up unless you're a tremendous success.

In April, we all went off to America to start touring. We did some shows supporting Joan Jett and some as a double bill with XTC. In one venue, the Ink Spots, this great classic group, were supporting us. We all felt we should have been supporting them. We played in one town called Coxsackie, taking a Sunday off there to have a nice traditional lunch, writing postcards featuring the name of the town, which amused us in rather a babyish way.

Then Ian Copeland told us he'd booked us into a show in South America with XTC. Unfortunately, Kim and Maz had come out to America with the wrong visas and had had to pretend that they were out there as our girlfriends, so they were unable to come on with us. But the rest of us flew to Venezuela, which was a whole new world to explore. When we arrived, it was pouring with rain, which was good news for Mike Paice, since the floods meant that all these strange creatures and insects appeared out of the drains. Mike is a nature expert and has since written the definitive book on the wildlife of the River Thames, and this gave him the opportunity to run and catch these huge beetles and insects while us ninnies were running and hiding behind the giant Pino.

The crowd in Caracas loved our music but there was a terrifying atmosphere in the hall. Instead of the usual few security men at the front urging the crowd back if it became overenthusiastic, they had these men with machetes, chopping at the audience. At the back of the hall, someone had set light to a huge bonfire and some others had a blanket in which people were being tossed twenty feet into the air. It was the maddest, happiest thing I've ever seen.

We all got on well with XTC but they were always arguing with one another. Their manager was particularly grumpy and kept making a point of telling them they weren't there to waste time and lark about sightseeing, they were there to do a job of work. Their record company, Virgin, had sent representatives down to help them do the gig and to show them around. However, what with the band members arguing and the grumpy manager ordering them not to enjoy themselves, after their shows had finished, XTC ended up catching the next plane back to Swindon.

We stayed on in Caracas, and Al Clark from Virgin Records took us out on his expense account. He didn't have to do it but he was stuck there and had the money to take XTC out for three days so, as they had gone home, he just took us instead. We went to incredible restaurants on the tops of the mountains, and to a fantastic nightclub. When I got back, I wrote to Al Clark to thank him, he had been so generous and charming. I went to the unusual trouble of constructing the letter like a blackmail note in a film, using cut-out newspaper words to write, 'Cheers – it won't be forgotten.' About a year later I started worrying that he might have thought it was a horrible threat instead of the thank-you I had intended. I hope one of the ways I've improved with the years is that I am clearer now about what I mean to convey than I was in my twenties. This book will be the test of that.

Mouthy in Montserrat

At this time there was an instance of Miles having an unwitting effect on my future. He had hired a director called Derek Burbridge to make a live film of the Police playing in a club in LA. I was going to be in the film anyway, as I was opening for them, but Miles suggested that I kick the film off and introduce them. I was hesitant; they were my friends and had always been supportive and loyal. I didn't want to let them down but I had no idea what I would say. Miles, however, reminded me of the side of me that used to get everything going on stage with Squeeze – boasting, making up huge lies, getting everybody to hold hands, kiss, whatever I felt like at the time. He told me that it was unusual and great, that I was a character. The word 'character' gave me pause; in the dog-racing world, if your dog's known as a character, it means he doesn't want to breed with other dogs. However, Miles persuaded me that it would be a great favour to him so I agreed to do it. I liked Derek Burbridge, and I find that when I get on with people and I enjoy working with them, what we make together is usually good. You've got to enjoy or be stimulated by the process in order to achieve something worthwhile. As a result, the film went quite well.

In July of that year Miles asked me to go back to LA to help with another film he was making, on his LA-based record company, IRS. Although I would be leaving the Millionaires at home kicking their heels at least it would mean that I could pay them, which had become an increasingly hard task. And, being Miles's artists, the Millionaires would be in the film eventually anyway. The IRS film included other artists too, such as the Cramps, REM, Wall of Voodoo and the Dead Kennedys. When I told my grandmother I was going off to film in Hollywood, her face lit up – I could see she was imagining me working with

Lauren Bacall or some other Hollywood legend, not with the Dead Kennedys singing their famous song 'Too Drunk to Fuck'. But there were some super people there and, although I felt I didn't really know what I was doing when talking to them, Miles thought I had a talent for it and told me that maybe I should do something on television. I couldn't spot it myself and, anyway, I wasn't interested in pursuing this line.

However, soon after this film, the BBC hired Derek Burbridge to direct a documentary on the Police, who were making their next record in Montserrat. They told Miles which of their interviewers would present the film and what line of questioning they would follow, but Miles told them that their suggestions sounded very boring. Instead he insisted that I should do the interviewing for the film, on the strength of these films I'd already made with him.

It was true that the BBC was quite earnest in those days and hadn't quite caught the punk spirit of rock and roll but I still felt a bit nervous at the prospect, and they probably did too. However, Miles told me I had no choice in the matter, and neither did the BBC, since he had told them they weren't getting the programme unless I did the interviewing.

So, we flew out to Montserrat, which is an enchanting tiny tropical island. Sir George Martin had built a state-of-the-art recording studio there but every piece of recording equipment had to have four duplicates, because if anything went wrong out there, that was it. Montserrat had one minuscule jail but nobody was in it or ever had been. John Lay and I were given Mini Mokes and drove off to explore in them, stopping off at a little bar perched on the side of the hill in which there were some locals playing dominoes. It was literally a ten-foot-square shed with a window looking out over the sea and a huge tortoise shell hanging on the wall. We asked for two beers. The proprietor of the shed explained that, as we were not members of this particular club, he wasn't allowed to serve us. However, for the consideration of $60, he could.

It was one of the most beautiful places I'd ever been to – the valleys, the flowers made it a paradise. When characters in *Star Trek* beam down to somewhere beautiful and it's a bit too beautiful and you know that one of them will get gassed by a horrid flower . . . that's what it was like.

When we arrived the Police were busy mixing 'Every Little Thing She Does is Magic' and couldn't talk to us for another week, so Derek Burbridge suggested we film bits of the introduction around the island in the meantime. We spent a week filming little jokes or visual gags, quite casually, but the end result was that the first four minutes of the film looked fantastic. It moved really quickly but it did take a week to do. The rest of the film took one day.

The broadcast was scheduled for Christmas, still a few months away, so I just forgot about it really and moved along. Nearer Christmas, the Millionaires supported the Police at Wembley. By then, Sting had seen the finished film, which I hadn't, and he kept saying that I had done something really different in it. I said with some embarrassment that I seemed to remember having been a bit cocky with it, a bit of a cheeky chappie, but Sting repeated, 'Well, I've seen it and I think you've got a new career ahead of you. I really do. A new career.' I didn't realize then that, in some ways, he was right – I would have.

Diminuendo

That Christmas Mary and I had a party at my flat at Dickie Dobson's to which Dickie and his wife, Maureen, came, and Mark Smith, who was back from his job at Radio Caroline, his girlfriend, Mary Lou, my friend Phil from Liverpool and Miles Copeland, which was rather sweet. It was a really jolly Christmas. I've got a photograph of it still and when I look at it I remember it as an old-fashioned Christmas, all of us round the piano having a laugh.

Afterwards, it was back to work as one part of having a group is that you have to write music for it constantly. Knowing this, Miles, with his usual gift of getting hold of equipment, managed to get me a four-track tape recorder out of some deal. This was really going to change things but, at first, it was no help to me because I hadn't a clue how it worked. I rang Glenn and asked him if he had any advice on how I could learn to operate it, and he did, some very good advice: read the instruction manual.

Once I'd done that, I found the tape recorder a very rich source of inspiration. I now experimented with all sorts of different bits of music and started doing my own harmonies and playing the drums. I wrote all these new songs in my own flat. One of them was 'Heartbreaking World', which Squeeze would later record.

I was quite happy writing songs in Dickie Dobson's flat and pottering around with my four-track. The Millionaires were still doing lots of shows but it was getting to be a bit like hard work. Certainly it was becoming more and more difficult to pay them all. Miles and I were both trying to think of ways to go forward; some movement was badly needed. However, at this very time, Pino suddenly announced he was going to have to leave the Millionaires, as he'd been offered a job with Gary Numan. Clearly, Gary Numan, who had records in the charts, was going to pay him a lot more money than I could. So, of course I just wished him good luck, as is the way with musicians, but I missed him. It wasn't so much Pino leaving that dismayed me, more that Gary Numan should seem a more exciting option than the Millionaires. I began to think of it as a realistic evaluation of our position. Martin and Mike were equally disheartened. We all saw it as an indication that nothing was as promising as it should have been, people wanting to leave the band rather than join it. We also knew it was going to be hard to find a bass player to match Pino and, since the band consisted of bass, drums and piano, it was especially important to find a good one.

Then Pino recommended a man called Taif, a small Welshman with ginger hair and a perky, smiling face. Being the opposite of Pino in size, he cost less to feed, which was a helpful start. Taif was a decent bloke and a talented bass player but I think he found it hard to keep his mind on the ball somehow. He was one of those people who could be described as hyperactive. When we first met him we asked him to tell us a bit about himself and he told us he had once spent a week in jail, following a pop festival. Somebody had put something in his drink there and, seeing a red-and-white-striped police car, he had mistaken it for a giant Raspberry Ripple ice-cream and had tried to eat it. He'd been taken off in a straitjacket by the police and spent a week in the cells. We were impressed by this story and all had a good laugh over it but, in hindsight, perhaps we should have listened a bit more carefully so as to have more of a clue as to what it was going to be like with him on board.

The plan was for us to do a big double-bill tour with XTC in America. Their record company liked us and, in combination, we could play sizeable places there. Our record company had got behind us and had arranged some press, TV and various promotions before we left England. Feeling in good spirits, we did a TV show in Manchester and were shown round the *Coronation Street* set. While there, we managed to place our record sleeve in the front of the Street's corner shop. When the programme aired, there it was, which was very exciting for me.

After a few days I flew to Los Angeles. The flight was very turbulent and there was an enormously fat man next to me who insisted on eating his soup even though it was spilling all over his huge beard. On my other side there was a young gay waiter who was going to Los Angeles to audition for an American version of *Fawlty Towers*. I thought being surrounded by these madmen might be a bit of a portent. Anyway, I got to Los Angeles and then the rest of the band arrived – they were all very excited to be there. We stayed in the Tropicana Hotel, which is a rock and roll landmark, the place where Sam Cooke was horribly shot. As it didn't have its own bar, from there we'd amble over to the little 1950s bar round the corner called Rudy's, which was like something out of *The Twilight Zone*. It was empty apart from a friendly Hispanic barman, a small man with a big black moustache and black hair, a medallion and a Fred Perry-type shirt.

On 14 April we were booked to play at the Palladium with XTC, our first big show. A few days before it Andy Partridge from the group came to me and moaned that he was bored with music; he'd been there, done it all, and there was nothing new in it for him. I found this strange, since the more you look at music, the more you find, and assumed he was just talking daft. But, afterwards, it did occur to me that, with the members of the group always arguing with each other and the bullying manager telling them that they had a job of work to do, his state of mind might be affected. In fact, I thought that he might be a little depressed and this was confirmed when, just before they were about to go on stage at the Palladium on the night, he suddenly announced that he couldn't do the show, or the tour, and was pulling out.

This left everyone and everything in confusion. The manager was beside himself but the drummer, who was a nice fellow, came to the dressing room and said he was sorry, he knew that this had left us in the lurch. He said that he was going to Australia to get married and that he and his fiancée were having a baby. So we all congratulated him and I gave him a huge cigar which Bob Garcia had earlier given me. My band and I then went to Rudy's bar to discuss the situation, and to get drunk. I was the band leader and

I had no idea what we could do. We had come all this way for a two-month tour, and the shows and publicity had been booked in each place. It was our one chance to launch in America and it looked like this chance had gone.

I decided to ring Miles to see what could be done. Together, we concluded that returning to England would be expensive and an outright disaster. The other option was to arrange some extra shows in between those in Los Angeles and New York, which had been booked and still remained. I knew that the last-minute shows we'd be able to get would be in some very strange little places and we'd have to drive miles to get to them and we would be spending loads more money from the advance, which was already dwindling fast. With the XTC tour, we had had a guaranteed amount which would have covered our costs, but now we were stuck. The Millionaires were a relatively small group but we would still have to book eight people each night into a hotel and the costs would soon mount up if we were covering them ourselves. However, given that going home would be even more disastrous, we decided we would stay and try to make it work.

Low Notes

The first extra show was in San Francisco. We drove quite a long way to get there and, instead of sharing a truck with XTC, as had been arranged, we now had to transport all the equipment ourselves. Then, because the gig had only been booked the day before, there was hardly anyone in the audience. This was the pattern on this particular tour, and it all began to seem a bit depressing. The pianos at the venues were often terrible too, which didn't help matters. I'd left Squeeze in order to be able to play my music, and to have to use all these horrible pianos was additionally dispiriting.

We would drive 530 miles to a bar in Oregon just to play in a hall to nice people who didn't even know who we were. Then we'd get up at seven o'clock the next morning and drive 600 miles to the next venue, all packed together in a small worn-out van Miles had lent us, with no air conditioning. To add to this, the nature-loving Mike Paice had found a snake somewhere and was keeping it in a jar in the van, which was causing some friction, especially with the girls.

Then Taif, who was a bit of a handful anyway, would insist that we stop from time to time at roadhouses so he could have a run around – understandable, since he was a very energetic sort of person. While we ate lunch, we would hear this *bompetybomp* and see him running past the window and then, two minutes later, he'd come by again. Eventually, after forty laps, he'd come in all out of breath, by which time we'd have finished our food and want to go. At one place, after his run, he took his time to order, which we found very annoying. At last he said, 'Oh, I think I might have a mushroom omelette.' The waitress said, 'OK', and then he said, 'What's in a mushroom omelette?' For some reason that simple question was the final straw and, without saying anything to one another, we all suddenly leapt on him and attacked him. It started off as a sort of joke but then it turned into a proper scuffle, and all the other customers started looking round. I suddenly wondered what on earth we were doing. It's well known that if you keep beasts cooped up together in unnatural conditions they start to get on one another's nerves and we had certainly reached that stage. Anyway, his mushroom omelette arrived (which had mushrooms in it, if anybody reading this isn't sure), and we sat outside getting our breath back while Taif devoured it.

We all felt that things were going from bad to worse. What would happen next? Miles's van broke down somewhere and then our next van got a puncture. Not only were all these little things contributing to the slightly depressed atmosphere but we were also drinking ever such a lot. We'd stay out drinking every night after we'd played and wake up with awful hangovers, which made everybody snappy with one another and everything more irritating than it should have been. We had rented a van from a company called Ryder, and the slogan on the back of it was 'Move it yourself with Ryder.' Perfectly harmless but, after weeks of looking at this slogan across hundreds of miles, 'Move it yourself with Ryder' was annoying us all. On top of that, the venues that we were playing at were becoming smaller and smaller, and none of the audiences had a clue who we were. The agent had done the best he could but shows are usually booked months in advance – booking at the last minute is almost always a disaster. We went to one place in Minneapolis, Duffy's, and there was a picture of me there playing with Squeeze from when Squeeze first toured. I couldn't help thinking then that Squeeze had moved on and we hadn't gone anywhere. I was trying to make my own music but, half the time, I didn't even have a piano. Instead of thinking about the music I was spending half my time worrying.

Anyway, back in Los Angeles we were met by the record company. We did this show there and it just wasn't quite working. We were all exhausted and rather depressed, and I could see the record-company representatives weren't knocked off their feet by it. I don't think the others realized quite what was going on but it wasn't a good moment for me. I knew that, without a record company behind you, things get really tough.

We all went back to Rudy's that night and we went totally mad there. The barman with the little moustache got out some pot and started smoking it, offering it to us because we were the only customers in that night. Then he started giving us tequila bangers and everyone started shouting. I remember sitting there in this *Twilight Zone* bar looking at all these people going completely mental, including me, thinking we still had another month to go.

When you're touring with a group, you've got to project an excitement about the music and atmosphere on stage and feel it yourself too. Because I was leading the band, I knew it was my responsibility not only to feel that way but to infect the other musicians with that excitement. In this instance, it was very hard. Sometimes you can deceive other people but you can't deceive yourself. You are the one person who can make a fool of yourself – and that was what was happening here to some extent. Half of me was telling myself, 'Oh, this is going to be fine. This is great,' but the other half knew that it was all really desolate.

We did do the odd show that was pretty good – there was one in Chicago where I improvised and played some boogie numbers, which went down very well. Everyone was lifted by this show, and I was especially pleased that it took place in Chicago, the home of some of my heroes – Albert Ammons, Pete Johnson, Jimmy Yancey, Lionel Hampton and Lonnie Johnson. But that was just one show and, on the whole, rather than inching up I felt we were actually spiralling downhill fast.

Then we got to Niagara Falls, and Martin Deegan bought a life-sized bust of Elvis, which we admired – until we found ourselves squashed in the van with it, along with the snake in the jar. Then, after all the care we took with it, carrying it around for the last month of the tour, the baggage-handlers at Heathrow Airport broke it.

At one point, Maz became ill, probably through nerves, and we were all still drinking too much. You have to be careful on tour not to overdo it. There's no sort of order to the days, you're always on the move. At one point I felt so desperate I just started swimming in the hotel pool and didn't stop until I'd done thirty lengths – practically the width of the Thames at Cliffe. Nothing in our situation had changed when I got out but at least I had released some of my energy after having been so cooped up in a van for so long.

At the end of that tour we played in the Bottom Line club and Joe Jackson came to see us. The first show was great but the second wasn't so good. Then we did an open-air show with Graham Parker, which went really well, a rare highlight in that whole dismal period.

One of the worst things that happened was that, during the tour, my grandfather, George, with whom I'd lived for so long, became ill and died. I'd always felt very close to him so this news made me very sad indeed. Not being able to be with him when it happened only added to my feelings of despondency.

On my return to England, it was clear that his death had brought on rapid dementia in my grandmother; the shock had made her lose her mind, which was tragic to see. She hadn't been hospitalized at that point but she was forgetting all sorts of things. This was very much my home as well as my mother's, and it felt like it was disintegrating.

So, I felt I was in a pretty bad place. The tour had been a disaster and the record had only sold about twenty thousand copies – it just wasn't happening. I had no money and couldn't really afford to keep the band going. I didn't know what to do. I spent a lot of time recording on my four-track, writing songs and thinking about what I could do. The Millionaires were doing one or two shows – we did what we could to earn money, as I'd had to stop paying everybody by the week. I was writing, but nothing much else was going on.

At some point during this time I met Kirsty MacColl for the first time. She was talking about songs and I played her a country-style one I'd written with Chris called 'Fingers and Thumbs', which she loved. She came up to my flat and sang it there on my little four-track, and I played her some of my demos. She had a deal with RCA to do five tracks and, out of the blue, she suggested I produce them. We had a week to do it, so we went up to Regent's Park Recording Company and started recording. For one of them, 'Shutting the Door', she wanted a trombone, so she asked Rico Rodriguez to come along. This was the first time I had seen Rico since the Police and Tommy Cooper show, and I was pleased to get to know him better. This was really the beginning of our working relationship.

Kirsty was a great friend and very entertaining and a brilliant person, and her death was a terrible tragedy. She was run over by a jet ski in South America and her family started a campaign to prosecute those responsible. I was pleased that I was able to contribute to the fund by using 'Shutting the Door' on my Friends album in 2002. Kirsty, without doubt, would have been one of the people on the album.

The original tracks were good and we liked them a lot, but the record company didn't and they didn't sign Kirsty – yet another project that didn't work out at this period.

Camera Test

Music is wonderful and very rewarding, but the music industry is pretty cruel and horrible. Sadly, the last thing it's about is nurturing talent or encouraging people's artistic ability in a loving way. People really have to do that for themselves. When a record label wants to drop you, they don't write you a letter cutting you off like the gas company does, but that's what it feels like. Instead, they let the manager know that they don't want to do another record – and that's what happened to the Millionaires with A&M. It was disappointing but we all already had the sense that it might happen. However, just before we parted company for good, I had one last call from A&M's TV promotions department: some television producers who had seen the Montserrat film wanted me to come up to Newcastle to do a camera test for a new television programme. The promotions man I spoke to didn't seem to think the offer amounted to much; in his opinion, it was hardly worth my while going all that way to do the test.

When I got the call, I was in my flat, wondering what I was going to do, knowing things weren't looking good. I didn't have any money and, now that the Kirsty MacColl record had failed to be taken up, people weren't queuing up for me to produce them. And, no other record company was interested in signing up the Millionaires. However, my view was that, since I had left the very successful Squeeze in order to make my own music, I surely had very little interest in trying for a television programme which, if I was accepted for it, would take up all my time and prevent me once again from making my own music. I put this to Miles, thinking he would agree with me, but all he said was that he thought the camera test might be fun and that he would negotiate a modest fee for it, which made it seem more attractive.

When I arrived at King's Cross I was delighted to find Paula there – I had no idea she had been asked up to try out for co-host. Immediately, it began to seem a more enjoyable prospect. On the way up to Newcastle we discussed what fee we'd require should we decide to do it – £10 million was our starting price but we decided to settle for five hundred quid. She didn't really want to spend the time going to Newcastle every week – she and Bob were getting quite serious, and she was writing a book as well as her column in *Smash Hits* every week. I was also in two minds, but we agreed it might be a laugh. We both assumed it was going to be one of those quiet shows that appears in the afternoon without causing much of a stir and that it wouldn't take long to record.

After arriving in Newcastle we went to the old Tyne Tees building and were taken to a studio and told that the producers wanted to see how we reacted with young people. Paula and I were only in our early twenties so could have been considered young people too, but neither of us thought of ourselves in that way. There were some students there, much the same age as us, who did seem like 'young people'. The BBC had a show at the time, *The Oxford Roadshow*, in which student types were asked their opinions on political and cultural issues of the day, so we understood the sort of thing the producers were after, but we had absolutely no interest in young people or their views. Paula asked one of the young people in the Tyne Tees studio what he did and, when he said he was a student, she told him he was a work-shy yob and he should get a job – what was the matter with him? He was almost in tears. The rest of the young people with whom we were meant to be blending in were insulted in similar fashion.

We were told to imagine we were introducing our ideal guests for the show. Since my ideal guests would have been John Lennon and Bessie Smith, in rather tasteless fashion, I mimed dragging their corpses on stage. The crew then held up notices with the announcements we were meant to make – but we failed in this too. I bumped into Paula at one point and she fell off her chair because she was laughing so much at our vulgar jokes, which were embarrassing the crew, who were quite a sensitive lot. We didn't seem to be able to manage anything; in the middle of one sequence, they just held up their hands and said, 'Thank you very much.'

On the train back John Lay, who had been in the control room, let us know that it hadn't gone that well. In our big-headed way, we thought it had. Anyway, we really had no interest in talking to young people sitting on beanbags or introducing music.

There was a tape of this camera test and Andrea Wonfor, the producer and creator of the show, told me afterwards that it was held up as an example of the absolute worst type of television you could possibly have. She watched it with some of her team and one of them said, 'This is the worst presentation I've ever seen in all my years with television,' and Andrea said, 'I think you're right, but I can't stop watching it. I've got to see it again. It's the most compelling thing I've ever seen. They're absolutely hopeless.'

When word eventually got back that they would like us to be the presenters, we thought that our initial impression had been correct – we'd obviously done incredibly well at the test. Our heads swelled so much at our cleverness we couldn't get through the door. We had no idea we were being booked just because we were so useless.

It was one of Andrea Wonfer's many gifts as producer that she identified that people would love to watch a programme that teetered on the edge of disaster, one of the consequences of having Paula and myself as hosts. Nowadays, television is like that all the time, with these endless reality shows but, looking back, I like to think there was something endearing about our unslick approach. We were being real in that we weren't just being nice to people we didn't want to be nice to and there was nothing earnest in our views of television or young people.

The other thing, of course, was that I knew about music. I might not have read all the music papers but I knew about it. And, as Paula said to me, 'You like all the old dead blues people and I like the sexy young boys. You've got the cred, and I've got the sex. So, between us, we've got it covered.' That was her view and I think there was something in it.

Anyway, once I had the official offer from the producers, I had to decide whether I really wanted to do this programme — *The Tube* — or not. Eventually, in spite of my reservations and after much discussion with Paula, we each decided to do it if the other would. Frankly, I needed the money.

Tyneside Times

The Tube turned out to be very important for a lot of reasons. In my story it was important as it made me a household name but, in a wider sense, it reinvented the way popular music was perceived and shown on television and that legacy remains.

Andrea Wonfer's first idea and the most important one was to have a programme that would be aired at half-past five on a Friday evening so the weekend would start at the moment of the *Tube*'s opening music, created by one of the world's greatest guitarists of all time, Jeff Beck. The programme was going to be live and have elements of *Ready Steady Go!* which was being remembered as a groovier show than *Top of the Pops*, probably due in part to nostalgia, since it was no longer on air. Andrea's choice of Paula and me as presenters was the other necessary if chaotic element in the mix. Rather like a good group, *The Tube* needed all its various elements to work.

However, just before the first programme was due to be filmed and simultaneously aired, Paula announced she was pregnant, which was a huge shock for those in charge. One of the reasons they'd wanted Paula as a presenter was that she was glamorous, Emma Peel to my John Steed, as it were. They wanted a sex bomb rather than a mum, forgetting that the two go hand in hand. But when they expressed their doubts to Andrea, she said immediately, 'She's a woman. Of course she can be pregnant. If she's happy with it, then we are too.' Exactly the correct response. Andrea was often the voice of reason among a lot of people who weren't thinking straight.

It was Andrea, along with the equally visionary Malcolm Gerrie, who had taken the idea of this pop programme to Jeremy Isaacs, the head of the new and as yet unseen Channel Four. He too had brilliant foresight and agreed to commission it. *Countdown* was to be Channel Four's first programme on air, *The Tube* its second.

As the big night drew nearer, I began to think it might be quite fun to do. The fact that it was to be filmed live might have daunted some presenters but was good as far as I was concerned since it made it more like a gig and therefore something I was used to. I knew I was happy to show off in front of the camera, as I'd already been on all the existing pop music programmes, including *The Old Grey Whistle Test* on BBC2. This was a good show but had a far more serious-minded ethos than that of *The Tube* and was on very late at night. When each song finished there wasn't even the sound of two hands clapping, just total silence and the bloke saying, 'Well, that was very nice.' When Squeeze appeared on the show, with a view to livening it up I had announced, 'We're sorry to interrupt this show but we're trying to contact the owner of the blue Ford Cortina in the car park, registration PEN 15,' but this little joke had met with absolute silence in the studio, and at home with the midnight viewers too, probably.

Music programmes, even now, are pushed into late-night slots. That's why *The Tube* was particularly innovative; at that time in the afternoon, it could touch the senses when they were still alert. Music does this far more than news or current affairs and, for that reason, I think music programmes should be on first thing in the morning. Still, five-thirty in the afternoon was a good start.

The Tube's first show was broadcast on 5 November 1982. The Jam were on, giving their now legendary farewell performance. This was advertised as a 'teatime exclusive', which it certainly was. That's how Andrea Wonfor and Jeremy Isaacs had been visionary: they had seen that music, when dealt with properly, could be included as part of mainstream television.

Although not everyone could receive Channel Four initially, *The Tube* did immediately have a huge effect on those who did see it. From the write-ups in the papers after the first show it was clear that something was happening. Some of the papers liked it, some didn't take so much to the disorderly style, but everyone was writing about it. The producers would have been quite happy for the more conservative elements of the press to take against it but, in fact, none of them really had.

One of the reasons people loved it was because it was real and spontaneous, just like the music. It was a music programme which was being presented by people who were part of the music world, so it seemed to be coming from the inside out. And that ensured it was a shambles, because the inside of anything is always a shambles. Only the façade of anything is controlled and, here, the façade had been lifted.

I only understood how differently *The Tube* was made when I came to make other television programmes. I hadn't really realized how much of a controlled team effort television usually is and, had it not been for Andrea Wonfer allowing Paula and me a completely free rein with our links and our presenting, I couldn't have stuck with it. I would have found the restrictions of normal television work too frustrating.

The Montserrat film, my only other experience of making a television programme at that point, had also been improvised. It wasn't the usual practice for presenters to be lippy in those days; they were rather sincere and earnest. However, I'd gone for the former style. When Andy Summers started to play something as an example, I'd pulled his lead out and said, 'Let's leave that to James Brown, eh?' Doubly rude, since I'd asked him about that particular style of playing in the first place. Now, this incident may have been one of the reasons Andrea asked me to audition for *The Tube*, but I don't want this book to be a celebration of rudeness. The one regret I have about my television career is that perhaps I did inadvertently open the floodgates for this brand-new style of television in which people are encouraged to be rude to one another. And, if this is the case, I'd like to use this book to apologize to the British nation. And for that matter, to Andy Summers.

Noda Taxis

Although the first show made an impact, *The Tube's* reputation had to build slowly, week by week. Television programmes are like records or concerts: you can't rely on doing just one fantastically and then sit back and bask in the admiration, you have to carry on and do lots more, and not all of them will be as good. Anybody under the illusion that one great success will do the trick has missed the point.

Paula and I got into a routine. We would meet under the big clock at King's Cross station on a Thursday morning to take the ten o'clock train up to Newcastle. I've loved King's Cross station ever since I first saw it in *The Ladykillers*. To this day I think of it as rather a romantic place, especially at that time of the morning. Then, it was much seedier, with many of the creatures of the night still hanging around – not that it's much more salubrious now, but one thing that has changed for the worse is that they've taken out the lovely clacking signs informing passengers of the stops on their journey and replaced them with digital ones. There are some great improvements to the quality of our lives in the modern world – I know somebody who had a successful cataract operation the other week which took twenty minutes, and the Channel Tunnel and mobile phones are really great – but these digital signs are a step down. I don't know why they got rid of the old ones, because the stations and towns have remained the same. The train's been doing that route for almost a hundred years; that's what's good about it.

After we'd met Paula would go and buy herself some magazines for the journey and sometimes she would kindly buy me some nudey glamour magazines at the same time. She knew I wasn't going to try and chat her up, because we were friends; she was one of my best female platonic friends. But being impeccably behaved, I assume she would buy me these just to give me an outlet should the need arise. I always accepted them politely; I thought it would be rude to do otherwise.

We would then travel up on the train together. I used to love the journey, having breakfast and passing through Cambridgeshire and Peterborough, and then on to Lincolnshire. I found this countryside rather romantic and used to say, 'Shall I just pull the communication cord so we can jump off the train and run across the fields and see where we end up?' Paula would answer, 'No, because we'd just end up at some really horrible fucking pub in the middle of nowhere that you'd like and I'd hate.' So we never did.

Then, arriving at Newcastle station would be like arriving in a 1950s film; there'd be porters with uniforms and trolleys, properly dressed gents on their way down to London for the day, some nurses, people from the armed forces, the odd beggar. It was like a traditional railway station fair, and you really knew you'd arrived in a different place. Newcastle seemed a very distant place in 1982; it had the distinctive feel of an old-fashioned city unlike any other. It still has that feel, but at that time there were great swathes of it untouched by the modern world.

I used to like exploring the pubs in the West End and sometimes tried to persuade Paula to come with me but, since she disliked both pubs and late nights, that never worked. Someone who did often accompany me, though, was Andrea's husband, Geoff Wonfer, another member of the team, who would direct film reports for *The Tube* from all over the world. He introduced me to one pub called the Rose and Crown, which I particularly liked. It was over the road from the studio and we usually went there after the show with a variety of guests. The landlord was called Jimmy. He must have been about sixty at the time, had grey hair and glasses and looked like he might have been an informer in an episode of *The Sweeney*, but he was very kind, as was his wife. He was quite stern, with a fantastic deadpan Geordie delivery. He would look after people but he would chuck everybody out bang on eleven o'clock. It didn't matter who they were – David Bowie, Miles Davis – they all had to be out by eleven o'clock sharp. One

New Year's Eve we did a special *Tube* show and, after it, we carried the piano from Tyne Tees into the Rose and Crown. I played and we all had a bit of a knees-up. But at half-past twelve Jimmy said, 'That's it, we're closing now,' and in spite of our pleading, he stood at the door waiting for everyone to leave. As they went through the door, he looked each person in the eye and said very fast in a completely flat monotone Geordie voice, 'All-the-best-to-you-and-yourn-for-the-coming-twelve-month,' and shook their hand. There was nothing groovy about Jimmy or his pub. He didn't want to be your friend; he was the landlord of the pub and that was it. That was why we liked him.

Once Paula and I got to the Tyne Tees building, we'd go into a script and planning meeting where there would be Avril McRory, Paul Corley, Malcolm Gerrie, Chris Cowie and Gavin Taylor, the director. Gavin, who nowadays directs the Montreux Jazz Festival, was lovely, somewhat like an airline pilot. He had bought a brand-new Ford Granada in 1973 and went on a caravan holiday to France once a year, so it had only done six thousand miles. He has that powder-blue car in his garage to this day. When she joined the show, Muriel Gray would grill him for hours on why he liked caravanning but he could never bring himself to discuss his holidays with us. He wore a perfectly cut blazer, and a blue shirt and slacks, was impeccably mannered and very respectable.

Back then there was a whole other element to Tyne Tees programming in that it had a most charming 1960s feel. They would do programmes about farming and other traditional subjects but, once *The Tube* got going, they didn't do much else but that. They were lovely people and there were a lot of what I would describe as middle-aged ladies, probably just my age now really, who helped out.

Paula and I were particularly fond of Avril McRory. She had a good mix of professionalism and kindness that we appreciated. At one of the early meetings, Paula asked Avril how she was, as you do, and she answered, 'Well, actually, my daughter won't tidy her room and my husband won't tidy the garage. I can't bear the house being in a state. If it's going to go on like this I won't be able to stand living there.' Instead of talking about the show we wanted to hear more, so we chatted a bit more about it, and the following week we asked how it was going. Avril said, 'Well, I've told my daughter she's got to tidy her room and my husband that he's got to tidy the garage or I'm leaving.' We thought that was a bit heavy, so we had a whole session on what she should or shouldn't do. One of her arguments was, 'No, I feel I must give them an ultimatum, because otherwise they just ignore me. What's the point of me being in the house if they don't listen to what I say?'

The other executives were trying to steer the conversation back to the show but Paula persisted: 'What are you going to do?' 'Well,' answered Avril, 'this weekend I'm going to say to them, "Right, that's it. Tidy your room. Tidy the garage. I'm going to the car and I'm staying there until it's done."'

At the next production meeting we asked what had happened after this ultimatum, ignoring the impatient looks all around, and Avril said, 'I went to the car and locked myself in, until about midnight. It was very cold but I had a blanket. My daughter came out. She knocked on the window' – Avril was almost cracking with emotion at this point. It was like being on a psychiatrist's couch but with the whole team there and awful bully Yates trying to wheedle all the details out – 'she knocked on the window and I wound it down.'

'And had she tidied her room?'

'No. She just said, "Dad and I are a bit worried about you so here's a Thermos of tea."' Paula thought it was so funny that even an hour later she was still falling off her chair with laughter.

By the time of the production meeting Paula and I were usually a bit tired from the train journey and found going through all the decisions a bit wearisome. But *The Tube* was like a big machine and needed to be planned carefully because of the time it was broadcast. If it had been a late programme, at this stage, it could have got away with being a bit more casual. At one of the meetings Paula suddenly announced that she needed a taxi. The same taxi firm was always used, and they were very friendly and on nickname terms with all of us. In this instance, the controller rang the production team an hour or two later and, in a very high-pitched panicked Geordie voice said, 'This is Noda Taxis. We're waiting outside the department store for Paula, and I don't know where she's gone. What do I do? Do I carry on waiting, like?' They were told they should wait and when, eventually, she came back, the producers asked what on earth she had been doing. She was meant to have been buying one thing and then returning, not running amok from store to store on a shopping spree, frightening Noda Taxis and holding us all up. She just said, 'So what – we're going to be here tomorrow, aren't we? Calm down and get back in your pram.' I used to love it when she was so naughty.

Gift of the Gab

From the beginning we had all sorts of guests on *The Tube*; they would fly the world and his wife up to Newcastle to appear on it. Whenever it was somebody really famous, like Elton John or Paul McCartney, there would be an extra air of attention from the crew, the cameramen, the doormen – in fact, the whole building seemed to raise its game. It really was a big deal to get someone of that stature into the Tyne Tees studio, and it was almost certainly only going to happen once in a lifetime. People would make sure the guest had a cup of tea and be especially polite when they were micing them up. The fact that all these musical legends had come all the way up to the industrial part of Newcastle made their visit all the more magical and extraordinary.

Miles Davis was one of these guests, and he caused the same vibration among the crew as Elton John or Paul McCartney. I met him very briefly before I interviewed him and it emerged that he wanted to promote his paintings. I was happy to stick to that subject, since it's always very difficult to talk about music.

Whenever we talked to any guest the producers always reminded us that we had to keep the interview to a minute. Frequently, we would be featuring a guest who could blow up a hot-water bottle or do some other novelty trick for which a minute was adequate. There were children and all sorts of people watching, so we were appealing to all tastes. But, for this great icon, Miles Davis, I protested that a minute wasn't nearly enough, so there was a bit of a kerfuffle as they talked this over. (He'd come all this way, yes. He was a legend, yes.) Finally it was agreed: two minutes. But even then Malcolm Gerrie had reservations and asked me, 'Eeh, kidder – is he really worth two minutes of prime-time television?' This was an expression I would get to know well. Obviously, in this instance, I came back with, 'Yes he is.'

The live interview started and my first question was, 'Well, Miles, you are one of the great musicians of all time and you are a great painter as well. You've got this new exhibition of paintings – do you connect music with painting?' He went, 'Y-e-h,' and he paused and then went, 'Ye-e-h,' again, really slowly. We used the green room for interviews and normally there would be a hubbub of noise but now there was total silence, everyone waiting for the great man's answer. Then he repeated the question: 'How do I connect music with visual art? Do I do that?' Throughout each interview, because it was live television, there was a floor manager signalling at me, 'Thirty seconds, fifteen seconds,' putting their hands together like a big cross – I never quite understood what that meant – then they would make a circle with their finger and thumb to indicate the last ten seconds and count down with their fingers, nine, eight and if you hadn't finished by then, they would do the 'cutting their throat' signal and then time really was up. In this instance, it was getting to ten fingers and he was still saying 'Y-e-h' and hadn't answered the question. I was starting to feel a bit panicked too. I may not be an expert interviewer now, but back then I was just a boy of twenty-three and didn't know what to do in difficult circumstances. We were down to five seconds, the floor manager was looking utterly desperate and then, at the absolute last minute, Miles said, 'Y-e-h. I would relate the two, most definitely.' 'Thank you, Miles Davis,' I said, and it was over.

Afterwards we went over to the Rose and Crown. Apart from relief that he had answered, I felt embarrassed we had insulted him by giving him such little time. I kept thinking, 'What's this all about? This is so frustrating. We're supposed to be daring and do what nobody else does. We should have just done an hour on him alone.' Finally I said, 'I was so worried we just didn't give you enough time.' But Miles Davis said, 'Man, don't worry. I loved it. I don't want to talk. It was great.' He then asked whether I liked his drawings And when I said I did, he asked which one I would like. There was one of two dancers, which I loved. He signed it and gave it to me and I still have it to this day.

TV Times

The Tube was the biggest show Tyne Tees had ever done and they had built a special studio for it with the money from Channel Four and they had fifty people working on it. Just to give an idea of how big it was, *Later* has twelve or fifteen, if that, and just one researcher who works on four other programmes at the same time, whereas *The Tube* had six permanent researchers. These researchers were always very friendly towards us. Seeing everything as if it were a Dickens story, I saw them as kindly people who, with their suggestions, were turning me into a gent, while Paula just thought they were patronizing silly old c—s and didn't hesitate in saying so.

The whole team at Tyne Tees was like a large family, with all the good and bad that brings with it. Newcastle people have something very nice about them, and we were really well looked after. They thought the best of us even when we weren't very well behaved and would have done anything to help us out. Also, they wanted us to look our best. A lot of them had been with Tyne Tees since 1961 and, when Paul McCartney came in to do the show, he told us it felt like being on *Ready Steady Go!* again.

Which of us would interview which guest was based on convenience and instinct. If I had some knowledge of the person, as with Miles Davis, it was felt I would probably be better as interviewer but, other times, such as with George Michael, Paula would choose to do it.

I tried to ask the guests about music and Paula would ask about sex. That was the difference between us really. Some people didn't want to be asked about sex and, likewise, some people didn't want to be asked about music. Sometimes Paula and I would tire of them early and break off mid-interview.

In the early days I used to think about the interview and the sort of questions I would ask beforehand. However, I soon learned that, if you ask one question and then shut up, the person will always talk – it's an old police interviewing technique. Before I discovered this, I'd ask a question and, if there was any pause at all, I'd immediately ask them the next, not giving the interviewee a chance to answer the first. Throughout the series, I found it hard to remember not only lines – if I was ever given any – but also who was who. I was always desperately trying to remember names and didn't even think of having a board held up with the guest's name on it. None of the crew suggested it either.

I wasn't an actor, that was the important thing. I have great admiration for many of my friends who are actors but I'm not one. Both Paula and I could only be ourselves and that, in fact, was the reason we were chosen. Being young and opinionated, Paula would rub some of her interviewees up the wrong way, but other people loved her. Apart from being very funny, she was also very beautiful, which was quite unusual for television at that time. And since she wasn't at all simpering but quite fearless, I think she quite scared some of the people at Tyne Tees. At one point, when we were rehearsing on the studio floor, she was swearing so much that the crew called for stage one of a strike. Before they got in touch with the union representative, Geoff Wonfor gathered them together and said, 'Look, you're going to seem a right bunch of tossers, if you say that a tiny little girl from the south of England is making you lily-livered and knock-kneed by using the odd swearword. What are you going to look like, eh?' They all agreed reluctantly and grumpily went back to work. Then Paula said, 'Right. Are you happy to come back now? Bunch of c—s.' She used to cheer me up no end.

At some point during the first series it was decided that some proper young people should be brought on board to help present certain features. There was still that insistence on the importance of 'Youth' being represented. I've always thought that people are people and age is of no consequence, but the *Tube* team didn't see it that way. Also, what with each show being one and a half hours long and the summer specials even longer, Malcolm Gerrie might also have felt that it was a bit much for Paula and me to do alone. He told us tactfully that, if we were John Steed and Emma Peel, we needed another figure – like James Bond's M. It was true that additional back-up was sensible, then, should Paula disappear on another day-long shopping trip, at least there would be a substitute.

To find these extra presenters a nationwide search was carried out, much like they do with the *X Factor* now. There was an announcement that anyone could come in off the street and try for the job. This, of course, was a way of getting extra publicity for the show and was a good idea but, unfortunately, the people they ended up with, although very nice, didn't have any real credentials. Thrown in at the deep end, they rather floundered, and the whole venture didn't work out. Paula and I appeared inexperienced and off the street, but she did actually have quite a lot of experience through her journalism and her writing, and through moving in rock and roll circles, and I knew about music and had experience performing live. We were a bit resentful of bringing people off the street. Nowadays, I'm much kinder to people, but then I had no time for any of that; I just wanted to cut to the chase. The one person who did shine through was Muriel Gray, and she stayed the distance. She is brilliantly talented and I think the world of her. She was quite clear-thinking, unlike a lot of people in television at that time. In fact, it was sometimes suggested that she was the only one of us who was any good, since she could string a sentence together and ask proper questions. She didn't arse about asking what people had down their trousers or drift off into her own world trying to figure out how the boogie went.

Paula left *The Tube* for the second series but returned for the third. At one point during the negotiations the producers asked her if it was Muriel who was putting her off coming back – they wondered if Paula felt she was a rival – but Paula said, '*No* – I want Muriel there. She makes me seem fantastic. You get rid of Muriel, and I'm going again.'

She was great, Muriel, but she seemed quite earnest to us in those days.

'Good Thing'

The Tube lasted five years so, all together over that time, there would have been 130 live shows at an hour and a half each, plus the specials – that's hundreds of hours of live television to fill. On each show there would be four live bands and some guests to be interviewed. *The Tube* team was always very happy to add what I would describe as 'novelty acts', but we would also look for new comedy acts for each show.

I'd become friendly with a man called Malcolm Hardee, who ran an alternative-comedy club called the Tunnel Palladium in Greenwich on a Sunday night. Throughout its time, performers such as Norman Lovett, Julian Clary, Jeremy Hardy, Harry Enfield, Jerry Sadowitz and Rory Bremner all appeared at the Tunnel Palladium before they were famous. It was very lively in this crowded pub, and people would heckle and boo off the acts that didn't work. However, if somebody went down well there, I'd try to get them on *The Tube*. The Oblivion Boys were very funny, and I asked them on. They came on in military fatigues at the very beginning of the show, barging me out of the way, and saying, 'We're in the TA. You know what that stands for?', and I said, 'No. What's that?' And they said, 'No nonsense.' Another act I got on was a clown called Daniel Rovai who balanced a bicycle on his nose.

Another evening, Glenn Tilbrook took me to see Vic Reeves perform at a tiny pub in Deptford. I thought he was so great we got him his first television appearance, doing his Square Celebrities. With a special set made for it, it was a take-off of *Celebrity Squares*, and he was on a Kirby wire so he could fly through the air asking questions. It was the most brilliant thing I'd ever seen. Once again, after the runthrough, Malcolm Gerrie started saying to me, 'Eeh, kidder, is he worth two minutes of prime-time television?' After a robust debate, shouting and pleading, I finished with the usual, 'Oh, go on – he is,' and so Vic was granted two minutes twenty seconds.

On the whole, we were allowed to do whatever we liked if we thought it was a good idea, so long as we stuck to the allotted time. In other words, it was like being an indulged child.

One Sunday night at the Tunnel Palladium a man called Les did an act in the interval, coming on stage and putting a load of cardboard boxes in the background, rather naïvely cut out to look like a New York skyline. He then took quite some time placing torches in these cardboard-box skyscrapers. Then he put these huge car-shaped boxes on his feet, three feet long and two feet wide. One was a New York taxi and one was a police car, and they also had torches in them for headlights. Then he put a record on and danced around with the cars on his feet, and the audience went mad with applause because he'd gone to such an effort. They thought he was fantastic and so did I. I booked him on *The Tube* immediately, but the producers were absolutely mystified why I'd got this person on. He died a death. Of course, the charm of it had been the big set-up on stage, but on television – in this instance I had to agree even before it was said, it wasn't worth a minute of prime time.

Anyone who came up to perform would stay in the Gosforth Park Hotel the night before. Apart from an eleven o'clock run-through, hosts and guests didn't really have to start until five o'clock the next day, so most people were up for a jolly night out in Newcastle. We had some fantastic nights with a variety of bands – Fun Boy Three, Eurythmics, Chaka Khan, Twisted Sister, Dexy's Midnight Runners. I'd see quite a few people I already knew, like Sting and Suggs from Madness. I also became very friendly with Robert Palmer, who used to send me compilation tapes of jazz and blues, the sort of music we liked listening to. There were a lot of different types of popular music, and we captured whatever the spirit of the time was.

The Tube was great because, for the first time, there didn't seem to be a separation between the crew and the musicians; the bands felt that everyone was in it together. Gavin Taylor may not have been groovy but everyone trusted him because of his impeccable character, like you would a doctor or a country solicitor. Sometimes the people making television shows have different criteria to the guests who appear on them, sometimes there's a feeling they want to make the guests appear foolish, but this was never true with *The Tube*: we just wanted to show people's talent at its best.

A big scoop for *The Tube* was getting Tina Turner to come on as part of her comeback. She brought with her a lovely gospel pianist called Kenny Moore, and he came to stay with Mary and me for Christmas. He had played on a lot of famous records but always as one of those background figures you never really hear about. At one point, we recorded a song together, which I've still got. To celebrate his visit, we took him out round the local Greenwich pubs and we had a bit of a singsong at one of them. I was having a lovely time, but I couldn't help feeling he was a little disappointed by this taste of south-east London life. I think he was expecting something a bit more glamorous from England.

At one point, I saw that Dr John was going to be in the country and suggested we have him on the show. I hadn't seen him since that time in Los Angeles, but this really cemented our friendship. We filmed him doing a piano version of 'Such a Night', which I think is one of the best versions there is.

The curious thing was, Jeremy Isaacs and Channel Four had hoped *The Tube* would emulate the success of *Ready Steady Go!* but had ended up with a totally original programme of their own that was hitting the mainstream consciousness and being watched all over the country. I got letters from all sorts of viewers, of all ages and types. One letter I was surprised to receive was from Reggie Kray, who'd been watching *The Tube* in prison. Someone on the show had mentioned the fact that I was wearing a Reggie Kray-style suit, and this had inspired him to write to me. In fact, I went to visit him at one point and found him most courteous. I told him I was trying to stop smoking and he asked me if I wanted an infallible method of giving up. When I said I did, he said in his soft, polite voice – 'Just give me your word you're going to stop.'

And so the first series went on. Part of Channel Four's remit was to bridge the gap between BBC2 and the people BBC2 didn't reach, audiences who weren't being served by existing television programmes. BBC2 was very good but, at that time, it was being watched largely by well-off people in the south of England, and that's where its programmes were being made. Not only was *The Tube* shot in Newcastle but it would also make films in various cities around the country, featuring local artists and bands, often before they were well known.

On 23 January 1983 we filmed Frankie Goes to Hollywood in Liverpool. There was a vibe about them already, although nobody knew who they were at that stage. Soon after this film they were to become household names. The night after our filming, we had a rather riotous night out with them, about which I can remember very little.

The producers had asked us if there was any subject we especially wanted to cover in Liverpool and I suggested that I borrow a motorbike and shoot some footage of me (which would then be speeded up) apparently breaking the land speed record riding through the Mersey Tunnel. At first nobody would lend us a motorcycle for this stunt, but then the more adventurous Hesketh's did. I was especially pleased to ride one of these for the film, one of the few motorbikes still being made in Britain.

Another city we filmed in was Hull. At that time, the Fine Young Cannibals were only doing demos, but we would help their career. Later, I was to play on their record, 'Good Thing', which went to number one all over the world – in fact, it's one of the biggest-selling records I've ever played on. Not so long ago Chrysler used the piano solo in their world marketing campaign. The Fine Young Cannibals used a riff they had taken from Solomon Burke, which Solomon had learned at his church – that riff keeps on coming back.

While we were in Hull I found a very nice tailor who made me a piano suit. It was made of black felt, with black and white keys stuck on top. It was quite possibly the hottest thing you could wear under any circumstances, particularly under the lights of television or on stage. One day it went missing, and has never turned up. Let's face it, it's not going to be easy to wear unnoticed, so I'd like to use this book as an appeal: I would like it returned. I haven't given it away and I want it back. Ringo Starr told me about being given a beautiful birthday card by Salvador Dalí, drawn on the night they met. Dalí wrote on it, 'Happy Birthday, Ringo.' Over the years it went missing and one day it turned up at a celebrity auction somewhere. Ringo rang up the auction and said, 'I want that back. That's mine,' and they said, 'No, it's not,' and he said, 'But it says "Happy Birthday, Ringo" on it – who else's can it be?' But it was no use, he couldn't get it back. Somebody will probably do the same with this suit – having nicked it, they'll sell it. Or maybe the thief is wearing it somewhere even now, sweating like a pig. Serves them right.

One of the other exciting aspects of doing *The Tube* was going away and filming specials abroad. Our first was a trip to St Tropez to shoot the glamorous Cannes film festival. John Reid, Elton John's then-manager, had a huge yacht there and, since Paula was a friend of his, he invited us all for a dinner party. Duran Duran were among the guests and so was Peter Blake, the artist. On arrival, I was alarmed to hear that we had to take our shoes off, since this was one of those occasions when I hadn't changed my socks for about a week. I was just thinking I'd got away with it, chatting to the other sophisticated guests and occasionally looking round politely to see where this unpleasant smell was coming from when Paula opened her big fat gob. Pointing at my feet she started saying, 'That's disgusting – can't we make an exception and let Jools wear his shoes?' The sophisticated gathering ignored this, as did I, but I did feel that I'd been isolated socially, a feeling that only increased at dinner, with sixteen pairs of feet under a grand dining-room table. If Paula had just kept her feelings to herself, a policy I recommend more than once in this book, they would all have thought Peter Blake was to blame. But it was me, they all knew it. There was no getting away from it.

Picking the Blues

Things started to change for me after the first series of *The Tube*. Before it, I'd been on the verge of being broke, flapping about trying to get money every week to pay a band and, suddenly, I had a regular fee coming in. Not only that but, by the end of the run, I found I was becoming a household name. I was surprised at this turnaround, because television wasn't an area I knew anything about, nor was it something I was particularly interested in. I knew about music but, at that time, I hadn't properly managed to figure out the music I'd been trying for, and that was still frustrating me.

During the first series the remaining members of the Millionaires had come up to Newcastle and we had played together on the programme. However, since we still hadn't managed to get another record contract, I now had to meet up with Martin and Mike and tell them we were going to have to call it a day. This was quite upsetting and I was a bit depressed by my lack of success in this area. But *The Tube* was a huge hit, so much so that Channel Four was desperate to give Paula and me more money to do another series.

In the meantime, Paula had been offered a lot of money to do a programme for London Weekend Television instead. This would be less stressful for her, because it would cut out the journey to Newcastle each week with her newborn Fifi and Anita the nanny. It would also give her more time to carry on with all her other writing jobs.

She told me that she was worried that she would be letting me down if she accepted it but I told her it sounded like a sensible move. John Lay added his own generous view that, as a consequence of her leaving, *The Tube* producers would need to keep me more than ever and it would mean more money for us.

Paula having left, the producers had to find somebody to replace her for the second series. Out of the many people who applied

Lesley Ash was chosen. We all got on very well with her when she came up for the audition, and she was professional. Although she wasn't edgy like Paula, she was equally gifted and beautiful and a successful actress too, which meant she could remember any lines she was given, something I very rarely managed. We became great friends and she was happy to stay up all night with us in Newcastle's nightspots. In fact, Lesley was keener on staying up even later than I was and, after Paula's early nights, I was now confronted with somebody who was twice the man I was, which I found rather exhausting.

At that time Lesley was going out with Rowan Atkinson, who was a huge success even then, an incredibly talented man. He would come up and visit and, in January, we all celebrated my birthday together in the Rose and Crown.

Geoff Wonfor was always very encouraging to Lesley and would draw her out of herself. She got quite nervous about interviewing people because she was an actress rather than a presenter. Put a script in front of her and she was fantastic but, when it came to interviewing people, she became quite shy. Music wasn't her specialist subject. I think she found it a bit stressful being thrown in at the deep end. But she knew that we were all there to look after her if anything got tricky, and some of the guests could be a bit awkward. When the floor manager said to Iggy Pop, 'Iggy, love, could you do that again?', he turned round menacingly and said, 'You motherfucker, what did you call me?' The floor manager replied, 'Well, "Iggy, love," like.' I realized there was a titanic clash of cultures and stepped in as peacemaker to try to iron the whole thing out, explaining that 'love' was just a Newcastle term of fondness. Iggy, though very talented, was a nervy man. He had a minder at the time, and his job was not to protect Iggy from other people but to protect him from himself. It was obviously necessary. On the return train journey from Newcastle that night, an elderly guard pointed out that we were in a non-smoking carriage and he could tell someone had been smoking. That someone had been Iggy. He became very distressed, and ran off down the train bellowing with anguish. His minder sprung after him, and later reported that Iggy had tried to throw himself off the moving train.

Another change that took place during this second series of *The Tube* was that Mary and I decided we could now afford to move up in the world and buy a place of our own. She was a clever businesswoman and a very talented barber so, with the help of Miles, who sorted out the finances, we bought some rambling commercial premises in Blackheath. Downstairs at the front was a small barber's shop, which you had to go through to enter the warren that was the rest of the building. There was a large flat, space for an office and, at the back, a recording studio. Mary and I were taken with the idea that it was a bit like *The Man from UNCLE*, where the spies would go into a small dry-cleaning office which served as a cover to the giant counter-espionage agency above. We decided to add to the mystery by calling the barber's shop Sid's. Sid would be the fictitious proprietor.

Living together above Dickie Dobson's had been fantastic, what with meeting all his various friends, who were truly colourful characters, but my late-night comings and goings were becoming increasingly inconvenient for him since he had to get up early in the morning to go to work. Equally, it was becoming restrictive for me, not being able to play my music at night. Also, the flat didn't have any running water, or kitchen or bathroom, and I had started to see Mary's point that this was a disadvantage.

My new studio room at the back of our new premises had once been the place where the corpses had been laid out during the years when Sid's Barber's had been Francis Chappel's, the undertaker's. This added something to the atmosphere of the room, as did the dark blue carpet I put all over its walls to keep the noise down. This carpet may have worked better at soundproofing than the newspaper I used at Dickie's. I am now able to provide another little tip to any reader planning to do the same: choose your colour carefully. When my friend Eddie Gittings came round and saw it he warned me that I would find the dark blue a bit much after a while – after all, blue was a depressing colour: why else would they call it the blues? He turned out to be right and now, if I go into a recording studio with blue walls, I advise them similarly: it's no use spending £1,000,000 on equipment and not thinking about the colour scheme. It's silly to pretend that the creative side of making music isn't a sensitive business because it is, even if the business side isn't.

I still, at this point, was using the four-track tape recorder but soon after moving I progressed on to an eight-track. I'd become fascinated with the recording process and wanted to figure it out so I could make my music sound as I wanted it to sound.

Steve Nieve from Elvis Costello's band had bought a machine called a Fair Light, which he suggested I give a try. Every year a new piece of huge technology comes out – 'With this you'll be as clever as Bach, as swinging as Count Basie and as brilliant as the Beatles' – which a load of mugs fall for. I'm not saying that Steve was a mug for buying the very expensive Fair Light – I'd done it with the Polymoog some years before – and, in all fairness, these things do have their own intrinsic sound. I was expecting a huge *Dr Who*-type instrument to appear, with wires sticking up all over it, but it was quite modest-looking. We had a curry and then, from eight o'clock in the evening until three o'clock in the morning, me, Chris Difford and Steve Nieve fiddled with this thing, trying to get it to create new music. By the end of the night, all we had got it to do was sample Tony Hancock saying 'The Bloke with the Biggest Hooter Survives'. In the end we had to give up trying to expand our musical horizons with it, and I can't say I've really bothered with anything like that again.

Now I have my own comprehensive recording studio in which I have been making my own records since 1990. With its Pro Tools and SSL desks, my present studio is too high-tech for me to work alone but I understand the principles, which have remained the same. For me, it was as important to try to master an understanding of the recording process as it was to learn how to perform live, and I enjoyed doing it.

At this same time Mary became pregnant, which we were both very excited about. What with this, the greater financial security and the new home, we were feeling quite settled.

The New Rock and Roll

During the first series of *The Tube*, I had seen *The Young Ones* for the first time and thought it was absolutely brilliant. I decided that we had to have some of the actors on the programme. Although *The Young Ones* was on BBC and we were Channel Four, the producers agreed with me that it could work.

Up until this point comedy had largely been of a showbiz variety, like *The Two Ronnies*, but suddenly there was this new alternative sort. Just as *The Tube* was breaking new ground, nobody had seen anything like *The Young Ones* or *The Comic Strip* on television before. Indulged, like us, by their producers, it was as if the lunatics had taken over the asylum. People either loved the result or didn't get it at all.

Ben Elton, Rik Mayall and Lise Mayer wrote *The Young Ones*, so I contacted them and ended up having a drink with Rik Mayall, near his rented council flat in the Old Kent Road. He was great, really full on and very funny and charming. I then invited him to the little fireworks party Mary and I were having in our new place, and he turned up with a couple of friends, one of whom was Roland Rivron, who was then a drummer rather than a comedian. We had a roof garden at the back of our new place, two storeys up. From it, there was quite a long drop down and behind it was a sharp-sloped, slippery roof. Anyway, after a few drinks, Roland suddenly announced that he could do this rather clever trick of letting a firework off from his head. Rik started to egg him on but everyone else agreed it was a bit dangerous to attempt this trick on an enclosed little roof terrace. And Roland said, 'Yes, you're absolutely right. I'll climb to the top of the pitch of the roof and let it off from the chimney.' So he scrambled up to the very top of the roof and, clinging to the chimney, placed the firework on his head and lit it. When it went off, we all applauded; it was probably the most dangerous thing I've ever seen to this day. We became very firm friends immediately.

Rik then invited me to stay at the flat he'd rented for the Edinburgh Festival but, when I got there, it was clear that there was absolutely no room. Ben Elton had one room, Rik the other and the comedian Andy de la Tour was sleeping on the sofa. Being on television, I got Andy's sofa and he got kicked off on to the floor. I then went around Edinburgh, which was like a whole new world. The big-haired music of that time never really got me going but this alternative scene seemed really exciting and entertaining. The comedians were making political jokes and taking their comedy into areas that previous generations steered clear of. There was a lot of vulgarity as well, so it was like the old music-hall humour in lots of ways but with its own originality, which was very attractive. And some of it was just surreal. One night back at the Tunnel Palladium's open spot a traditional comedian from Dagenham came on with his well-rehearsed mother-in-law jokes, and got booed off after a few minutes. The act that followed was called Fiasco Job Job and consisted of two men wearing sunglasses, mortarboard hats, luminous gloves and tights, and university gowns. One of them had a hose which he span round and round above his head and the other one bobbed up and down so they looked like a strange machine. Through the mouthpiece attached to the hose one shouted, 'Fuck off, German, fuck off, German,' and the crowd went mad with applause. I saw the poor traditional comedian staring in bafflement: how could it have all gone so wrong?

Fiasco Job Job were too weird even for *The Tube* but Rik came up a few times to appear and I also appeared in an episode of *The Young Ones*. We all seemed to be in one another's programmes all the time, and it was rather a wild time. For example, one evening Roland was showing off and cycled down the stairs of the Groucho Club, just to prove he could do it. He couldn't – he fell off and broke his wrist.

I also got friendly that year with Robbie Coltrane, and he remains my great friend to this day. Robbie came up and performed on *The Tube* a couple of times, as did Malcolm Hardee and the Greatest Show on Legs, who performed their famous naked three-man balloon dance. Harry Enfield did his first spot down at the Tunnel Palladium, so he came on *The Tube* after that. He performed dressed as a centurion, his first television appearance.

However, even the television world was very much divided into people who understood the humour and people who didn't. Dawn French and Jennifer Saunders came on the show and, when somebody on the crew asked me who they were, I told them that they were two Neapolitan street girls I had rescued and brought to Newcastle for my own purposes. Two members of the crew laughed at that and the other two looked completely blank. That was how the world seemed to be divided at the time.

Having Dawn and Jennifer up was very jolly but it was an early example of the trouble that would follow from pushing the show to the edge. On this occasion, after the French and Saunders piece, I walked off the set saying, 'Get off the show, you're rubbish,' as had been planned. At that, one of them shouted back the unplanned and almost out of earshot 'But what about all the blow jobs?' We got a lot of letters complaining about that. At half-past five in the afternoon it's not the sort of joke most people like to have in their front rooms. Faced with the indignant producers, I said that I too was appalled and suggested Dawn and Jennifer apologize to us all, adding for good measure, 'And I'll see to it that we never have them on the show again.'

From the first series of *The Tube* onwards there had always been risky moments. I'm afraid that waiting for things to go wrong was one of the reasons many people watched the programme. The very first controversy involved my promotion of a *Tube* poster which was available to buy. In trying to persuade viewers to send in for it, I helpfully added that the cardboard tube the poster would arrive in could be a useful receptacle for numerous items, from elephants' farts to hamster droppings. After the show Paula and I were called to the producer's office; he had something serious he wanted to talk to us about. Sensing trouble, we decided to pretend we hadn't received the message and leg it out of the building on the assumption that, a week later, whatever the problem was would have been forgotten. However, when we returned the following week, we were summoned in again and told we had to write a letter of apology to the Independent Broadcasting Authority. Even at the time, I couldn't believe the fuss that was made over that joke. It hadn't been that funny and, on those grounds, I was indeed guilty but, when you think of the things people get away with nowadays, it all seems a bit of an overreaction. I suppose, in all fairness, half-past five was still thought of as children's time but it was, I thought, childish humour.

As the series progressed there were a growing number of instances which drew the attention of the IBA. There was the time when somebody's snazzy new keyboard suddenly made a really loud noise and on air a voice was heard to scream, 'For fuck's sake.' We ignored that one and carried on. Then there was the time when the Urban Warriors were on, playing drums on a car using an iron pole. An indignant viewer wrote in and asked whether this wouldn't encourage people to go out and smash up cars, about which Geoff was very scornful: 'Eeh, man. What a ridiculous idea – it's just a bit of entertainment.' However, before the IBA could even get going with a reprimand, he parked his new Jag outside Newcastle football ground and it got pummelled with metal bars by someone who had seen the show.

What with the steady stream of complaints and niggles, by the time of my inadvertent slip of the tongue in the very last series, there was a big folder on the head of the IBA's desk. In fact, he probably couldn't see out of the window for *Tube* complaints. When I first heard that the IBA had their eye on me I was rather flattered, as I assumed it was like CBS or RCA or some other record label. I didn't know that it was the body responsible for maintaining standards of decency on television. But where are the IBA now, when they are most needed? Everything seems to have gone out of the window. Looking back, I can only think that they should have shut us down altogether and prevented the start of this tidal wave of rudeness. If we were the first little drops of water through the dyke, they were like the Dutch boy in the story, sticking their thumb in to try to protect the citizens from the flood. Unfortunately, in their case it was to no avail, although they hung on in there until they were flattened by it.

New York Suite

For the second series we went and made a film in New York. In those days, when we filmed our specials abroad, as well as the presenters who, on this trip, were Lesley and myself, we had a full film crew of two lighting men, two sound men, the cameraman, the assistant, the researcher, the director and the producer. Nowadays, one person will do the lot, but this was the old days of television. Geoff Wonfor, the director of these specials, along with Andy Matthews, the editor, could make television films that looked like features, and these foreign specials were rightly acclaimed. I didn't realize how lucky I was, having people like that to work with. Sometimes, when you explain something to a director, they don't listen to what you have to say or refuse to budge from their set ideas but Geoff, Andy and I always felt as one, and this trip to New York only strengthened our creative bond.

The researchers had decided that, for this film, we should concentrate on the grooviest New York discos. I like listening to live music being played and I like records but discos leave me cold. Every disco looks the same to me, whichever city you're in. There's always a load of flashing lights, noise and undrinkable beer, and you can't hear yourself talk. This was certainly the case on this trip; we went from one to the next, each being the newest and the most fashionable place, with a great queue to get in, but then it was completely empty once you got inside. I felt we weren't really hitting on anything that couldn't be found in any big city in the world.

One day after filming Geoff and I went for a drink on 52nd Street, which was round the corner from the hotel. Once, there had been all these jazz clubs where the legends had played but now half of it was demolished and there were only about three clubs left. We went into one of them and it was like being back in 1950s

New York. The barman told us that the following week the rest of 52nd Street was due for demolition. We rushed back to the crew and stressed the importance of capturing this legendary place on film before it went for ever but the researcher stubbornly insisted that the whole schedule had been worked out already, that there was another of the newest discos we had to film. I then tried to explain my view, which was that one of America's biggest contributions to the modern world was its music. Jazz, the amalgam of sounds and influences from all over the world, had flowered in this particular street in New York and now the place where this seminal artistic achievement had first come to light was about to be demolished – and we had a chance to capture it on film before it was lost to the world. But they wouldn't budge from their irritating discotheque idea.

Geoff and I left that meeting in a frustrated fury. From then on we realized that we really only wanted to work with researchers who were open to new ideas. There was no point working at cross-purposes.

One of the youngest *Tube* researchers was called John Cummings, and he had always been the least groovy of them all. He always wore a tweed jacket and had started in current affairs. From the start, Paula and I had been drawn to his refreshingly methodical way of thinking and his lack of interest in rock and roll craziness. Soon after this trip John became our chief researcher. From then on, our location and foreign films became far more successful and won many awards. John also became a great friend of ours, and it is satisfactory for me to report that his rise to success was so great that he now lives in Monaco as a tax exile.

I learned another very valuable lesson on this trip. I went to visit Lesley in her room at the Plaza only to discover that she had been given such an enormous suite, it was like walking into St Paul's Cathedral. I'd never seen anything like it. My room in the same hotel was the size of a shoebox. She told me that actors' agents always put a clause in the contract that their client has to have a large suite. I adopted this tactic on all our subsequent foreign trips.

*

One of the really good things about filming in New York this time was meeting and interviewing Stevie Wonder. 'For Once in My Life' was one of the earliest records I'd ever bought; I had played it again and again, until cracks appeared in it. I'd followed his progress, every musical direction he took, from that time. Everything he did I liked and found fascinating. I loved the way he played the drums and the way his music went in such different directions. He is a true giant of music.

Waiting in the room to interview him, I was feeling rather nervous and, as there was a piano there, I began to tinkle away on it. Suddenly there was a hand on my shoulder. It was Stevie Wonder and he said, 'That's nice, what's that?', and I replied, 'It's just a song I've been working on.' He said, 'I've just been writing something too – I love it when things are half-written', and I moved away from the piano and he started playing me this fantastic song. When he'd finished, I was rather surprised as he put his hand out and ran his middle finger very gently over the edge of my profile, from the top of my forehead, my nose, upper lip and then over my chin. Then he said, 'Oh, I thought I'd seen you before.'

We chatted and he talked very eloquently about all sorts of things. I wanted to know some hard-core information about his recording process. There was one great song called 'I Love Every Little Thing about You', which he played for me at the interview, and in it there was one chord change I couldn't work out, so he showed it to me. Then he invited me to his concert that night at Radio City. I went along and was very well taken care of, sitting at the mixing desk at the back of the hall to watch it. The concert was fantastic and his version of 'Blowing in the Wind' there inspired the version Ruby Turner does for my Big Band.

At one point all the lights went down and he started singing a ballad. He paused and the curtain fell behind him and everything grew romantic. A sofa was brought on to the stage as well as a bottle of champagne in a bucket with two glasses. He asked whether anyone would like to come and share it with him. Out of all the girls who ran forward he picked one out and, without any help, led her to the sofa, poured her a glass of champagne and sang to her. I said to the sound engineer, 'That's amazing – does he do that every night? Will I see the girl backstage afterwards?' He said, 'Yes, and you'll easily spot her.' When I asked how he said, 'Just look out for the girl covered in champagne.'

My son George, after hearing that Michael Jackson was in trouble for having licked a boy's head on an airplane, said that he, as a fan, would find it an honour to have his head licked by Michael Jackson. That's how I felt about Stevie Wonder: it would have been an honour to have had champagne spilled all over me, and I'm sure the girl felt the same way. I began to think it was rather good being on *The Tube* if it meant I could meet all my heroes.

We were told that, the following night, we would be filming in Alphabet City, which had the reputation of being a bit dangerous. A few of the younger members of the crew were a bit worried by this but the lighting man, Ken, a lovely, decent man, like everyone's dad, reassured them; it was going to be fine. When we got there it was just a bit sad, with a few vagrants and junkies hanging about. There was one poor fat man who was standing in a corner without any trousers on, just sobbing. He had glasses but no shoes or socks on. It was one of the most heartrending things I have ever seen. The Geordie crew, led by Ken, rounded on the researcher and said, 'Man, we cannot film the poor man like that.' They disappeared and, two minutes later, returned with a pair of trousers they'd bought. Ken gave them to the man and we left to film something else.

You see these documentaries of people starving in Africa and you think, 'Well, the crew must have had something to eat. Give them your sandwiches,' or the wildlife films where the gazelle's about to be killed by the lion – why don't they shout and warn it, but they never do. But we did. And I take my hat off to the crew.

Our next foreign trip was to Japan the following year, and the crew once more bonded together with one idea in mind – but in this case it was to avoid Japanese food. To provide a taste of home, they tracked down an English pub, the Pig and Whistle, and remained there throughout. I liked sushi and Japanese food generally but there were some aspects of the culture I did find harder to understand. We had ordered a bus to pick us up at the hotel at nine in order to go and film at the Nissan factory. The bus arrived and some of us got on. The rest were ambling out but, on the dot of nine o'clock, the bus closed its doors and set off, leaving these latecomers standing on the pavement. I stood up and asked the driver to stop but he had been instructed to set off at nine and so that's what he was going to do. It wasn't in him to allow for British casualness.

While we were there, we filmed Culture Club, who had a big Japanese following. It was then I discovered that Boy George had been expelled by the same headmaster who had expelled Glenn Tilbrook, and for the same reason — refusal to have a hair cut. By coincidence, this headmaster, Mr Dawson, had managed to expel the two most talented pupils ever to attend his school. Or perhaps it wasn't coincidence: my co-author tells me that Renoir was attacked by people all the time — even when he walked in the forest, the deer used to attack him. There was something annoying about him because he was a genius. Certainly Dawson reacted in this way against Boy George and Glenn Tilbrook.

Towards the end of our stay in Tokyo, I was walking round the smaller streets and came to a dark and rather sinister market at which I was the only non-Japanese. In one strange secretive corner was a print shop and, although it had its blinds down, it had a beautiful black and white abstract picture in the window. All of a sudden a face looked out from behind the blind. It was a very old Japanese man with a beard and a silk duffle coat without the hood. He beckoned me into the shop and, speaking a little English, said, 'You wish for beautiful painting of tiger?' He pointed to it but, really, it was rather sentimental-looking, as was the one next to it, a vividly coloured sobbing child. I said politely, 'No, no I quite like that, but the thing I really want —', but he interrupted me with, 'I show you one more. I have one more of lion. The lion he hunts.' Again, the lion looked a bit soppy to me. Finally I explained that the one I really liked was the beautiful abstract work he had in the window but he looked at me strangely and told me that was the sign that said 'Closed for lunch'. I quickly pretended I'd known that all along, and was so embarrassed I ended up buying a rather nice picture of a lot of people naked in a bathhouse. So it was a success in the end. I had a suit made on that trip as well, so I enjoyed Japan.

All the big cities – Manchester, Liverpool, Glasgow – had their own musical heritage, so the producers of *The Tube* thought that, as well as filming in these different cities, it would be nice to broadcast live shows from them. They wanted to continue to emphasize that London wasn't the centre of everything.

The Manchester scene was going on so we decided to film there first, at the now legendary Hacienda Club. This show was the occasion of Madonna's first ever appearance on British television. On the same show we interviewed *Coronation Street*'s Pat Phoenix and her husband Tony Booth. Tony Booth, now the father-in-law of Tony Blair, was drinking at the time so he was a bit wild, a full-on sort of a character, but Pat was charming, a very beautiful and elegant woman. On the way in, she took time to sign lots of autographs. Finally, she came in and somebody asked her why she had spent so long outside with them. She gestured to her smart fur coat, saying, 'You see this? They paid for this. I wasn't going to rush them.' I loved her and I loved her attitude.

Tony Booth was a bit of a handful though. I asked him whether there was anything he particularly wanted to talk about and he said, 'I can talk about anything?' in a challenging sort of voice. Poor Pat was trying discreetly to restrain him but he wouldn't be held back. 'Right. If you really want to know, I'll tell you what I want to talk about. Blue cheese. I want people to know that the blue bits in blue cheese are the most carcinogenic things there are. The Milk Marketing Board is trying to silence me, but I don't care. I'm going to say it anyway.' So, Madonna performed 'Holiday' with her two male dancers and, being ahead of her time, wearing a radio mic. I thanked her and introduced Tony who, for his allotted minute of airtime, gave the Hacienda audience the benefit of his knowledge of the dangers of blue cheese.

'Biggie-Wiggie'

All this travelling abroad was exciting but it was also quite exhausting and time-consuming, and going up to Newcastle meant I had
to get up early in the morning, and that wasn't something I was
used to doing; I was more used to working late at night. The
workload of filming was really heavy at this time – and somebody
introduced me to cocaine. I would like to give my views briefly
here, in this short chapter: there are lots of things that are very bad
for you but they tend to have at least one or two good aspects to
them. Cigarettes, for instance, smell great, look great, feel great,
the packaging is great, you look more glamorous with a cigarette
– everything about smoking is great apart from the fact that it kills
you after disabling you horribly. That's the bad bit. Obviously
there has to be a good bit, or nobody would smoke, would they?
Now, with cocaine, I actually think the truth of it is that everything
about it is bad. It's hard to see any positive aspects to it at all, other
than the ability it gives you to talk non-stop rubbish to your friends
or to people of a similar disposition. You hear about drug-fuelled
orgies but, if cocaine increases the desire for such activities, it
doesn't help your ability to engage in them. It also has an insidious
effect in that you think you are only taking a bit, then you take a
bit more, then you laugh a bit too loudly, talk a bit too much, and
then three days later you fly into a fury at somebody who's simply
opened a door for you.

I was very fortunate because my cocaine experience was very
brief. One time, just before I was about to perform, I suddenly felt
that I was having a heart attack or going mad. A doctor was called
and he told me it was a panic attack brought on by having taken
cocaine two days previously. That terrified me so much I never
wanted to take it again.

I'm no drugs tsar but I wouldn't advise anybody to touch it in the first place. Not only does it make you grumpy and twitchy but music sounds worse with it too. Anyway, that's enough advice on that matter; and now let's move on to the next chapter.

Mushroom Men

During the last part of the second series Paul Young came up to play on *The Tube*, and that was a little bit odd for me. His band now had Pino and Kim and Maz in it, and I did feel a twinge, seeing that my old band was now half his new band. They were having huge hits, produced by Laurie Latham, who produces all my records now. I did wonder what I'd lost.

All my life I have enjoyed music in a number of different ways: the act of listening to it, the act of playing it and the act of performing it. I need all these elements in order to feel satisfied in my life. I was still doing the listening part but very rarely the performing part. To make up for this, I would spend all the time I wasn't working on *The Tube* writing and recording in my new little studio room. During this time I released a rockabilly single under my own name called 'Crazy Over You', on which Gilson, Pino and Boz, who is now the guitarist for Morrissey, played.

Soon after this Matt Johnson from The The rang me up and asked me to put the piano on a track they were doing. I went over on my Velocette Venom to his studio near Brick Lane and he played me a track called 'Uncertain Smile'. There was a long bit in the middle of the song and he asked me to do the piano solo for it. I rather enjoyed doing this and it seemed to work quite well. Later that year the album came out and 'Uncertain Smile' was one of the last tracks on it. I decided I would sit down, play the whole record all the way through and wait for my section on 'Uncertain Smile'. It got to the song, and then the bit in the middle of this song, but my piano solo had gone. I was so disappointed. I really felt it had something, Matt had liked it at the time, and I'd liked it. But then, continuing to listen, there at the very end of the record were two piano solos, which Matt had taken and edited together to stand alone. Matt did a brilliant job on the whole record, and it is still one people listen to.

Another musical venture caused less of a lasting stir. Since I was still seeing quite a bit of Glenn and Chris, Glenn asked me to join his new two-man group, The Mushroom Men of the Sixty-Sixth Trip. I was happy to do this and, as a group, the two of us went and did a gig in a tiny club in Wardour Street. In addition to our weird get-up, I had something called a Moog Liberator hanging round my neck, a bit of a daft name as it was always going out of tune so didn't liberate me at all. We'd written a song with this drone which went, 'Mushroom men and the sixty-sixth trip, mushroom men and the sixty-sixth trip, mushroom men and sixty-six, mushroom men and the sixty-sixth trip, there's the mushroom men and the sixty-sixth trip'. The Moog Liberator had this weird electronic sound, and our hippy audience ended up in a Conga-type line, following us out of the club, through Soho and back again, all to this mushroom-men chant. It was a proper sixties happening but taking place in the eighties. Glenn and I had always liked music's abstract expressionists, such as Captain Beefheart or the Stardust Cowboy, and we were just having a go at that really. Chris was a bit sceptical, but that kind of experimentation often leads to interesting ideas or new paths. It didn't in the case of the Mushroom Men.

Meanwhile, MTV in America had taken a liking to the video Geoff Wonfer had shot of my song 'Crazy Over You'. We had originally intended to shoot this video in glamorous St Tropez but had ended up in the public toilets of Newcastle's meat market. To make up for the loss of glamour we had featured Rik Mayall and French and Saunders as a backing band. Since MTV had been playing the video consistently, when they invited me to go over to America and guest host for a week, I felt obliged to accept. I suspected it would be a case of having to be perky all day long, alone in a blackened TV studio, and I was proven right.

Anyway, by the end of my stint I was glad to get back to London, where I received a far more attractive invitation. The week before I'd left, Glenn and I had got Vic the pianist from

the Royal Standard pub round to my studio and made a recording
of his playing, and now Vic was inviting me to come and play a
duet with him at a working man's club in Charlton. You get an
invitation like that, there's no question of refusing it.

Channel Four didn't have that many programmes that were popular, as it hadn't quite worked out what it was doing. *The Tube* was
the exception and was really hitting its target. Because of its success
I had now become a celebrity, something I hadn't been before. I
hadn't planned this and I was a little worried whether it was a
good or a bad thing. But, whether I liked it or not, I was now
a household name and, because of the age of the audience we
attracted, I was seen to be a happening, groovy one. I have never
paid attention to whether musicians were young or old, groovy or
otherwise, I'm only interested in their work. That's how I felt
about *The Tube* and my role on it but I had missed the point, since
we now had a huge audience of young people who trusted what
Paula, Lesley and I were saying because they could see we weren't
phonies. They might not always have liked us but they knew we
were real – and we were. And that meant that the industry wanted
to get hold of us, to use us for their evil purposes.

There was a body, unknown to me at the time, called the
Manpower Services Commission. They had conducted a lot of
market research with unemployed youths in Sheffield, asking
which public figure they would most trust, and many of them had
replied: Jools Holland. Whether it was right or wrong, the outcome
of this market research was that corporate bodies were suddenly
interested in me.

The Manpower Services Commission then had this mad idea of
making a waxwork replica of me, indistinguishable from the real
thing but with a blank where the mouth was. They would project
my talking mouth on to it and put it into colleges and unemploy-
ment offices around Britain. When they first rang John Lay with
the idea, he said, 'Oh, you're bonkers. Get lost,' but just as he
was putting the phone down, his enormous ears heard the tail end
of the mention of a large figure and he whisked the phone back

up like lightning with, 'Well, we might talk about this a bit further . . .'

So I went to a boardroom at the Manpower Services Commission, an executive world I had never encountered before. I told them I didn't want to say a lot of old bollocks to people, but they told me they just wanted me to say that manpower training schemes were available and there to help. I then had to go and have my head cast by a Russian sculptress and her sinister team of helpers. The finished object was like an automaton. I think my hands moved as well. I don't think a single young person could have been inspired to go on any opportunity scheme because of it. But this strange creation made me realize I must be catching on. For the first series of *The Tube* they had produced a lifesize cardboard cut-out of me in the studio and I had been impressed enough with that, but this – what next? Jools the Action Man doll?

Along with this celebrity life, I was still very much part of south-east London life. I would go with Vic Wing, a marvellous fellow, absolutely spotless character, who still works with me, through post-nuclear sites in New Cross, climb across wasteground and scamper over cars to find an old Rover gear box for forty-five quid. And I still remember the joy of going round to Vic's house, pressing on the door bell and the sound of 'Hitler has only got one ball' ringing out.

Occasionally I would go with my Kentish friends Colin and Rosie Strickland for a trip out to Broadstairs, stay in a lovely Dickensian hotel and go to the no-longer-existing Dumpton Park dog track. Some people would want to go to St Tropez, St Moritz or somewhere horrid like that but I was really happier going to fantastic Broadstairs. As well as being involved in the world of dog-racing, Colin also had links with New Orleans jazz; I think the two worlds go hand in hand. He would bring over musicians such as Kid Thomas to play in the Hammersmith Palais. Kid Thomas was born in the 1890s and was a contemporary of Louis Armstrong. He was from the true dawn of the jazz age. For this particular show Colin included a band of similarly aged veterans, adding Britain's own great saxophone player, Sammy Rimington, and me. Colin put everyone's date of birth except mine and Sammy's on the poster; we were only whippersnappers from the twentieth century.

My best friend, Mark Smith, was working then as a chef at the Prince of Orange, a wonderful jazz pub in Rotherhithe, so we would spend lovely evenings eating his delicious food and listening to other fantastic musicians. One night Mike Paice did a gig with Dr John there, one of the best shows I've ever seen.

People always try to categorize the music of the eighties – mine varied from Squeeze to the Millionaires, Fine Young Cannibals, The The, Kid Thomas, Sammy Rimington and Vic the pianist. This is what I was playing, writing for, listening to, dancing to, making love to and being part of.

At this time I often used to visit my grandmother in hospital, and she always seemed pleased to see me, but her dementia was becoming so bad she couldn't remember anything properly. My mother and I wondered if perhaps she could come to live with one of us, but it would have been impossible because neither of us would have been in a position to look after her properly. It would also have been unfair on Mary because I was away so much it would have been her that was left with the responsibility.

They had a piano in my grandmother's ward, and that Christmas my mother took me so I could play for all the patients. My grandmother had really become very distant by then, almost a vegetable, but she lit up at the sound of the music, a really miraculous thing to see. Both my mother and I were amazed. I don't know how much my grandmother knew or didn't know, but I was struck once more at what a powerful force music can be.

Boaster Not a Toaster

The Tube was always top in magazine polls for music programmes and was recognized generally to be a great television success but, in 1983, we got a *TV Times* Award, which was a really big deal for us because the *TV Times* only dealt with mainstream television. It was like getting a BAFTA – quite a thing.

The award night itself was a big, glitzy affair: photographers were taking pictures all over the place, Robert Mitchum had been flown over to pick up an award, Leonard Rossiter had won one too, and Selena Scott was there, looking absolutely dazzling. I had been to film premieres but this was the first time I was among those being celebrated.

Lesley and I were at a table with Rowan Atkinson and Roland Rivron. We agreed that I would do the talking when we went up, to receive the award but discussed what I should say – I had no idea. Looking back, it should have been obvious: I should have thanked Andrea Wonfor, Malcolm Gerrie and Jeremy Isaacs, who had given me my chance in television. Because I was young and stupid I didn't realize that at award ceremonies like this one, your only responsibility is to thank the other people involved and then get off – not to try to be clever. While I was thinking of smart and funny things to say instead, Rowan suggested a gag: I should say, 'I haven't got long, so I just want to thank one or two people . . .', and then produce a very long piece of paper, one that almost reaches the ground, and just keep reading. The more names read out, the funnier it would be.

That was a very good idea but, instead, I listened to Roland, who said, 'Why don't you just thank Billy, the prop man, because you haven't got time for anyone else and, to cap it all, you can wear these.' Then he removed a box from his pocket which had a label on it saying, 'the world's funniest glasses'. It was a pair of comedy spectacles and the bit that went over the nose was a big penis. Roland put them on and we did all laugh, agreeing that these were indeed the world's funniest glasses. Rowan, a professional comedian and one of the funniest men in the world, expressed his doubts about whether this gag would work quite as well on stage but I ignored his professional advice and continued to listen to Roland.

He continued confidently, 'Tell them you are going to read a speech – people often reach for their glasses to read their thank-you speech – and then it will be doubly funny as you're only reading one name out, Billy the prop man. And wearing the world's funniest glasses. You'll have them howling with laughter.'

Geoff Wonfor was sitting in the audience near the back and afterwards gave me a full account of my acceptance speech. Lesley and I came on stage and I said, 'To all at Tyne Tees, I would like to thank . . .' I got a piece of paper out and then I put on the world's funniest glasses – to complete silence. Apparently, I looked rather pleased with myself for a moment. As he was near the control box Geoff heard the director screaming, 'Wide, cut wide, no close-ups,' and then I went on, 'Thanks very much to Billy, the prop man.' There was a rather confused ripple of applause, I took the award and Lesley and I left the stage to the sound of our own echoing footsteps.

In the wings, waiting to go on, was Robert Mitchum. I said to him, 'I don't think that was a good idea,' and he said, 'Son, I've made a lot of mistakes, but it doesn't matter. Fuck 'em. You just enjoy yourself.' However, there was a floor manager by the side of the stage who was particularly pernickety about everything, and he didn't share Robert Mitchum's laidback view – in fact, he came up seething with rage and screamed, 'What did you think you were doing?' He took it as an insult to the show and therefore an insult to him; I'd made a mockery of the event – even with what I had been told were the world's funniest glasses. Finally, I was able to return to my table where I said to Roland, 'That didn't seem to go very well, mate.' He agreed.

Anyway, at the end of the evening, as Lesley and I were going

out, she stopped off to chat to Leonard Rossiter. At that point, I
went up to Robert Mitchum, who was at the bar, and we chatted
about our love of jazz and swing music. I then asked him if he
minded giving me his autograph. He said, 'Oh, it will be a pleasure,
son.' However, realizing I didn't have any paper for him to write
it on, I pulled out my expired credit card and asked him to sign
that instead. He said, 'Sure, son. There you go.'

At this point, this floor manager, befuddled with rage, took it
upon himself to get really carried away. He had seen me getting
Robert Mitchum to do something with a credit card and now he
came marching up with two security guys and said, 'That's him.
Hold him until the police come.' I started to protest: all right, my
joke wasn't that funny but surely it wasn't a criminal offence. But
he said, 'You've insulted the show and now you're attempting
to defraud Robert Mitchum. The police have been called.' I
explained what had happened, but he wasn't having any of it.
Mercifully, Terry Wogan came up and said, 'Listen, calm down.
He was just having a laugh. Just forget it,' sorting the whole thing
out in a very fatherly way. I will never have a word said against
Terry Wogan – what a truly great man he is.

We had a bit of a chat and he told me that he'd just interviewed
the Prime Minister, who at the time was Margaret Thatcher, and
told me she was a chainsmoker. Another showbiz evening.

Afterwards, we went for dinner with Andrea and Geoff Wonfor
and Mike Bolland, the man who had commissioned *The Tube* for
Channel Four, and a few others. The first thing Geoff said was,
'Well, how do you think that went then?' Looking around the
table, I realized everyone was averting their eyes. I made a vow to
myself that, if ever I was given an award again, I would stick to
the customary thank-yous.

Our next award in fact came for a film that we shot in Jamaica
some time after this disastrous evening. I'd always loved Jamaican
music and I had worked with one or two Jamaican musicians, but
this trip gave me a chance to understand their music and culture
properly.

We filmed Josey Wales, Massive Dread, Yellowman, the fantastic

Dennis Brown and the Wailing Souls. For one scene in the film I threw myself into a swimming pool fully clothed; we then ran it backwards. We also filmed a video for a song I had written with Chris Difford, 'Black Beauty', which was actually about a car. We filmed it in the street and everyone was dancing, because it had a ska beat on it, which was great to see.

I'd inadvertently inhaled some extremely strong Jamaican mari-juana while filming in the streets of Trenchtown. Everything went into slow motion. I was standing next to a man called Alvin, who was telling me that, if I were to smuggle two white women into the hotel for him, he would send two cases of weed to my address in London. There was nothing about the idea that appealed to me – especially the two cases of drugs arriving at my London flat and getting me flung into jail. But he kept going on about it, telling me there was no danger nowadays, nobody bothered to check these things. While he was talking this relentless gibberish some red ants who had climbed up my leg without my noticing all bit me simultaneously. Feeling paranoid anyway because of the herb, I tried to slap my leg to get rid of them, but they bit even more. There was nothing for it but to tear off my trousers altogether and whack them off my bare legs. This was somewhat embarrassing in the tough streets of Trenchtown, where I had been trying to blend in and, afterwards, I had to go and lie down to get over the incident.

I wouldn't recommend anyone to experiment with this strong Jamaican herb because of the effect it can have on your feelings. If you are of a certain temperament, it can make you very paranoid and send you off your rocker completely. If you are just feeling mildly embarrassed, it will exaggerate that sensation, and that was certainly what happened in this instance.

Also on the trip we met the great Lee 'Scratch' Perry. There was a toaster on the pillars at the entrance to his house, and he pointed it out and said, 'I'm a toaster not a boaster,' and I said to him, 'Well, I'm a boaster not a toaster, mate. Nice to meet you,' and we got on very well. If he thought the ambience was wrong he would change the colour of the room or the colour of his studio. In fact, if he didn't like the colour of other people's studios, he would take it upon himself to repaint them in garish colours in the middle of the night, without bothering to consult their owners first. He certainly wouldn't have stood for the blue carpets on the walls of my studio.

Bearing in mind that Jamaica was once a British colony, there was something in the attitude of Jamaican people together, a sort of cheekiness and group humour, that I imagined was just like that of eighteenth-century London. There was an air of danger too – another similarity. We'd been filming in a club and, as we came out, the enormously fat chief of police, who was called Bigger Ford, shouted to the crowd, 'Get back, get back. The film crew is coming out now. You get back,' and he waved his machine gun, pushing people about. He was a frightening great giant of a man mountain and was acting very menacingly. Someone in the crowd piped up, 'Oh, him like trowing his weight about!' Bigger Ford swung round looking furious and, as he did so, everyone immediately assumed an expression of complete innocence, glancing about to signify their disbelief that anyone could possibly have said something like that. Seeing it done en masse like that was so beautiful and heartwarmingly funny.

We all loved our time in Jamaica and were very pleased with the finished film. However, when it won an award at the New York Film Festival, I wasn't invited to go and pick it up. They sent somebody else. I wonder why that was?

Baby Baby

Back at home, our baby was about to be born and, since my great friend Mark Smith had a lovely holiday chalet at Greatstone-on-Sea, Mary and I would spend some time down there. We would go on trips to Dungeness and the marshlands, have a lovely time walking on the shingle beaches and visiting the great listening wall. We really had the feeling we'd escaped from everything there, and I still think the marshlands of Kent are one of the most beautiful and romantic parts of the world.

Mary and I tried to think of names for the baby. Apollo and Vesuvius were two that Paula had suggested, and I was rather keen on Meadlux. Little Walter was another that I liked particularly, but I did worry that he might grow out of it. In the end we decided on the name George. On Saturday 14 April 1984, the date that Mary was due to give birth, we were doing a *Tube* five-hour special. Rik Mayall and Chris Difford were up there for it, and Rik had bought a drum kit for the baby – a nice annoying present for the parents. At the end of the show I got into John Lay's car and raced back to London, just getting back in time. George was born at 11.45 p.m. Mary and I were so happy. He was a delightful little fellow and all the family on both sides eagerly came to have a look at him. Everyone agreed he somewhat resembled Mary's wonderful mother, Joan, and coincidentally, he had been born on Joan's birthday. This, for us, was the biggest event of the year.

Soon after George's birth, *The Tube* was due to film a special in the north-east on Bryan Ferry, and Gilson drove me to Heathrow for my flight up to interview him. I had been seeing a lot more of Gilson who, since the disbanding of Squeeze in 1982, had had a difficult time and was now driving cabs to earn some money. Falling on hard times had helped inspire a rediscovery of himself and he had stopped drinking. This had turned Gilson almost overnight from a beast into a saint. I had always loved him; it was almost impossible not to. He was always trying to do the right thing, even though drink had often turned him into a big animal and, worse, away from his music. But now I had such admiration for his strength in giving it up, and his playing was so much better for it. We started to discuss doing the odd one or two shows, just he and I together.

I then flew up to Newcastle with Bryan's wife, Lucy. We were going to film Bryan walking along Bamburgh beach at sunset but, as we arrived at Bamburgh village early, I decided to go to bed for a while. I woke up later that afternoon having had a very vivid dream which had left me with a certain feeling of unreality. I had a cup of tea to try to wake up and put my head out of the door of the hotel, taking in the picturesque chocolate-box village, with a little green in front of it. As I was leaning in the rose-covered porch, I noticed that the pub was owned by Mr Holland and his brother, and another Mr Holland was the licensee. I thought that was curious. Looking out again, I saw two cars at completely opposite ends of the green very slowly approaching one another at the village crossroads. I didn't really take much notice – I heard a dog barking gently in the background and the sounds of the sea in the distance – the cars were just sort of pootling along. And then, *smash*! They crashed straight into one another at the little crossroads. It was so peculiar. How could they not have seen one another? It was a big open village green. I was the only witness, so I ran over in case anyone had been hurt. In each car was an elderly couple, and no one had come to any harm. It turned out that the people in one car were called Holland and the people in the other car were also called Holland. It was such an odd coincidence I wasn't really sure whether I'd woken up or not. I felt this strange dream-like incident must mean something and signal the approach of some monumental change. I had no idea of what that change would be and was no clearer about its meaning by the end of the day.

We filmed Bryan on the beach, which went quite well, and afterwards, he told me he and Lucy were going to dinner with some friends of theirs who lived near by, Ned and Christabel Durham. He asked me if I would like to go too, and I said I would. They were up in the Bamburgh beach car park and Bryan took me to meet them. I was impressed by Christabel's new silver Alfa Romeo Spider and by the fact that, instead of facing the most picturesque view in England, they alone in the car park had chosen to reverse the car in to face the dustbins. We all got on famously straight away.

We followed them back to where they lived, a huge, beautiful house in the middle of nowhere. Very romantic and somewhat spooky-looking. Over dinner they mentioned that they wanted to give up smoking, which I had just done – I'd given it up now I had George. I told them that I used to watch my dad and my uncles smoking, and I didn't want George to do the same with me. Apart from that serious subject, we all had a laugh and Ned gave us some extremely good wine from the cases his father, Lord Lambton, had laid down at his birth. Sixty-one had turned out to be one of the best years for Bordeaux and it was certainly going down extremely well that evening. Christabel was very attractive and she made me laugh a great deal. Like in the song, 'Where or When?', it was almost as if we knew each other already, although we'd never met before. Bryan, Lucy and I then left and flew back to London. I thought no more of it at the time, but things were to develop.

Mr and Mrs Showbiz

At King's Cross station first thing in the morning Paula, Anita and Fifi would all look rather rough. In fact, they would look like Eastern European refugees, trailing around with their last tatty possessions. Telling them this never improved their mood, and Paula would say again how much she hated this weekly journey to the distant province of Newcastle. This was one of my favourite aspects of *The Tube* and I felt sure that, in her heart, she loved it too and was glad to have it back in her life having now rejoined us for the third series.

Paula always bought second-class tickets for herself and Anita but they always sat in first class with me. Why she persisted with this petty con trick I don't know. Perhaps she took the old-fashioned view that the ticket collector would turn a blind eye to a lady travelling second class with a first-class gentleman so as to avoid causing the gentleman any embarrassment. Maybe that would have been the case in the 1920s before the trains were nationalized but, in the 1980s, it just meant that every week there would be an argument and I would be landed with paying the difference. Paula always used to say I was a true gentleman because I would open car doors for her, always pay for her dinner and, of course, pay for her and her entourage's elevation to first class. She said she had learned from me that it was very important she never carry any money with her, because somebody else would then have to pay. I'd often told her that myself, but I'd meant that somebody from a film or TV company – not me – would have to fork out.

We usually talked about what we'd done in the week. She always assumed that I'd been in a pub all week and I that she'd hardly moved from her bed. Paula loved Muriel, as did I, but she would sometimes ask, 'Is that Scottish woman and her voice going to be up there this week?' Having been away for the second series she now thought that Muriel was given more lines than she was or, as she put it, 'I've had my links cut down like young soldiers on the front line.' Being such good friends, we were happy to travel in silence but, occasionally, I'd point out some of the more interesting aspects of railway station architecture. To be honest, I don't think this held any great appeal for her. I'd notice her hand move over a page of one of her glossy magazines and then her eyes would lower and she would unobtrusively turn it over.

Now Paula was travelling with Fifi and Anita, litter would accumulate around them and, because we were on the telly together, Paula and I were seen as a couple. Even my mother seemed to perceive us as televisual man and wife and had put a photograph of us together on the top of her piano, which put Mary out a little and Bob, too, when he came round for a party once. Passengers often looked at me crossly as if I were responsible for my family's mess. I would usually try to pick all the litter up, but I'd often fall asleep and the debris would once more start to build up around us, annoying the other first-class passengers anew.

Having arrived at Newcastle, Paula would leave Fifi and Anita at the Gosforth Park Hotel and we would go to the planning meeting. Once the bands had been decided upon, another whole team of researchers would come with ideas for the show; these ideas weren't always to our taste. In their continual attempt to appeal to the young, they would sometimes decide to cover a rather dull subject such as leg-warmers, something they thought young people would be interested in. A lot of people in television are happy to go along with whatever suggestions are put forward, but Paula and I weren't as easy as that and we began to get a reputation for being a bit stroppy. The researchers were quite sensitive – if we didn't like their ideas they would often be on the verge of tears because, for them, it meant failure – so we started to use excuses. Paula used to say, 'I don't think Bob's going to want me to do that.' This was a good argument so I would use it too. Bob was very useful as this stern figure with impeccable judgement lurking in the background. Occasionally, Paula would

1. Self and Paula Yates striking
a pose to promote *The Tube*

2. Self, Paula, George and Mary in Blackpool

3. Self and Lesley Ash, in New York

4. Stephen Fry, self and Stanley Unwin and a member of the Tyne Tees production crew in Portmeirion, filming a spoof of *The Prisoner*

5. Self with George Harrison in Hong Kong, filming *Shanghai Surprise*, 1985

6

7

8

6. Self with Fats Domino in New Orleans

7. Learning from the master. Stevie Wonder, in New York

8. Discussing Rory McEwen with Van Morrison

9. Self and the Genius Ray Charles in his studio in Los Angeles

10. New Year's Eve at the Hootenanny: self (holding Lucille) and BB King

11. Joe Strummer and self take a break from recording at my studios

12. Self and President Bill Clinton, prior to the pressed flower incident

13. Early twentieth century: Mark Flanagan, producer Laurie Latham, Christopher Holland, Boaster, Dave Swift, Eric Clapton and Gilson Lavis at Helicon

14. Accompanying Amy Winehouse on *Later With Jools Holland*

15. The remains of the vehicle from which we narrowly escaped death

16. Self and Christabel

17. Rosie, aged three

18. Self, Mabel and Velocette Venom 500 outside the studios

19. Amateur architect in front of one of his elevations

23

23. Surrounded by our
loved ones, on our wedding
day, August 30, 2005

switch to 'Jools thinks that's a really fucking stupid idea,' but the insult we'd keep as a last resort was 'That would make it look like a pop programme.' Nobody could understand why that was a bad thing; they all thought that's what we were making. Andrea Wonfor was very supportive of us in these meetings, in spite of the fact that we were probably a bit of a liability.

Some of our own ideas sounded good in theory but didn't go down too well in practice. At one point we decided to hold a competition, just in order to find out how many people were watching *The Tube*. We had a hamster on the show and informed the viewers that he belonged to the King of Pop, Michael Jackson, and that his name was William. The competition was to guess this hamster's size and weight. We told the viewers to send their answers to us on a postcard labelled '*The Tube* Competition. Guess the size and weight of Michael Jackson's Willy.' Anyway, we all laughed, thinking it was rather funny. However, on Monday morning, everybody was hauled up to the Channel Four offices in Charlotte Street. It was explained that this sort of thing was unacceptable at that time in the evening. I found it all quite tiresome. We hadn't been advocating violence or anything corrupting, just making babyish jokes.

When the meeting was over we'd go back to the hotel. The hotel was never that busy so we would often have the swimming pool almost to ourselves. They had a jacuzzi, too, but Paula was wary of catching something, partly because she accused me of peeing in it. I would suggest that it was more likely to be Fifi, which she would indignantly deny.

Paula was such an absolutely wonderful mother, devoted isn't the word for it. I often used to try to tempt her to come out to various dives and places I'd got to know in Newcastle but she would always prefer an early night in with Fifi watching *Top of the Pops*. In those days, she didn't let a single spoonful of drink cross her lips. I didn't know this then but, as soon as she did have a drink, her personality would change dramatically for the worse.

I'd visit their room momentarily before going out and I would find it rather nice and cosy, with the smell of milk and beans on

toast and the television on. Nevertheless, after about ten minutes
I'd get bored and go out to join the night creatures of Newcastle.

She did come out once, when Rik Mayall persuaded her to join
us. Rik was a very charming fellow and very attractive to the
ladies, but I was a bit insulted that, after all these years of refusing
to come out with me, she joined us in the pub as soon as he asked
her. That night someone tricked her and put a tiny bit of alcohol
in her drink, but she tasted it immediately and spat it out. Then
she gulped her soft drink down and sat there looking around like
a beady bird, waiting for something exciting to happen – the walls
to fall down or a floorshow to begin. But we just sat there and
chatted, which was what being in the pub was about. She just
couldn't get her head around the point of this at all.

I've always found the breakfast smell in hotels revolting, however grand the hotel. To avoid this we used to go to Tyne Tees
and have our breakfast at the canteen before doing the runthrough,
walking through the show but without the audience or bands so
that the cameras knew where they had to be.

The Tube was sold all around the world, so it did have a big
audience. The American channel it was shown on sometimes asked
us to do special links and introductions for them. Paula started one
off by saying, 'Right, you big fat Yank bastards,' but before she
could carry on somebody said, '*Stop*'. Whoever it was then came
down from the control box upstairs and suggested a slightly different approach.

Before the show there were a lot of last-minute rehearsals,
because you had to be in the right place for the camera. In those
days we had to hold the microphone; when you shook someone's
hand, you always seemed to need a third hand for something else.
On one occasion I asked if it was possible to get a mic that you
could pin on to your clothes but immediately a voice came over
the Tannoy: 'Jools is refusing to work with the stick mic' – it
looked as if stage one of strike action would be called for once
more. Paula was delighted – 'Oh, making trouble again?'

At lunch Paula always nagged me because she thought I didn't
eat enough. She ate huge meals of the sort all-in wrestlers would

eat but remained this dainty little thing. She was very energetic, always working on or writing something; perhaps that's how she burned it all off. We'd spend the afternoon in her dressing room together, look at what was on the show and try to think of amusing things to say. Muriel would come in and say to Paula, 'My God, you look incredibly beautiful tonight – I'm looking horrible,' and Paula would say, in a rather unreassuring way, 'That doesn't matter.' We would have to encourage Muriel though, because she wasn't confident. Confronted with Paula, it would have been hard for any woman to feel confident.

Paula was absolutely angelic-looking anyway but would take her time over make-up and, if she ever had even a tiny spot, she'd be furious and start bellowing, 'Who gave me this?', trying to find a culprit to blame and sack. The tiniest bit of powder would cover it completely but she'd look at me, on the verge of breaking down, and say, 'Look at this. What good is this? A sandbag on Vesuvius.'

The countdown to the programme would begin, which was nerve-wracking for everyone, what with 5 million viewers watching and the whole thing being live. Somebody asked Paula whether she got nervous, and she said, 'I do, but Jools is fearless.' Then she qualified this compliment by adding, 'The only reason people get nervous is that they worry something is going to go wrong, but Jools would never realize that anything had gone wrong because he's too stupid to notice.' I did notice the occasional mistake, such as the time I and the film crew went into Marc Almond's dressing room, not knowing there was another person in there, without his trousers on, thus exposing his private areas to the viewers.

Sometimes we'd shoot outside, for which we'd have a selection of outdoor gear, bearing in mind we would be on air from November until April and have summer specials. Shooting outside meant that the different seasons were reflected but, up there on the banks of the Tyne, even in the height of summer, it was never going to be Barbados. Once, not realizing we were on air, the first thing viewers heard was Paula saying, 'Oh, I'm freezing my bollocks off here.' However, the good thing about it being live was that if you made a mistake it didn't matter – it was over and done with. You had to move on.

We used to open the programme with, 'It's Friday, it's five thirty, this is *The Tube*,' in a jokey imitation of those clichéd television openings. Rik Mayall and I were having a drink one evening, and he suggested doing a version for us himself, along the lines of, 'It's Friday, it's five thirty and the pubs are open,' and then being sick into the camera. All the *Tube* team liked this idea, so he came up to Newcastle, where we discussed it further and rehearsed it. In the final live version, he had huge slurps of beer in between each part of the sentence – 'It's Friday glub, glub, glub, it's five thirty glub, glub, glub the pubs are open, glub, glub, glub. Ugghugh.' And he collapsed as I came into shot with, 'I can't apologize enough' and the titles started to roll. We all thought this was rather a jolly start to the show, a new way to draw people in, and it was a bit of skilful acting on Rik's part, after all.

However, during and after this particular show, the phone didn't stop ringing at the Duty Office at Channel Four. One woman thought it was the most disgusting thing she had ever seen on television, another man in Oxford was going to contact his solicitor and call the local police. I wondered if he would then ask them to dispatch a squad car from Oxford to Newcastle to make an arrest. I had no idea how upset everyone would be but, as usual, I fell back on 'It wasn't me, it was Rik. We won't have him on again.'

Strangely enough, after the same programme we also had a number of complaints that we had censored too much. The Red-skins had been on and, half-way through their number, they stopped and this Durham miner got up to say his piece. Nobody had told the production staff or the people in the sound room, so his microphone wasn't turned on. He was speaking for thirty seconds but no one could hear a thing. It was the time of the great miner's strike and people assumed that this was censorship of the worst sort but, of course, we would all have been thrilled to let him speak if we'd been told about it beforehand. Everyone was affected by the atmosphere present in England at the time – there were so many conspiracy theories, train strikes in sympathy with the miners, whispered instructions about where to go in order to demonstrate on their behalf, but this silence was nothing but a technical mistake.

After the show Paula immediately took off whatever she had been wearing and changed into something casual. I'd change too, but Paula often remarked that I would just put something even dirtier on. I might have taken offence at this, but she was very good to me and always added that she didn't mind if I was drunk or smelled.

British Airways had changed the time of their Newcastle to London flight from seven o'clock to seven thirty, so all the *Tube* people could now take the plane back. The show finished at seven so Paula and I and all the other people on the show would get there fifteen minutes before it took off and just run on to it.

After we'd landed I would drive Paula back to her house, passing the fantastic illuminated sign of a bubbling Lucozade bottle at Hammersmith flyover. At this point, before I could express my appreciation, Paula would always pipe up, 'I know what you're going to say – "I wish I had that sign on the side of my house."' Then we'd get to Chelsea Bridge with all its pastel-coloured lights and she would say, 'Oh, isn't that beautiful' and I would just raise my eyes or, if that didn't feel dismissive enough, answer, 'Oh, shut up, you old bag.' Sometimes she'd point to a flat somewhere with just blankets up at the windows and naked light bulbs and say, 'Doesn't that look depressing? Can't they even have side lights, or shades – just to make it prettier?' I would agree with her but then get home and look up to see the same bare light bulbs hanging in our house.

After I'd greeted Mary and George I used to pop out for some real ale and, later, watch the taped programme back. Paula used to suggest scornfully that I did this in order to smother my screen image with kisses but, in fact, it was just to see if there was any room for improvement. There always was.

Count Me In

I've since played bigger and more prestigious venues, but the concert I played in Southampton on 10 November 1984 was a very important milestone for me. I walked on stage alone and, to the large and rowdy audience of students announced, 'Ladies and gentlemen, please welcome to the stage – my Big Band' – and on walked Gilson. The two of us played the same sort of thing we play now and the crowd went completely wild – almost overly wild, crowd-surfing to our piano and drums. We were so excited by their response and by the act of playing that we decided to do more gigs. It was Malcolm Hardee who had booked the South-ampton concert, following a conversation I'd had with him about missing playing live and, after this successful venture with my Big Band of two, he started to book us more shows. It was the begin-ning of my current career. Throughout 1985 Gilson and I did concerts whenever we could, including a benefit for the miners at the Albany Empire. The two of us didn't have to rehearse that much; we'd just play and let it happen.

During the years I was doing *The Tube* I sometimes questioned why I had taken myself away from playing live: it was a strange blip, because television programmes come and go but playing stays with you so long as you're physically and mentally up to it. There's a difference between audiences watching you on television just because you happen to be on and audiences who have paid to come and see you. In the end you have a different relationship with them; they've chosen to be there with you, therefore you have a bigger responsibility to them. If you're a musician, you have to play live consistently to make it work. It's like exercise, like walking or boxing, you've got to stay in trim.

I had no idea that from these modest early roots this band of myself and Gilson would gradually evolve into a genuine eighteen-piece Big Band, selling nearly 2 million records thus far and becoming one of the most successful Big Bands ever to come out of Britain. But enough with this boasting of the future and on with the story.

To celebrate the new age of television and technology, the Independent Television Network had decided to broadcast a Europe-wide edition of *The Tube* on 4 January 1985. It would be live, five hours long and, for the first time, linked up with all the European stations and their millions of viewers. They planned to call this show *Europe A-Go-Go*. Paula and I were very dismissive of the idea and especially the name but everyone else was very excited. The French would contribute and the Belgians and the Dutch and the Swiss and the Germans and the Spanish and the Italians – all the constituent nations of Europe would have a part to play. There was a feeling that music was the means of communication that could cross all language barriers; this still holds true today. There was a positive, optimistic feel about the broadcast, despite the remarks from Paula and myself.

So each country depicted their local scene, sharing their culture with millions of viewers. At the end of each one, the show would return to us at base. I was proud that our notoriously uncouth and offensive show had been chosen to represent Britain's culture.

Soon after this show we decided to film in Blackpool as we all, with the exception of Paula, thought there was something rather romantic about empty holiday seaside destinations off season. Mary and George were getting the train up from London to meet me there, and I had a pleasant drive from Newcastle with my television family of Paula, Anita and Fifi.

At Penrith I suggested stopping for a cup of tea. Penrith was the sort of place I find tremendously mysterious, imagining suppressed sexual tensions behind every closed net curtain and unrequited love in every cul-de-sac and public bar. Paula was less taken with it. We went into this faded old three-star hotel for tea, as Paula hadn't liked any of the cafés I pointed out. The hotel was almost like something from *Dad's Army*: the ancient armchairs had doilies on the arms and all the other guests were as old as the chairs. A rather nice, gangling white-haired waiter with a shiny white jacket and bow tie came out to serve us. After he'd brought us our tea, he asked, 'Would your wife like some more toast?', and Paula said, 'Well, she's on her way to Blackpool so why don't you go and ask her, you stupid fuck.' She had what I would call these blurting moments. I said to this poor crestfallen waiter, 'She's very tired,' and he nodded and said, 'I understand, sir, a tired wife,' which she found even more annoying.

We arrived in Blackpool, which was freezing cold and covered in snow. We went to film the ballroom dancing and giant theatre organ in the glamorous Tower Ballroom. David Bailey had come up to take some photographs and at one point he started giving Geoff tips on how he should do the shots. Finally, Geoff said, 'Look, mate, you take two or three photographs a minute, I take five hundred frames a second. When you get to that level, talk to me. Until then, I'll direct the film.' Bailey found that quite funny, and we got on very well. He took my camera off me and took a few shots with it; I was amazed at how much better these few quick photographs were than the others on the film.

On 12 January the members of Squeeze got together again, as we had agreed to perform a one-off fundraising show for a local charity at the Saxon Tavern pub in Catford. We'd been talking about it for months but, on the day, we didn't rehearse very much, just sat together in the afternoon and played. We all knew what we were supposed to be doing and it felt really natural and enjoyable. When we did the concert that evening the whole place was heaving and the crowd wildly enthusiastic. Miles met us in the bar after this show and told us that A&M was desperate for us to get together and do another record. Also, if we did and toured America again, it would be even more successful than our previous tours.

The next day Miles dashed off to the States to meet Jerry Moss, the head of A&M. Once word of a potentially huge deal got out, there seemed to be interest everywhere. When a popular group's been apart and comes back together, people like it all the more, and this atmosphere of anticipation and enthusiasm infected us all.

Walking to New Orleans

Following the success of all the films we had gone out and shot in various cities in Britain and worldwide, Andrea Wonfer asked me if there was any city I would particularly like to film in. I told her that the city I loved almost above all others was New Orleans. Its music had had such a profound influence on me, starting back with Louis Armstrong and Jelly Roll Morton, going right up to the present time with Dr John and Allen Toussaint. Then there were the Neville Brothers, Fats Domino, Lee Dorsey and all the music in between, including the Cajun music of French-speaking Louisiana. Andrea suggested I go out there to research and, on my return, she would get the money we needed for a film. This is another reason to feel grateful for Andrea's visionary approach since it's very hard to get the money to do anything on television nowadays. If possible at all, it involves a very long-winded process, which is why I haven't really bothered in the last few years. It's easier, more stimulating and really much more fun to play music.

Having received the go-ahead from Andrea and a verbally agreed, and then very handsome, budget of about £200,000, we now went and spent a few weeks in New Orleans in order to research the material for the film. Quint Davis, who runs the Jazz and Heritage Festival out there, was very helpful and introduced us to a lot of people. Once these people realized that we really loved and knew about the music, they were enthusiastic about being in the film. We met Rockin' Dopsie – the Cajun king – at Lafayette, and Allen Toussaint, who had produced hits for Lee Dorsey and many other fabulous musicians.

Quint then took us to Fats Domino's house. He had this huge mansion on a hill with a speckled drive, and on the drive were all these people working on row upon row of powder-blue Lincolns. They were all his relatives, as it turned out, but he was rather dismissive about them. Strangely, it was they who lived in the big house – Fats preferred the shotgun shack at the bottom of the hill where he'd always lived.

Fats was one of the most charming people you could ever hope to meet. I'd always loved his music and had been to see him a few times. He'd always managed to have his own unique sound, and it remained consistently his own across the different eras of music. Some people use pick-up bands and musicians whenever they need them but Fats had kept the same New Orleans Rhythm and Blues Band throughout, which had helped to keep his sound consistent. They sound so great, those bands when they play; I always get a lift listening to them.

Anyway, going back down the hill to Fat's shotgun-shack home, we found him cooking Cajun food, wearing his dressing-gown and a hair net. He offered us some but, having just eaten, I rather rudely turned it down. He then put some in a Tupperware container for me to take away and, in his thick old-style New Orleans accent, asked, 'Tell me, son, so what's this all about then?'

Instead of just saying, 'We're making a film about New Orleans celebrating its music, could you be in it?', I talked him through the whole outline. I started with Robbie Coltrane selling me a ticket to New Orleans and me setting off from the London docks. The planned Lee Dorsey opening, travelling to Lafayette, crossing the Bayou on the ferry and listening to Cajun music and Rockin' Dopsie. I explained the idea we'd had of hearing a gospel choir on the radio and then driving past a field and seeing it singing there in the flesh. And the Neville Brothers, Allen Toussaint and Dr John in London. It took me about forty-five minutes to explain all this and, at the end of it, I said, 'So that's about the size of it – would you be in the film?' Fats gave me a smile, and turned and said to his manager, 'I can't understand a word he's saying.'

My heart sank. The manager put his hand over his forehead, frowned and said, 'Well, Fats, he's doing a film. I mean, I don't know what to say, Fats. He's doing a film.' Fats repeated, without enthusiasm, 'Doing a film? Oh.' It wasn't looking good, but Quint Davis, with a flash of inspiration, said, 'Here, Jools – play Fats that thing you played on the piano the other night,' so I played with my left hand a thing I'd learned off Fats, 'I'm Ready'. Fats' eyes lit up and he started playing at the top end of the piano alongside me. As he did so, he said, 'I'll be in your film. I'll be in your film. That's my music. You've got my music.' This was proof once more that music is far superior as a means of communication to the blunt instruments we call words I am using to write this.

Having gathered all the research material, that summer we went back out to New Orleans and filmed it. Before we went, we asked Stephen Fry to do the voiceover and filmed Robbie Coltrane, George Melly and Rik Mayall for the London section. We also included Stanley Unwin, a jazz fan, one of the greatest British actors of all time and the inventor of a unique made-up way of speaking. Stanley, if he were telling you the story of Goldilocks and the three bears, would say, 'This is the storylode of goldieloppers and the three beardilobes.' He started our film by referring to Louis Armstrong as 'the king of trumpiblow – deep joy'.

I knew Sting had written a great song called 'Moon over Bourbon Street,' and I also knew that if he was in the film singing it the programme would get a lot more viewers. I had learned that if you involve a mainstream artist in your programme, you have a good opportunity to introduce their audience to lesser known, but equally great, music. As much as I loved Rockin' Dopsie, not many people had heard of him. Sting was completely rushed off his feet with big international projects, but he generously took the time to come down, and we filmed him in the Woolwich foot tunnel at seven o'clock on a Sunday morning when it was empty. That was a big boost.

Back in New Orleans, it was boiling hot. Mary and my mother came out to join me for a while. Everything went to plan and Lee Dorsey, the first person we filmed, was fantastic. We filmed him in his scrapyard and car-repair lot. In the film, he cuts the top off my car to make it a convertible and later performs 'Working in a Coalmine'. He took me to his neighbourhood bar afterwards for a drink. This, as far as I'm concerned, was a dream bar. It was full of people of his age, in their early sixties, with sixties and seventies

New Orleans R&B records on the jukebox. If I lived in New Orleans, I would have made that my local and that alone almost tempted me to move there. And, with Lee Dorsey himself, I felt a real complete sympathy. Maybe it was the interests we shared in scrap metal, auto repairs and great music. He's no longer with us but his classic records, for example, 'Working in a Coalmine' and 'Everything I Do, Gotta be Funky', are plundered and sampled all the time.

We filmed Johnny Allen doing 'Promised Land', and Rockin' Dopsie, whose correct title is actually Good Rockin' Dopsie. If you're 'rockin'' that's all right but if you're 'good rockin'' that's like becoming a sir or a lord on the bayoux in musical terms.

Then we drove all night to go out to Mamou, Louisiana, where all the French-speaking Cajuns live. There was something heavy in the atmosphere there. I couldn't quite put my finger on what it was but everyone seemed to be drunk at eleven o'clock in the morning. Their music was great but these were wild people and we were a long way from anywhere. I had just bought something in a shop and these three drunk men came out of a bar as I was walking round the corner. I was wearing a black shirt and a dark suit I'd worn throughout the filming and, apparently, I cut quite an odd figure in Mamou at that time of the morning. The three men looked at me and said, 'Hey, man, you looking like a preacher. You a preacher?', and I answered, 'No, I'm not a preacher, chum.' They didn't look as if they understood a word I was saying and said, 'Well, we don't like the look of you.' I didn't like the look of them either: one had webbed hands and another the pointed teeth of a ghoul. As they lurched towards me I thought, 'Hello, we're gonna have a row here,' and I realized it was too late to reason with them and explain the Christian principles of peace and non-violence. So I prepared for close combat and screamed the traditional south-east London response, 'Fuck off, you tossers.' Luckily, Geoff heard my cry, and he and the film crew came running round the corner and saved me just in time.

To this day I think that *Walking to New Orleans* is the best thing I've made for television. It stands out because it reflects the music and my love for it. It manages to capture the atmosphere of New Orleans at a time when there were still a lot of great people there who are no longer with us.

People knock America, but in the twentieth century it changed popular music beyond recognition. New Orleans played a vital role in this. In our film, we just wanted to give viewers a feeling of the music and atmosphere without using too many words and explanations.

Some of this charm and individuality has now gone from New Orleans, destroyed not only by the terrible floods but also by the rise of corporate conformity. Instead of being charmed by the simple sight and sound of someone playing in their front room, now you're left with the uniform din of the expensive karaoke or sports bars which have sprung up. When we made the film, there was still a lot of the old style left. Mind you, every time you return from some enchanting place, there's always the suggestion from some clever Dick 'that you should have seen it twenty years ago . . .' So I'll refrain from going on in this way here.

Down the Tube

Back in England, there was a lot going on. Things had improved financially and Mary, George and I moved to a bigger house in Blackheath. Mary was pregnant with our second child, which we were both very excited about. Then my musical hero, Little Richard, came to play on *The Tube*. I had always loved not only his amazing piano playing but also his gospel, shouting style of delivering a song, a huge influence on the Beatles in their early days. Paula had to put up with my great enthusiasm throughout the journey to Newcastle and, as she was very much less excited than me, all she would do was turn back to her magazines with, 'Yeh, typical of you to like somebody like that . . .'

Since Little Richard was a Seventh-Day Adventist, he didn't want to record after dark, so we had agreed in his case to do a pre-record. He announced that he wanted to do 'He's Got the Whole World in His Hands' but he didn't want to play the piano for the recording so he asked me to do it. I played it one way and he said, 'No, no, do it my style.' I changed it and to my great relief he said, 'Yeh, that's it.' The whole crew was mesmerized by him and, at the end of the song, started clapping spontaneously themselves, quite a rare occurrence. It really worked beautifully and we then recorded it, ready to put into the live show.

Before Little Richard left, we had a photograph taken of us all together, and in it I was beaming because I was so pleased to be standing next to him. What can't be seen is that he had playfully grabbed hold of my buttocks for the shot. I could have seen it as sexual harassment in the workplace but I chose to shrug it off as experience and, in fact, from Little Richard, an honour.

That evening, as we waited to go on air, Paula started to read out certain passages from his autobiography which, unlike this one, was filled with incredibly racy details. Towards the end of the last-minute countdown to the live show, Paula said, 'There's a whole chapter about a man with a fifteen-inch dick up his arse . . .' I looked up and the floor manager was furiously mouthing the words, 'You're on, you're on.' Clearly, Paula's observation had gone out live. I said, 'So sorry. Good evening and welcome, children.' As the show continued I was thinking, 'Oh, here we go again. Oh why, why?'

The reason I like music is that it's like being an author or a painter; apart from having to wrestle with your talent, it's you alone making the artistic decisions. In television, you have to deal with so many people – 'What do you think of this? What do you think of that?' Jeremy Isaacs, the head of Channel Four, was always supportive of *The Tube* and defended us against the Independent Broadcasting Authority whenever we got into trouble with any of our offensive moments such as this one. He said to me that with television, you're in the hands of other people all the time – even he was. And I thought he was in charge of everything.

Occasionally I would play with some of the guests on *The Tube* and was pleased to play on various occasions with Pino and the drummer from Go West, Alison Moyet and Eric Burdon, and Howard Jones. I was becoming frustrated because I didn't have the time to concentrate on my own playing. Introducing groups was all very well, but you can get any old show-off to do that.

However, this same year, this wonderful jazz collector and enthusiast called Bobby Furber organized a jazz charity event and asked Gilson and me to perform at it. The charity was very excited because he had persuaded Princess Diana to attend, one of her very early public engagements, which meant that there was huge press interest.

The night arrived and I came on with my Big Band duo and we played a song called 'Bumble Boogie', which went down well. The cream of British jazz was there and, after everyone had played, we all lined up to meet Princess Diana in her black velvet dress. Humphrey Lyttelton was the MC for the evening, chosen because, as well as being such a talented musician, he has perfect manners.

There were so many of us, and Humphrey Lyttelton was doing such a good job of remembering everybody's name, I was quite aghast. I think I'd have fainted if I'd been shown this whole line of people and told to introduce them. If it had been my family I would have forgotten their names under those circumstances. His task was in no way helped by Spike Milligan who, annoyed by the presence of Princess Diana, had taken it upon himself to pop from one end of the line to the other shouting towards her, 'You're not jazz. *You're not jazz.* Not J-A-Z-Z.' His point, which I didn't share, was that she wasn't an authentic jazz enthusiast and shouldn't have been there. I felt that she'd come along to listen to and support us and that was good enough. The Royal Protection officers were there but, seeing that this rude man was the familiar figure of Spike, they weren't quite sure what to do. Humphrey behaved perfectly, as if he were an equerry to Queen Victoria, and both he and Princess Diana ignored this eccentric abuse and carried on. Years later I met her again when I performed at the big Prince's Trust concert with Eric Clapton and George Harrison. Over the years I had observed first-hand the wonderful work of the Prince's Trust and was very pleased to be able to support them in any way I could. At the reception after the show she came and asked me to play the song I'd played at the jazz charity event, as she'd really liked it and wanted to learn the left hand of the piece. Luckily I remembered which song it was and, with her sitting beside me on the piano stool, I played it for her again, happy and honoured to demonstrate 'Bumble Boogie' to such an enthusiastic amateur pianist.

By now I had begun to feel that the spirit had gone out of *The Tube* to some extent or, at least, my enthusiasm for it had diminished. We constantly had to find new things to thrill and shock the audience, and an hour and a half was a lot to fill, twenty-six weeks of the year. We had to find three groups, plus a couple of acoustic acts, plus specialty acts, plus someone for the comedy spot. And then there were the films we'd do on location around Britain, exhausting not just for me but for everybody. The show had become such a success but at this point I felt it had reached its zenith and it couldn't really go anywhere. Before every programme Paula and I would broadcast live trailers, which would air at quarter to five, asking the viewers to join us at five thirty. For the filming of one of these trailers, I was very tired, not having slept the night before, and was standing there vacantly waiting for action. When they gave me the go-ahead I said, 'Join us later on *The Tube*, be there or be . . .' and then instead of saying 'square', which suddenly sounded stupid to my tired mind, I added '. . . a completely un-groovy fucker!' As it slipped out, I thought, 'Oops. That was a mistake . . .'

Now, there wouldn't have been a problem if it had been late at night but, unfortunately, this live trailer went on air straight after *Noddy*. A lot of very gloomy and earnest faces met me at Tyne Tees after that show. And, not surprisingly, the tabloids had a field day with 'Foul-mouthed Git Upsets Tots' headlines. There had been so many other controversies with the programme generally but this was thought to be the last straw.

That week I had to write many letters of apology, which I was happy to do because it genuinely had been a regrettable slip of the tongue on my part. I hadn't been concentrating. I wouldn't have deliberately run the risk of the whole programme being taken off air and causing everybody to lose their jobs. And I wouldn't have wanted to swear in front of the tots watching *Noddy* either. Mary Whitehouse wrote to me on behalf of her National Viewers and Listeners Association, and I wrote back. In my letter I said that I was really sorry, it had been an inadvertent slip of the tongue due to tiredness, and it wouldn't happen again. I had such a charming and sympathetic letter back that, really, feeling so much in agree-ment with them on so many things, I considered joining their association.

The following week, when I returned to Tyne Tees, the gloomy faces remained. Even the doorman looked disapproving; there was a feeling that my link might have lost us the show. Even Paula was being annoying – 'Oohh . . . you've got to go and see the headmaster. You're in a lot of trouble.' When I got to the meeting

I found that not only were the usual production people present but the managing director, the accountant and all these Newcastle grown-ups, every single one averting their eyes from mine. I've always been amused by the word 'carpeted' – imagine emerging from a room covered in a nice Axminster suit – but, in this case, the carpeting meant the *Tube* executives saying they had no choice but to suspend me from the live programme for six weeks. The series was coming to an end anyway, and it was agreed that I would come back after the suspension for the last three programmes.

I remember saying, 'I can't apologize enough,' but I was beginning to get a bit tired of all this apologizing.

Three-Finger Exercise

With all the rumours of Squeeze re-forming, there had been many signs of interest from record companies in both Britain and America, and Miles had been talking to many of them on our behalf. Although Miles was still managing me, there remained a bit of ill feeling and mistrust towards him as far as Chris and Glenn were concerned. Furthermore, I don't think Miles was entirely confident Squeeze would stick with him even if he did get them a deal. But we did need somebody to pull the whole thing together. Eventually, A&M offered us the best deal, and we agreed we'd stick with Miles.

We wanted Laurie Latham, who had recently done so well with Paul Young, to produce our first record back together. He was living in Brussels at the time; however, since I was suspended from *The Tube* for six weeks, I was free to go there, and we all rather liked the idea, because Brussels wasn't too far to drive, it had lots of restaurants and would be an inspiring and different place to be. So, in our various vehicles, the reformed Squeeze set off in convoy to the Continent.

Laurie was a great producer and has since produced all my Big Band records. But, with Squeeze, as he had done with Paul Young, he laid each sound and instrument down bit by bit, which sounded great on the final record. However, this process was painstaking and, one day in the studio, as he was overdubbing a tambourine with Gilson, I was a bit bored and decided to play a joke on Glenn. I put a newspaper over my head, cut some eyeholes out in order to look as if I was an SAS person and crept up behind him in the furtive manner such a person would employ. He did jump when I shouted, 'You're under arrest,' but he also overreacted, picking up a rolled-up Venetian blind and hitting me with it, accidentally

catching the forefinger of my right hand. Suddenly, there was
blood squirting everywhere.

Neither of us knew what to do, so we decided to go and ask
Laurie, since he was the record producer and the grown-up. As I
started to explain, showing him my finger, the whole of the top
of it lifted up like a grease gun in a garage, and blood spurted all
over the mixing desk. Far from helping, Laurie went, 'Ugh. Don't
squirt it all over here. Go and see a doctor. I don't know. I'm not
a doctor.'

Glenn felt so awful about it that he took me to the hospital and
waited with me there. Unfortunately, that week there had been a
lot of football rioting and hooliganism in Brussels, which had led
to ill feeling towards English patients with injuries on the part of
the hospital staff. I could see that everyone assumed I myself had
been injured in the course of rioting and I tried to explain – 'Artist,
piano, finger, urgent' – but they ignored my mime and told me to
take off my trousers so they could give me a tetanus injection in
the bottom. I tried to say that I thought this was unnecessary but
I did what I was told. Watching, Glenn's shoulders were shaking
but he was making no sound; I think he was very upset by the
whole thing. Anyway, credit to the brilliant Belgian medical services, they sewed my finger up well and put a big metal splint on
it, leaving me with this huge pointing finger which the Belgians
took to calling Monsieur le Digit.

We had almost come to the end of recording by now but I still
had some keyboard overdubbing to add, which my injury now
prevented. However, our good fortune was that both my brothers,
Richard and Christopher, had turned into very accomplished
musicians. As children, they had listened to Squeeze practising in
our family's front room and, once we had left to go to the pub,
they'd have a go on all the instruments we'd left behind. They had
formed a group called the B Sharps, which had already had one
single on Miles's IRS label. Since I knew that Christopher could
play in the same style as me, I asked him to come out to complete
these overdubs, which he did brilliantly. The finished record was
called *Cosi Fan Tutti Frutti*.

We went on to do a huge concert in Dublin with U2 – a great change, we all agreed, to our first one in the Hope and Anchor with its three-men-and-a-dog audience. I had my finger in a splint still, which limited my ability, but I announced to the huge audience, 'I've only got one finger but it points beautifully, will you join me?' The crowd followed suit and, seeing all these fingers lifted in the air, I felt I'd invented a new gesture.

By now, my six-week suspension from *The Tube* had come to an end and there were still three more programmes left to make, and a summer special. However, Squeeze was now lined up to tour America, so I was unable to do the last *Tubes*. They asked the talented Malcolm McLaren to step in instead and, before we left for America, Squeeze actually appeared on *The Tube* as guests, which was quite a novelty for me. Just as we were about to play, we noticed that the sign put up behind us with our name on it read, 'Sqeeze.' We did point out the spelling mistake, but by then it was too late to do anything about it.

Mary was getting bigger with Rosie but, what with recording in Brussels and now this tour of America, I was rarely at home. In fact, it was a very busy summer and a very hard juggling act for Miles to balance, but he managed it.

The first concert on our American tour was at the Pier in New York. Then we played the Nassau Coliseum, which is an enormous stadium on Long Island. People were going bananas for us, suddenly remembering how much they'd loved us. It was quite odd, having played these small shows with Gilson, to be now going out into these enormodome stadiums. I'd look out from backstage and there'd be huge articulated lorries and tour buses, one for the crew, one for us; it had suddenly become a very big operation. With the size of the crew, it was unbelievable we made any money at all. It was like taking the Roman army on tour.

I was still in America when I heard that Mary was about to go into labour. I flew back immediately, in a panic – and on 1 October at 3.38 a.m. the most marvellous thing happened to us for the second time, which was Rosie being born. I was really thrilled to bits with this little baby. I went to pick her and Mary up from Greenwich Hospital in my 1964 Mark 10 Jaguar, with its superb fold-down luxury picnic tables. I remember tucking Rosie up on one of these picnic tables and driving her home on that because she was so small.

Mary and I had recently become friends with the artist Brian Clarke. We had met him at the house of our friend, the writer and broadcaster Joan Komolosi, and immediately got on well with him. As well as his abstract paintings, Brian Clarke did stained-glass works of a monumental scale all over the world and was a huge success. It was inspiring talking to him about his work. Just after Rosie's birth he invited us all to a villa he had rented in Italy, just outside Rome, owned by a man called Dado Ruspoli, who had been part of the *Dolce Vita* set. Dado was going out with one of the ravishing beauties of our age, the talented clothes designer Bella Freud, who also became a great friend at this time. Vivien Westwood was there too, and I remember her saying, 'Oh, are these your children? George and Rosie. What odd names.' I thought they were probably the least odd names you could possibly have. Another guest was this extraordinary author called Hugues de Montalembert, an aristocratic Frenchman who had been blinded after having acid thrown into his eyes during a robbery in New York. He wore wraparound steel glasses and had the most incisive wisdom.

Hugues was a tremendous success with the ladies with his devastating looks and his air of mystery and, also, I suppose, his slight vulnerability. I sat next to him at lunch and he was an incredible conversationalist. What fun to be holidaying with sophisticated, international folk. At one point I turned to Vivien Westwood, who was on my other side, and George, who was sitting on my lap, stuck this springing eyeball sucker toy he was playing with on to Hugues' steel glasses. I felt that George had rather let me down in front of my new international friends. I made my excuses but, as George was only two, we all laughed about it. Poor Rosie had colic, so she cried most of the time but, apart from that, and the springy eye incident, this holiday was a very enjoyable family break.

'Architectural Number'

After this tour of America, Squeeze was getting a lot of attention, which meant more work for us all, and doing *The Tube* again would only make more demands on my time. It was all getting a bit much and I wasn't able to concentrate very much on anything let alone trying to concentrate on my own music.

Before I could make any decision about what to do, and before the series had even started, I flew out to Hong Kong with a *Tube* film crew. George Harrison's Handmade Film Company was making *Shanghai Surprise* with the newly married Sean Penn and Madonna and *The Tube* wanted to shoot a Making Of documentary to feature in our next series.

I didn't really get to talk to either of them but, one afternoon, I watched Sean and Madonna shooting a scene. As I did so, George Harrison suddenly appeared and came bounding over to speak to me. At first I was really starstruck. Not only had I always been a Beatles fan but I'd also always been a huge fan of George Harrison in particular. I loved his solo music and identified with his frustration at being a songwriter in a group which already had two great songwriters in it.

I had met all sorts of people in my life and had been thrilled to interview Paul McCartney but, because the Beatles were such a phenomenon, to find myself chatting casually with one of them was odd at first. It must be like that for them all the time, like being a member of the Royal Family, and everybody either smiling inanely or behaving oddly towards you. However, after about two or three minutes, we really got on very well and made one another laugh. At the end, he said, 'Listen, stay in contact,' and he gave me these numbers and said, 'Give me your number and when we're back in England and I'm having a party, I'll let you know – come over. It'd be great to see you. Let me know what you're doing.'

At that point he had to go over to where Madonna and Sean Penn were loudly complaining to the producers about the hounding they were receiving from the press. The producers were listening and sympathizing, but one of the pair said, 'You have no idea what it's like! We can't move out of our hotel. They're on to us wherever we go.' I then heard George say, in his completely deadpan way, 'Well, I was in a group once meself, and we had a little bit of that, you know.' They both completely ignored this and kept rabbiting on about their concerns. Nobody noticed except me. That was the beginning of a good friendship.

When I got back to England I was still very busy and there were further bits and pieces to do for *The Tube*. By now, I felt my heart was really not in it any more and I found any demands it made on my time simply annoying. I wasn't sure it would continue for much longer anyway, but I had to make a decision before the next series began. After some more consideration I informed the producers of my decision so they would have time to find a replacement.

We had already arranged to do a film in Wales, and I suggested Portmeirion as the location, partly because *The Prisoner* had been filmed there. The idea of making a spoof appealed to me, a story about my resigning in the style of *The Prisoner*. I'd always liked the programme when I was a lad, although it had been a mystery to me why anyone would want to escape from such an enchanting place.

I wrote the basic outline and then we improvised. My original storyline was that Stephen Fry, playing the role of *The Prisoner* character 'Number Two', wanted to close the place down and let everyone go but would do so only if I would tell him why I was leaving *The Tube*. However, every time I started to tell him my reasons, he would interrupt me before I could get going on the explanation. We also filmed with heart-throb Hugh Laurie and British screen legend Terence Alexander, who represented the men from the ministry and the television suits from upstairs. We spent quite a lot of time filming the opening titles, which intercut with the original titles from *The Prisoner*. The cult series was being reissued on video at the time and the production company allowed us to use all these bits of footage from it so it looked like the only people left in the village were myself, Patrick McGoohan, who played the original Prisoner, Stephen Fry and Stanley Unwin. I'd just say to Stephen or Stanley, 'This is the situation,' and they would take it from there. Stephen Fry was brilliant. He gave a long improvised speech and, at the end of it, I was horrified to hear Geoff Wonfor say, 'Oh, that wasn't bad, man. Can you do it again like?' But Stephen did it again, word for word. Not only did it cut in very well with the original *Prisoner* footage, I felt it was a rather satisfactory way to leave *The Tube*, the running theme 'Why have you resigned? Why are you leaving?'

One outcome of this trip was to reinvigorate my interest in architecture, something I'd had since a child but not had time to enjoy in recent years. On my visit to Portmeirion, I became friends with the poet Robin Llewellyn, the grandson of the original designer, Sir Clough Williams-Ellis, and he gave me information about its history, which was to stand me in good stead when I came to design and construct my own small village of studios in Greenwich. Portmeirion had been built quite cheaply just after the war when there hadn't been many materials or much money available, and the whole place has a musical quality to it, in that Williams-Ellis would take architectural phrases and improvise, as musicians do all the time in their work. He had part of a classical building in one corner and, in another, a gothic arch with a temple on top of it, but all of it was done charmingly and with great wit and taste.

My years of doing *The Tube* had come to an end and I felt a mixture of nostalgia and relief – it was a bit like leaving school. Squeeze had another big American touring commitment lined up, and Channel Four wanted another *Walking to New Orleans* type film, this time on Memphis. And, in between all these things, Malcolm Hardee had booked some more gigs for Gilson and me. I was grateful for all this activity because it made me look forward rather than back. Had I had time on my hands, I might have felt more sentimental. And, much as I'd enjoyed my time there, it was quite a relief not to be on that train to Newcastle every week. Soon after this *The Tube* ended; Channel Four shared my view that the show had run its course.

Everything was changing, and not only in my professional life. There was to be another lasting legacy from my time at *The Tube*. For right or for wrong, for better or for worse, by the end of my time there I had started to see Christabel Durham on quite a regular basis. At the time, she was living apart from her husband, Ned, but still in the same house in Northumberland I'd visited that evening after the strange afternoon in Bamburgh. She would come to Newcastle to visit me and to watch the show being made. I found her completely irresistible; she made me roar with laughter and I was beguiled by her beauty. Without saying any more on the subject for now, this brings us swiftly on to our next chapter, which I will call '*Casca il Mondo*', or, for those who don't speak Italian, 'The World is Falling Apart.'

Casca il Mondo

In June, Christabel decided to come with me to Plymouth, where Gilson and I were playing at a charity event organized by Lenny Henry. John Lay drove us down and we played just one or two songs. We stayed the night in the Holiday Inn and set off the next day in our rented green Vauxhall Cavalier. I was sitting in the back with Christabel and John and Gilson were in the front. At about 11.30 a.m., travelling east along the M5 near Exeter, John suddenly said, 'What's that?'

I looked up and saw that, coming towards us in the fast lane, was a late 1960s maroon-coloured Austin 3-litre. John Lay jammed on the brakes, which was the most sensible thing to do, and I adopted the aircraft crash-landing position, not through training, through panic. The others were so mesmerized by the sight of this Austin 3-litre coming towards them they just kept looking at it. Then there was this huge crashing noise and I realized we'd had a head-on collision in the fast lane of the motorway.

After this horrible sound of smashing there was silence. Then, the most terrifying thoughts occurred to me: would the car burst into flames? Would a lorry plough into the back of us and kill us all, just as had happened to Bessie Smith? I shouted to everybody, 'Get out, get out of the car.' The car had been crumpled my side and the door wouldn't quite open properly. I said to Christabel again, 'Get out,' and she said, 'I can't move, I've broken my leg.' In the front, Gilson had hit the dashboard and had his arm twisted round and John Lay was collapsed over the steering wheel, covered in blood. I thought, 'Well, this is it. John's dead.' In a panic, I managed to get out of the car and helped Christabel out too. I tried to get Gilson out but he had broken his arm badly and found it hard to move. Very fortunately, just behind us, there was a breakdown vehicle, which had pulled up and turned on all its yellow lights to stop the traffic, and a police patrol car was on the scene within seconds.

Christabel and I slumped against the Armco barrier of the central reservation. The helpful motorway-maintenance men were asking me what had happened and I started explaining and urging them to get an ambulance as my friends were dying, if not already dead, in the car. Gilson was being examined by one of the policemen and, seeing me sitting gesticulating to these two blokes, he thought I was giving an interview, an illusion he harboured for many years. By now other motorists had stopped and, in spite of some of them saying he shouldn't be moved, I suggested that we'd better try to get John out of the car, since I didn't want him to die from our lack of action, if he wasn't dead already. As we were trying to inch him out, this rather helpful woman said, 'I think we'd better leave him, he's dead.' John suddenly came to and hissed at this woman, 'I'm not dead, you stu'id 'itch.' Half-conscious, he couldn't pronounce the 'p' or the 'b' because he couldn't move his lips.

Since we couldn't move him, I could only think to say, 'It's all right, there's an ambulance on its way.' Finally an ambulance did arrive and we were all taken off to hospital. I'd hurt my back, cut my face and was very shaken but I hadn't injured myself nearly as badly as all the others had. John had to be rushed into the emergency rooms, and Christabel and Gilson too. I was left lying there just feeling really bad, everything going round and round in my mind. They brought in the confused old man who had been driving the other car. His name was William Williams, Bill Bill. I'm not one for road rage but when he started to blub, I thought, 'Why are *you* blubbing? I'm the one who should be blubbing because of what's happened to my friends.' That was the only time I really felt furious, like giving him a piece of my mind, probably through shock.

Then I passed out and, when I came round, I was in a hospital bed opposite John Lay. He looked in a really bad state. He'd broken his foot and his whole face was bandaged up, so you could only just see his eyes. The steering wheel had completely smashed his face in. Christabel and Gilson were elsewhere in the hospital.

The nurses and the doctors came in to tell me that the hospital had had quite a few enquiries from the newspapers and they wanted to know if I was OK to do a photograph. I told them I wasn't but, in spite of this, an hour later these photographers appeared. I was still quite groggy but I tried to explain that John was the real victim, the one most badly injured, but they weren't interested in him, because he wasn't on the telly. They took my photograph, saying, 'Could you give us a thumb's-up, Jools? Nice wacky one for the kids?' I looked at John, and all I could see through the bandages were his eyes rolling. Then I blanked out again, because I'd bashed my forehead and they'd sedated me. When I came round the following morning, it was obvious the crash had been in the papers because a bunch of flowers had arrived from the kindly surrealist actor Stanley Unwin, adding to the strangeness of the whole episode.

I decided I had to leave the hospital and get a train back to London. I couldn't really walk and, in fact, it took a month to recover from my injuries, but I knew I had quite a bit of explaining to do.

The aftermath of the crash was that Gilson, like the Six Million Dollar Man, had to be rebuilt. For ages he couldn't move his arm at all and it was weeks later that he rang me, in great excitement, to tell me he'd managed to touch his nose. This from the great Drum King whose solos were as interesting to watch as to listen to − I found it very poignant.

John Lay's face was very badly injured and they had to set it, break it after six months, and re-set it. All the while, he had to wear a steel brace on his head and face, which meant people pointed at him and stared. Christabel, with her broken leg, was recuperating in Northumberland and, as John felt too self-conscious to go out in London with this great head brace on, she suggested he come up and stay so he could wander round the fields there in solitude. As well as being in great pain as a result of this crash, effectively, he had to go into hiding. Willie Williams ended up with a broken wrist and a relatively undamaged Austin 3-litre (which says a lot about the pressed-steel unit construction of the car's chassis and body, as opposed to the modern car's more flimsy build quality).

And of course, it also brought things to a head where Mary and Christabel were concerned. I had been trying in my head to work out what was the best thing to do for a long time, and when to talk to Mary. I was in love with Christabel but didn't want to hurt Mary. The crash, ultimately, forced me to tell Mary how badly I'd been behaving, having an affair with Christabel. At first we tried to patch things up and I agreed not to see Christabel. I found I was unable to do this.

It was a painful and difficult moment in our lives, which Mary and I both privately resolved. Her generosity of spirit and my continued affection for her meant that we continue to this day to be great friends. We both worship our children and hold one another in the highest regard. She is now married and has two more beautiful children, one of whom is Christabel's godson. Mary has always been completely dignified in her behaviour, which is more than can be said for me. However, I will now take a lead from Mary, say no more on the matter and return to the subject of music and my career.

Musical Conviction

Not everything was going wrong. Malcolm Hardee was continuing his efforts as my agent, and informed me that, following the rumours of my death in the crash, ticket sales had doubled. However, the theatre managers, on hearing my name, would often ask exactly what it was I'd be doing on stage. This led me to the horrible realization that I was now better known as a TV personality than as a musician. It made me all the more determined to go and play, to show people what I could do.

I told Gilson he'd be back with me as soon as he was better; he knew as well as I did that, in our business, the show must go on. However, without his unique talent, I would have to add a bass player; I could no longer rely just on piano and drums. This is how the Big Band started to grow. I asked Keith Wilkinson, the bass player from Squeeze, to join me and, having auditioned many other drummers, I ended up asking Roland Rivron to stand in for Gilson until he had fully recovered. Many of the drummers who had auditioned were technically brilliant, but they didn't quite have the swing you need for my sort of boogie-woogie – it's easy to play but hard to play right. It doesn't matter whether you're playing thrash metal or Mozart – you need technique *and* feel, both of which Gilson possessed in abundance. You don't want to be limited by your technique, but you don't want such virtuosity that it actually gets in the way of your feel. Roland was known at that time as Rolando the Gypsy Prince, and also as 'the quietest drummer in London'. This was useful in the jobs he did at night-clubs and restaurants, which needed soft background drumming. I wasn't really sure about his technique but his feel was fantastic. Some readers will be wondering where the exotic name 'Rolando' came from. He won a competition playing in big bands when he was sixteen, and his family agreed he should go professional and join the Musicians' Union. Roland went to the local representative's dusty semi-detached house in Park Royal. The aged, chainsmoking MU rep opened an ancient ledger, and asked, 'Age?'

'Sixteen.'

'I'll put eighteen, so you can work in licensed premises. Instrument?'

'Drums.'

'I'll put drums and percussion. Name?'

'Roland Rivron.'

'Stage name?'

'I haven't got one.'

'I'll put Rolando.'

Roland is still listed as Rolando, drums and percussion, in the MU directory.

As John Lay was away in Northumberland recuperating, Malcolm announced that he would take over as tour manager. This wasn't ideal, since one of a tour manager's most important duties is the driving and Malcolm had recently been banned. He told me he'd be happy to use his fake licence, but I thought this was unwise. So, I ended up doing all the driving myself and Malcolm sat beside me reading a book. Roland and Keith Wilkinson sat in the back of the car. Roland couldn't read on journeys because it made him feel sick, so he took on the duty of valeting his corner of the car, which did remain spotless. In the car he was known as 'the stewardess (male)'. At every red traffic light he would jump out and clean the windscreen, then ask us for money.

At the start of this tour, just as we had reached the first village, Malcolm ordered us to stop beside a skip. He pulled a tatty expanse of rag from it and announced that, rather than pay daft hotel prices, he would pitch this tent in the hotel gardens and sleep in it to save money. I argued that the hotels wouldn't let him do that and, furthermore, this so-called tent stank of piss, but he was adamant. The tent was loaded into the boot of the car, which made all our bags stink. I loved Malcolm but, as a tour manager, he was, frankly, a bit of a liability.

We played in the 100 Club, the Leadmill in Sheffield, where Edwin Starr came and sat in with us, as did Richard Hawley, the guitar player from Pulp. We then played in Matlock, near Derby, so pretty on that summer's evening, and the crowd were just wild. All our venues were charming little places and doing my own music again was very enjoyable. Whereas Gilson would do a drum solo at the end of the show, Roland preferred to do the letting-the-firework-off-the-top-of-his-head trick as a finale, an exciting fusion between jazz, rock and roll, punk music and wild self-expression.

Malcolm suggested that it would be nice to do a benefit for the poor inmates of Dartmoor prison, and we agreed. In his younger days, Malcolm and a friend had stolen a Rolls-Royce in the West Country and had crashed it. The car had belonged to a prominent politician so they'd received longer than usual sentences. They were driven down to Exeter prison in a Transit van and, when the prison officers got out to open the gates to the prison, Malcolm got out too, and wandered off to the neighbouring park. He spent the night there and, the following morning, just as he was about to set off and take a train back to London – his great escape – a young woman pushing her baby in a pram alerted the park police to the fact that there was a suspicious-looking man lurking in the bushes. She quite rightly assumed that he was up to no good. The park police didn't believe his excuses and took him to the police station and, although they didn't recognize him as a criminal on the run, in the end he broke down and told them, because he just couldn't bear them not being able to guess what had happened. He was then given a longer sentence still.

We arrived at Dartmoor prison for our gig on a very sunny afternoon, and dark, sinister shadows were being cast by its gigantic Victorian walls. Inside, it was just as old-fashioned; huge warders took us past the barred cells to the hall where we were to play. Malcolm, being Malcolm, had smuggled in about 150 packets of roll-up tobacco to give away as gifts to the prisoners.

The prison chaplain, who was organizing the event, was a lovely fellow. He looked like Arthur Lowe's Captain Mainwaring in

Dad's Army but had the gentleness of John Le Mesurier's Sergeant Wilson. He had quite thick glasses and was bald on top but had thick grey hair sticking up at the sides. He wore a tweed suit and a vicar's collar and you felt he was there for no other reason than to help his fellow man. As we came in, this vicar saw that Malcolm had a huge stash of tobacco stuck up his jumper but chose to ignore it.

When it was time to do the show, the vicar introduced us to all the prisoners, who were sitting on the floor cross-legged. The warders were all down the side. A lot of them had dogs and big truncheons, and were looking out for the first signs of trouble. At the back there were a couple of prisoners who must have been bigger players in the crime world, because they had on expensive gold watches and were sitting on chairs.

We started to play and it all went quite well. However, then we came to our last number, 'Nut Rocker'. There is a particular bass line at the end of this song which always gets audiences going, and this time was no exception. Suddenly, all the prisoners stood up and went mad dancing and shouting along. It was unbelievable – like a scene from *Jailhouse Rock*. It was frightening and funny at the same time, and the prisoners themselves were laughing. The warders, however, were not amused and not sure what to do about this dancing. They started menacing them to make them sit down, and the prison chief signalled frantically for us to stop, but we couldn't because we were in the middle of a number. We stopped when the song was over, and then Malcolm Hardee took it into his head to run on to the stage and shout, 'Thanks very much, everybody. I'm afraid that's all we've got time for.' Then he started tossing the packets of tobacco at everybody as a leaving present. This caused a huge riot as the prisoners surged forward to grab them. The warders came on to the stage and started pushing people back with these great big sticks, but it looked like it was getting more and more out of control – the men were shouting and swearing and fighting each other for the tobacco.

Since the warders were losing control, the nice prison chaplain was then pushed up on stage. His glasses were a little skewwhiff and what hair he had was all over the place. We were stuck in the middle of all the fighting and swearing and couldn't get off the stage because there were so many warders with truncheons all around us. The vicar said into the microphone, 'One, two, one, two,' and then in kindly fashion, 'Now, come on, lads, let's calm down, let's calm down.' But at that moment the prisoners started screaming unprintable foul abuse at the warders who were trying to take the tobacco back. Meanwhile, Malcolm was kicking more tobacco off the stage into the scrum and making things even worse – and over all the shouting and fighting, the vicar started to say, 'Come on, lads, let's keep this chittle-chattle down.' At this point they managed to clear a path and lead us out. Behind us, we could hear the noise of the riot and the voice of the vicar through the microphone: 'Come on, lads, bit less chittle-chattle. Don't let's spoil everything with this horseplay.'

After this gig, we did some more shows near by and were able to visit the places Malcolm had been allowed out to on his weekend paroles. He would show us where he'd gone for cups of tea and treat us to stories of his bravery. It was an enjoyable string of dates. By the time we'd returned to London in the autumn of that year, my separation from Mary had become more formalized. Since the car crash, I had been staying on and off at hotels and had been on tour much of the rest of the time, but now I moved out, one chapter closing, another chapter opening.

The Groovy Fellas

Now that *The Tube* had finished, Miles took the view that I should embark upon another television programme of some sort. Both Paula and I kept turning down proposals for further pop programmes. She was toying with the idea of a history of underwear, and I would have quite liked to do a history of the piano. In the end, what emerged for me was *The Groovy Fellas*.

This idea had initially taken hold during my touring days with Roland. We came up with the plan of taking a recently landed Martian on a tour of Britain, explaining its workings to him. An alien visitor would have quite a different take on all aspects of our culture and, with Roland acting as the Martian, we felt that such a programme had possibilities.

It was decided that, although Geoff Wonfor was a brilliant director and we'd worked together well on the *Tube* films, a different director would give this a new look and feel. Tim Pope had made some great videos with the Cure and, whenever I'd met him, we'd got on well, so it was decided that he'd be the perfect director for *The Groovy Fellas*.

Channel Four then put up the funds for the programme, not really knowing what they were going to get for their money. They would have been used to this since that's how *The Tube* had always made its films abroad. The only information we gave them was that it was going to consist of six half-hour programmes in which we would show a Martian around Britain. Originally, we had thought to feature music, particularly the bands and local music of the regions we were filming in and, looking back, it might have been better if we had done this. However, we thought that the original premise would give us material enough.

We asked John Gwynn and Elaine Kemble, who had done such a good job producing and researching *Walking to New Orleans*, to do the same for this project, along with another rather helpful Scottish woman called Isobel McKiver. We all decided that we wanted a very strong image, having always liked those 1960s television programmes, in which either the heroes or their cars were so distinctive. To achieve this distinction for ourselves, Roland and I had identical suits made at my Savile Row tailor, with unnaturally huge chalk stripes. We had two each made. The television company tried to take them back at the end; Roland returned his but I hung on to mine.

For the car, we bought an old Rolls-Royce, planning to convert it into a Batmobile-type vehicle. However, a thorough conversion would have cost too much money, so we got this bloke in a little workshop to cut the roof down six inches and remove the hubcaps and bumpers. This left the car looking rather odd – the windscreen wipers were now too big for it, for example – but we added to this by spraypainting it gold from its original blue. Roland had a little aerial on his head which rotated, and the first programme opens with him completely naked other than this aerial, walking down the road having just landed from Mars.

We had to film in sections to fit in with my recording and touring schedule, which meant that the series took longer than usual to complete. Although we were largely making it up as we went along, each programme had a distinct theme. In one, for instance, we showed the Martian what the British people did for jobs and why; in another, how they ate. To deal with the concept of money, we stood on the corner of Bond Street trying to give money to passers-by and then took the Martian dog-racing, where, having gambled his money away, he then asks the bookmaker if he can have it back to try again. Unsurprisingly, the answer was no – even to a visitor from another planet.

The final programme was devoted to the question of why we are here. We asked Jeffrey Archer, we asked Tony Benn, we asked the Archbishop of Canterbury, we asked the Chief Imam, we asked the head Buddhist, we asked random people in the street. We asked everybody we could, and the programme ended with the question: what is the point of it all?

In some ways *The Groovy Fellas* was a good early example of reality television, since we would go into people's homes and ask them to explain various aspects of their lives to us. Amazingly, lots of people were perfectly happy to be on television explaining, in all sincerity, their point of view to this Martian. We came across some sad and some funny stories. We made a point of filming bits of Britain which we knew were disappearing – Routemaster buses, red phone boxes or car dumps, scrap-metal yards and small, local shops. These were commonplace at the time but we all felt they would soon be gone, stamped out by the fascist corporate hand of modern Britain. Our Look and Learn interactive approach was pretty daft, but some of it worked well.

We did one episode where the Martian wanted to know what a child was. Since Rosie was the most charming-looking child you could ever hope to see and as she, of course, knew Roland, we all thought it would be fun for her to be in the film. So we put her in this little red coat and, as we drove past, Roland stopped and said, 'What's that? A small human?', and picked her up and put her in the boot of the car as a souvenir. However, it was felt that this was sending out the wrong message, so it never made the final cut. I still have the footage, which is a nice keepsake of Rosie at that age.

Roped Off

During the last part of 1986 and the start of the following year I spent a lot of time with Squeeze, recording our next record *Babylon and On* in a variety of studios in England and America. The first single to be released from it was 'Hourglass'. Because the other members of Squeeze felt that I had a lot of visual ideas and knowledge, the decisions concerning the video were largely left to me. I asked Ade Edmondson to direct it. I loved Cocteau films, with their strange surreal camera tricks, and asked Ade if we couldn't do a whole video like this. He had a much greater knowledge of cinema than I did and was able to come up with lots of surreal vignettes. It worked really well and won numerous awards, including one from MTV, which was a small silver statue of the astronaut Buzz Aldrin, which John Lay took and kept on his mantelpiece.

Ade then made another video for 'Trust Me to Open My Mouth', our next single. For this, we had a giant set made to look like a huge face, with this great mouth which would open and we'd all come out of it. However, the production was a bit too expensive for the song, which wasn't quite up to being a hit. I did take one of the giant teeth away as a souvenir, liking the idea of having it as a chair. But, once it was estranged from its big mouth, it just looked like a lump of polystyrene, so I threw it away.

Babylon and On turned out to be very successful but, as it had taken such a long time to record and because we had used such expensive recording studios, we now found ourselves in need of some money, so Miles arranged another American tour. This time round, we flew straight to Atlanta, which pleased me, because I have always liked the South. When people down there said, 'Have a nice day,' it seemed they really meant it, so I always replied, 'Thanks very much. I shall.' It used to annoy everyone else in the band but I used to tell them to savour it – nobody in London ever bothered about the state of our day.

However, once we arrived, it turned out we weren't staying in charming old downtown Atlanta but opposite this huge sprawling shopping mall. There being nowhere else to explore in the area, we ended up having a morning in this mall, buying pointless items. Chris Difford bought a diver's watch which was luminous and worked at 400 fathoms below the sea, although he'd never swum further than the length of a swimming pool. I bought all this art material with which to do lino cuts and sculpting and many other crafts besides, none of which I could do on tour.

We had a rehearsal in the afternoon, which went quite well, but the man who ran the rehearsal studio then came shopping with me. Annoyingly, since I had a hangover, I listened to his advice and put down the big diary I was planning to buy in favour of a smaller, neater one. What a mistake – not all of my day-to-day observations fit on the page and I had to cross over to the following day's. I really learned not to shop on a hangover from that, and not to take anybody else's advice. This well-meaning man had no idea what interesting things were going to happen to me that year – a lot of things did.

We were now spending an enormous amount of time in the extremely expensive tour buses we had hired, the sort country stars buy for themselves. Basically, they are very luxurious, huge, fully stocked up with food and drink and kept tidy by the driver. The bunk rooms in the middle had deluxe beds, air conditioning and lights and, at the back, was what was known as 'the throne room', which had a television in it and comfy sofas. We had asked especially not to have buses with the tinted windows which prevented fans and nosy Parkers looking in because we wanted to be able to look out. BB King told me that he never liked to drive overnight because he feared you were more likely to crash in the dark, but we didn't mind doing this occasionally so we could wake up where we wanted to be.

The bus became like home and we treated it as such. During a particularly long journey I drew a version of an ornate doorway from the Sistine Chapel on the ceiling of my bunk. When he saw it, the driver said the company might have to charge me for it but really I felt I should be charging them for providing a work of art.

In Florida, because it was raining so hard, the show was postponed and we had a day off. We decided to stay in a motel, picked because of its large swimming pool. That evening, to our amazement, also having a drink in the hotel bar was Ken Dodd, with a friend who turned out to be the head of the Showmen's Guild, the official body of Britain's fairground proprietors. We got chatting to them and, from their long experience of showbiz, they stressed the importance of being unique: after all, as Ken said, 'There's only one Beatles, and only one Jimmy Clitheroe – the Clitheroe Kid.' We couldn't argue with that.

After doing our massive MTV spectacular on the beach the following afternoon, we had the evening off and decided to go dog-racing. I assumed that, like everything in America, the racing would be bigger and better than its equivalent in Britain and certainly more glamorous, but it was a very poor show indeed. For a start, instead of six dogs per race, they had eight, which made winning all the harder. I didn't win a penny the whole night. And, unlike England's dog tracks, where there are colourful characters – the bookmakers, the nobs, the yobs, the lot – it was a most cleansed and sanitized experience, quite pedestrian compared to going to Walthamstow.

In Dallas, instead of getting back on the bus for another overnight drive, I decided to stay to see Dr John play. The club in which he was playing was pretty wild and the audience were all-night-tripper types like him. I played a couple of duets with him, one of which was 'Mess Around', and the audience went mad. The following morning I flew to meet the band at our next destination, and they were saying, 'You should have been on the bus, it was great. We pushed so and so out of his bunk,' which made me feel all the more pleased I'd decided to stay to see Dr John.

In spite of the luxury and its size and layout, it still was quite close quarters living on the bus. Occasionally people would have private moments in their bunks and others would think it amusing to barge in on them. The unattached chaps could bring girls on if they wanted but, if they did, they'd be stuck with them – you could hardly call them a cab from the next state. That sort of thing was best left for when we stayed in hotels. But anyway, people's wives and girlfriends would come out for a week or so at a time. Christabel came out for our show in Pennsylvania and then travelled with us on the bus to the Amish town of Intercourse, which lent itself to some very enjoyable souvenir shopping.

From time to time we would go in our bus as a group to local clubs. This was always gratifying, as the sight of our gigantic gleaming tour bus pulling up outside would put any ordinary celebrity limo to shame, and bring out the manager, the chef – in fact, anyone connected to the club. Once they were all there, ready to greet whoever got off this huge bus, the doors would open with a *shhhh* and we would step down to a great welcome and applause. Sometimes parties were laid on for us, which would only mean a special roped-off corner for our friends and ourselves. This always amused us and, back on the bus after one of these occasions, Chris suddenly produced a rope which he'd nicked as a souvenir and cordonned off his bunk with it. He was so keen on being roped off he told us he was going to rope off his room back in England too.

Before one gig in Buffalo, upstate New York, there had been a huge blizzard, and there was this poor guy living outside our hotel in a tent. We decided that, if he had a couple of hundred dollars, he could have a hotel room for quite a few nights, until the snow had gone. We had a whipround, collected the money and gave it to him. This kind of gesture can sometimes backfire, but it didn't matter to us, because we were back on our bus and on to the next county.

Charleston, North Carolina, was very pretty, so Gilson and I got up early and walked round it, visiting a beautiful eighteenth-century church. Then we had a lovely drive through South Carolina – its tumbledown motels, the moss hanging down into the swamps and the weatherboarded mansions all made it look so filmic.

Having driven through miles of beautiful but deserted scenery, we decided to have a fireworks stop and asked the driver to pull over at a layby. Delighted to find that America had none of the safety restrictions Britain has on the buying of fireworks, Glenn had bought these rockets as big as missiles. Someone else had won a large pink cuddly rabbit called Bunny at a truck stop and, having fashioned him a safety hat out of an old polystyrene cup, I tied Bunny to this gigantic rocket and we launched it off one of the trucks carrying our equipment. It went straight up in the air then crashed down, setting light to the prairie grass. We'd potentially started a forest fire – it was the most irresponsible thing we had ever done. We ran over with fire extinguishers and put it out, stamping all over it. However, someone found Bunny in the ashes, and this inspired us to have another go, not thinking enough was enough. This time, Bunny and his rocket almost hit a man on his motorbike, so we ran into the bus and drove off.

We all had things we particularly liked to do on tour. In Tucson, Arizona, which was a sort of great dusty cowboy place, I bought a book called *Ernest Norlins Teaches You How to Draw Perspective*. It was a children's book, but perspective was something I'd never learned before and, once I understood the basics, I couldn't stop doing it. Ernest Norlins' first chapters used illustrations of endless desert roads going nowhere with mountains in the distance and a car and a lamppost to practise with, which was exactly the sort of landscape we were driving through. I mastered those and then the book progressed to very tall views looking down towards distant objects below so, when we reached Kansas City, I requested the highest room in the hotel in order to attempt the next lesson. I enjoyed all this so much that, from then on, I always asked for the top floor. Rooms on the top floor of hotels usually had the added advantage of being surrounded by empty rooms, so you could not only practise your perspective but also have noisy parties without causing any complaints. At other times I'd do abstract painting or learn Bessie Smith songs.

We were enjoying the tour but it was also hard work, and we

were feeling very far away from London. In those days, there were no mobile phones, so you'd have to wait until you were at a hotel to ring people and then get up early to ring London.

There were all sorts of people wanting to manage us, hanging around or suggesting merchandising deals, because we were quickly selling out big stadiums. John Lay, who was once again our tour manager, was dealing with all the new business that was coming in. When you're in that situation, other jobs and offers keep coming in. You get to the end of the tour and a promoter will say, 'Just do a club here, one more show here' – there's always something else. That made it harder and harder to get back home; there was always another reason to stay, something else to do.

By the end of the American tour I was missing London and my trips out to Kent. I would speak to my children on the phone and keep telling them I'd be back soon. And, finally, just as we were set to return, Miles told us about this Budweiser advert he wanted us to do. We all protested that we were exhausted, longing to get home and, anyway, we all preferred English beer. But he told us that this 'Bud's For You' campaign would not only bring in a lot of money but had also been done by Frank Sinatra, so it was a great thing. So we did that final job and then thankfully returned, exhausted, to England.

The Case

I was pleased to get back to London and to all the familiar sights and sounds of Greenwich, and even more pleased to see my small children again, who were now a little bit bigger. After we'd been on tour for a long time there were so many details to attend to and things to sort out. I had work to do on *The Groovy Fellas* and on my own music. I was also trying to get planning permission to convert some old stables into a recording studio, which would, although I didn't realize it then, grow into its own small Portmeirion-style village. It would also become the place where my orchestra would record, both as a unit and with many great artists, music that millions would buy. But, for now, my recording studio was set up far more modestly in the myriad of rooms behind *The Man from UNCLE* barber's shop. Mary and I had both moved to separate houses in Blackheath and the children were living with her.

It was rather a turbulent time for all of us. With so much going on, it was hard to keep everything in order, everybody was moving around, possessions were stored all over the place. One of these items was a case of jewellery which belonged to Christabel that I'd said I would put in the bank for safekeeping. With all that was going on before I left for America I hadn't done this but had just left it in a briefcase in my office, which was rather daft. And now, back from America, I found that the case was missing. I reported it to the police, who at first didn't seem very interested, although they took down the details. I even told them that somebody who had keys to the office must have taken it since there was no evidence of a break-in – but they didn't pursue this lead either.

However, Christabel then saw what appeared to be some of her missing jewellery for sale in a shop and called a policeman. It turned out that it was hers but, even before the investigation had really begun, my father came forward and admitted that, in a moment of madness, he had taken it from the briefcase in the office and sold it to a jeweller.

We understood he'd been very tired and emotional and at a low ebb, having recently been made redundant, but he was the first to say that this was no excuse, and he was desperately sorry about letting us all down. We were not angry, just disappointed. My father had clearly been in a precarious state of mind, and Christabel and I both hoped that the charges could be dropped, but the value of the jewellery meant that charges had to be pressed and the inevitable court case was set for June.

It was a particular pleasure to see my small children at this time. Both George and Rosie got on very well with Christabel's young son, Fred, and in the evening I would tell all three of them stories. I made up this character called Peter who had a little red car in which he'd go off and have adventures. Then I introduced a badly behaved character called Naughty Billy and they loved him so much more than Peter that he took over. The worse he behaved, the more they wanted him; it was an interesting insight into human nature.

In the day I would take them round the corner to my favourite place, Frank's café, which was always filled with local musicians, scrap metal men, local police and crooks. There we would feast on stuffed hearts, beef with pickles and exhibition-standard home-made chicken pie in the private room I was given, being such a regular. It was a very rare example of an English café that made all its own food – pies, steamed babies' heads and no breakfasts after eleven o'clock. In Frank's, you pointed to what you wanted, it was put on a plate and you went upstairs to eat it. It kept me fed through that period and, had I known a few years ago that it was going to be sold, I would have bought it myself and kept it going.

Meanwhile, I was being introduced to another side of life, as we would sometimes go and stay with Christabel's friends and relatives, many of whom lived in great family piles. Her cousins Lord and Lady Hesketh turned out to be two of the kindest and most generous people I've ever met. I was interested in meeting

Lord Hesketh not only because a Hesketh bike was used in our filmed attempt to break the land-speed record through the Mersey Tunnel but also because he was the last man independently to finance a Grand Prix-winning Formula One racing team. I was keen to meet such a great modern-day hero. He lived in this extraordinary Hawksmoor house called Easton Neston, a perfectly proportioned palace.

The first time I went there Imran Khan and James Hunt were among the guests – James Hunt had won for the Hesketh team in the Grand Prix. It seemed to be a very glamorous lifestyle Christabel's family were leading. We ate a delicious dinner in a grand dining room and, at the end of it, I stood up to go and was told to sit down again, since it was a great tradition that the gentlemen wait behind and smoke a cigar after the ladies had left the room. I wasn't quite sure what we gentlemen were going to discuss; I imagined somehow that it was going to be the political situation in the Sudan or some other high-powered topic, suitable for such erudite company. I comforted myself with the advice I'd been given ages ago, which was: if you don't know what to say, just nod wisely. But, in fact, one of the other guests started the conversation going with, 'You know, I think it's almost impossible to perform oral sex upon yourself.' James Hunt then remarked, 'I was once racing and had a dreadful crash where the car landed on top of me and practically forced me into that position.' I am pleased to say that the ladies were shielded from that type of conversation, but I found myself quite at home and liked all them very much. As well as my old friends, I now had a whole group of stately ones to add to my circle.

Whenever I could, I was filming sections of *The Groovy Fellas*, and the rest of the time I was trying to see my children and friends and hardly finding the time to do so. Since I was going away such a lot, I employed Kathy Coleman as my secretary, and she was a great help. She would come into the room where the recording-studio equipment was being stored and sit in the corner managing calls and making arrangements for me. We were all looking forward to building a proper office where she could work in less chaotic surroundings. I'd get back to London for a while and then we'd be off filming again in various parts of England, Scotland and Wales, staying in hotels all the while. In fact, 1988 turned out to be one of the most hectic and busy periods of my working life. But, with all the turbulent events going on in my private life, this workload probably helped – or maybe made it worse; who knows?

On 27 June, Christabel and I went to court for my poor father's case; we really had thought that, now the majority of the jewellery had been recovered, that would be an end to it. Christabel's view was that, since we had forgiven him, perhaps the court could too. However, it became clear they weren't going to let it drop; sentencing was adjourned and he remained free in the meantime, because he clearly wasn't a menace to anyone. He and I took George to Broadstairs and had rather a nice short break there.

In the odd spare moment I would sometimes go to the Tunnel Palladium, which was still going strong. One evening it featured a new act, Chris Lynham, who would stick a Roman candle up his arse while pirouetting to 'No Business Like Showbusiness'. I was pleased to see that nothing had changed down there – it felt like one small bit of stability in those chaotic months.

Major Scale

The fourth single to be released from *Babylon and On* was '853-5937', which charted in America. Reforming Squeeze had increased our popularity and in order to take advantage of this, we once again flew back there for another tour. We started in Milwaukee and, because we were now doing such big shows, not only did we have to do production rehearsals with all the lights and sound but the size of the crew on the road was that of a small army. We had our tour bus, three huge Pantechnicon trucks for the equipment and two Silver Eagle buses for the road crew to sleep in. Nowadays I might take the same number of people on the road but most of them are on stage. Then, there were only six of us on stage and the rest were technicians.

In some ways we had to adopt the Japanese approach to time-tables when travelling in this vast convoy: if anyone was late, the whole team would be delayed, so there would be fines and abuse for anyone who lingered and held us up, and very few meal stops allowed. However, because of the time it took to set up these bigger shows, we usually had a day off before the concert itself. It would work out at a day or even two days off a week, which makes quite a difference when you're away on tour for that long. And we did end up in the weirdest places. One of them was this place called the Melody motel, in Batavia, upstate New York, which we all rather liked because being there was like being in a fifties film. It had old diners and stock-car racing tracks and, best of all, was the motel itself with its red neon flashing sign and little chalets with Venetian blinds, a small bar and a jukebox.

One evening at the Melody motel, I got a phone call from Miles telling me that NBC Television had been on to him about a new music show from the makers of *Saturday Night Live*, and they wanted me as co-presenter. Of course, Miles was very enthusiastic about the prospect, but I had to stop him, just to point out that I had far too much on already; I didn't think I could physically fit any more in. He just repeated that it was the opportunity of a lifetime: 'You're mad even to consider not doing it, don't you see that?' I told him there were only so many minutes in each day, and I seemed to be using more of them than there actually were. Anyway, in the end, I gave in and agreed to meet up with the producers before leaving America.

There were still quite a few concerts to do and the following one, in the open air in Harrisburg, was a highlight. It was a very hot summer's night and the stage was by a river. The stage lights attracted all the bugs and insects from the water and, like most other things in America (apart from dog-racing), they put our English versions to shame. Dragonflies the size of eagles swarmed on to the stage along with thousands of others and, when I looked at Glenn, it was as if I was looking at a huge alien swollen with insects, and Chris the same. Every time any of us opened our mouths, insects would crowd in and almost choke us so, in the end, we had to leave the stage. The audience was booing, so we decided to try again but, as soon as the lights went on, the same thing happened. Luckily, just before it got ugly, I remembered the film *Night of the Lepus* in which giant killer rabbits were set to invade a small American town. In the film the population was saved by the hero, who got the townsfolk to drive to the other side of a high-voltage wire and turn on their headlights, thus diverting the giant killer rabbits away from their target. I decided to try the same tactic. There were thousands of people and I shouted from the dark stage, 'Has anyone seen *Night of the Lepus*?' This didn't get much of a response, but I just bellowed the instructions to them anyway. People who had cars near the edge of the field around the gig went to turn on their headlights. At first, only a few bugs flew towards them but, as more were switched on, the exodus began. We finished the gig to huge cheering, looking out on to a sea of Chevrolets and Pontiacs, their lights covered in these insects. I was as surprised as anyone that my quick thinking had saved the day. But, with the teamwork between us and the audience, the bugs were beaten and the concert was one of the best of the tour.

In New York, we played first at the Meadowlands, a great big stadium in New Jersey, to an audience of 14,000 people, and then two nights at Madison Square Gardens. All together, we probably played to 50,000 people in that one week. It was a week of big vibrations. After each show we would celebrate in an Irish bar we had always liked. It was all rather giddy and exciting – being in New York, playing these enormous venues and knowing I was about to meet up with a producer to discuss a possible show on American television.

However, the thrill of playing at these monster places was stopped short by a phone call I received telling me my father had been sentenced to fifteen months in prison. Before I'd left for America we had all discussed it and come to the conclusion that this sentencing procedure would be a matter of routine, that he would receive a suspended sentence. However, there was little I could do now and, on the telephone to my family, we all agreed there wasn't any point in me returning to England early.

At the Madison Square Gardens after-show party, I was not aware of the good it would bring, nor of the mysterious way in which the Lord works. The prison sentence broke my father's black hole of darkness and depression, which had first been brought on by his having been made redundant. While serving his sentence, he was helped by the chaplain, who told him that he was fortunate in that he had people outside the prison who cared about his welfare. So many of the other inmates had no one. Furthermore, my father was able to take the time to concentrate on his Latin studies. In the end, he served five months and was then granted parole.

My father was always a regular pub–goer and he is now a regular churchgoer too, much loved by the congregations of both, and a model of wisdom, forgiveness and humility. The great thing about my father is that, as well as being an existentialist Christian, he's never boring. The judge could not have known the sentence he handed out would help my father consolidate his good-humoured faith nor realize that he would also be sentencing my father to a lifetime of people reading about the incident every time they read about me. Most people serve their sentence and twenty years later it's forgotten about. Certainly, I didn't think I'd be writing about it myself one day as I'm doing now. However, it's played a bigger part in my father's lifestory than mine and I hope that, now twenty years have passed since the scales of justice fell, we can put all this behind us.

Soon after this I had dinner with Bryan Ferry and our friend Johnson Somerset and, when I told them about the NBC programme, they both grew very enthusiastic, which raised my spirits again. Then they went on to tell me how great it was living in New York, but this was less appealing to me; in fact, the idea of leaving my life in London and living in New York seemed unthinkable to me and made me feel a bit gloomy.

The first person I met with to discuss the programme was John Head, who was very nice if a bit vague. He had seen *Walking to New Orleans* and felt it hit just the right wavelength. I did say that that had been a programme about one place, hard to replicate every week, but they said that was just where they were coming from. John worked with Lorne Michaels, the man behind the phenomenally successful *Saturday Night Live*, which had introduced such stars as John Belushi, Steve Martin, Bill Murray and many others to the public. He was going to be the producer so John suggested that our next step was to meet up with him.

I thought it all over on the way back to my hotel. I liked John Head and appreciated that he knew about music. I had also liked the fact that there were going to be so many good musicians attached to the show, such as David Sanborn, the top saxophone player. By the time I reached my palatial hotel suite I was feeling quite excited about the project, and then the telephone rang. My grandmother had died.

I flew back to England for her funeral. Whereas I would usually be pleased to be going home after a long and quite riotous tour, this time my grandmother had died and my father was in prison, so the circumstances were far from ideal. I may not be one to go on about my feelings but, looking back, the Bessie Smith line just about summed them up at this time: 'When you see me laughing, it's just to keep from crying.'

Town and Country

However, not everything was a disaster — Malcolm Hardee was still acting as my Big Band's official booker. He now said that Gilson and I should play in Edinburgh. It was hard to imagine how we would find the time to do this, in between the continuing Squeeze mania and the filming of *The Groovy Fellas*, but we managed. The year before, when Gilson was still recovering from the car crash, Roland and I had played at the Assembly Rooms in Edinburgh, but this year Malcolm arranged a bigger venue. Keith Wilkinson joined us for it, making it a Big Band of three.

The club in Edinburgh was rather strange and had a big screen behind the performers which could be made to display any message. At that time, the message usually read 'Free Nelson Mandela', but Malcolm fiddled with it and managed to add 'and my dad' for my benefit, which was nice of him. We played there for three weeks and, whereas the year before the crowd had been quite small, this year it had grown considerably, which was encouraging — there was a varied mixture of people, of all ages and sexes, united by their love of boogie-woogie.

There was a TV festival in Edinburgh at the same time so I was able to go and see some of my friends from Tyne Tees and Channel Four who were up there for it. I still found the TV world a little alien: there was one woman there who had just been made Head of Sport for one channel and she kept telling everyone that it was her job to make sport sexier. I had assumed that it was her job to make sure that each season's sport was covered but, apparently, additional interference of this sort was needed. I didn't really understand that approach and, from what I'd heard, the high-ups at Channel Four were finding what we'd made of *The Groovy Fellas* equally baffling. Tim Pope told me that he had shown the commissioning editor the cut so far and, at the end of the screening, which he had watched in complete silence, this man kicked over his chair and said, 'This is the most formless rubbish I have ever seen.' I had comfortingly said to Tim that a strong reaction was better than no reaction at all. During the festival I ran into Lenny Henry, who had also seen an early cut. He told me it was the funniest thing he'd ever seen and, just as I was thinking I would pass on this compliment to Tim to boost his confidence, Lenny added, 'The most hilarious thing is that you managed to get the money to make it.' So I didn't pass it on in the end. We still had lots more formless rubbish yet to film.

Christabel, her son Fred, and George and Rosie all came up and joined us for the last week in Edinburgh. On the way back, we thought we'd stop off and stay with her husband, Ned, in Northumberland. We also had Mark Smith with us and, of course, Gilson and Keith, so there was quite a crowd of us. However, Ned has always been extremely hospitable. As well as cooking us a rather disgusting mushroom dish, he also generously produced some more bottles of 1961 Haut Brion wine from his cellar, which we gratefully scoffed.

I was sitting next to Ned's mother, Belinda, known as Bindy; I had never met her before. Towards the end of dinner she suddenly turned to me and announced, 'I've been thinking about this. Why don't you just butt out of the whole situation? Just Butt Out.' I didn't really answer and, since it was quite late, went off to bed. The next morning, I had to leave early for an appointment in London and, when Bindy got up and asked where I was, Ned answered, 'He's butted out like you told him to.'

Bindy was highly amused that I'd taken her at her word, adding, 'What — he was prepared to drop Christabel just because I asked him to? I was rather hoping we would become friends.'

And, indeed, after this unpromising start, Bindy and I were to become great friends and would spend many happy hours exploring the stranger parts of Northumberland together. I also became great friends with the whole of the Lambton family, and we would spend holidays together at Cetinale, the Italian home of Ned's father, Lord Lambton. He was very kind and took us on numerous cultural trips to little-known churches and various sights in Tuscany. Sadly, Lord Lambton died recently. He'd led a full and colourful life, and the papers wrote quite a bit about him. One article alluded to drug-fuelled bacchanalian orgies which apparently took place at Cetinale during the holidays. I regret to say that I saw no evidence whatsoever to support this suggestion, and can only say that if they did happen, it must have been when I had popped out to buy the paper.

The next segment of filming for *The Groovy Fellas* was the money episode and featured a visit to the Bank of England printing works to watch £10,000,000 being burned. Roland fainted at this sight, and I felt rather the same way. We then travelled on to film in this little village in Cumbria. Having already quizzed an ex-bank robber on how to do it, the plan was for Roland the Martian to go up as if to rob the little bank in this village, find it shut, give up and go to the pub. Now, I am able to give another handy tip to my readers here: if planning to film this sort of escapade, always alert the locals and the authorities beforehand. For this sequence, Roland got out of our adapted car carrying a sawn-off shotgun, shouting in preparation, 'Lie on the ground. Give me all your valuables.' Before we knew it, we were surrounded by a huge armed response unit and carted off to Carlisle police station through all the roadblocks which had been set up to apprehend us. Once it was clear what had happened, we were all carpeted by the chief constable. We apologized and said it was all Channel Four's idea. It was all over the press of course.

Soon after this I was once again back off to America to talk some more about *Sunday Night*. At passport control, one of the immigration men said, 'Hello, Jools. See you're in trouble again, eh?' I didn't know what he meant. As far as we were concerned, Roland and I were innocent victims in that particular misunderstanding. And I didn't like this 'again' business.

'Hamster's Wheel'

Had the offer from America been to be in a series like *Friends* or a daytime argument show, it would have been of no interest to me and, in any case, I wouldn't have had the credentials to do it. But *Sunday Night* was to be a music show, with people on it who I would love to meet and listen to, and it promised to be very good. However, I did say to Miles again that, what with all my Squeeze, Big Band and *Groovy Fellas* commitments, it was impossible to see how I was going to find the time. But Miles was very confident it could be done, as people who don't have to do it themselves often are.

Finally, I decided to go ahead with it. They arranged to shoot the opening titles and told me I would only be needed for a few hours. That sounded easy until I remembered that this would mean having to get to and be in New York for those few hours, but they told me they would fly me out on Concorde in the morning and fly me back first class in the afternoon. At first I agreed with my friends that it all sounded very glamorous, as if I were a participant in a particularly strange edition of *Tomorrow's World*, testing what it was possible to achieve in just one day in the modern world.

On 7 September, I flew out there, met sax legend David Sanborn and the musical director Marcus Miller, who were on the show too, and we filmed the opening titles. It was good to meet them both, and David became a great friend of mine but, almost as soon as I got there, they were taking me back to the airport to catch the next flight home. And the opening titles ended up so cartoonish I felt they could have saved themselves the £15,000 and used a cardboard cut-out of me – or perhaps that animatronic version of me from the Manpower Services Commission. On the street outside the studio, there had been a man shouting out, 'Belts, belts.

Three dollars for two. Double your money. Double your money.'
Because I was so tired, on the flight back I became preoccupied
with what he meant: did you have to double your money by
buying two belts and then sell them on for $6 . . . ? Anyway, six
hours later, I was back in London, taking my children swimming
in the local baths and meeting my friends for a drink. Then I got
another call: I had to fly back to New York to meet with Lorne
Michaels. I did ask if we couldn't just talk on the telephone but,
no, it had to be face to face. I began to feel that, rather than being
glamorous, it was already seeming a bit like hard work.

Lorne Michaels had his office at the top of the Brill building.
Since the 1930s songwriters have used it as a centre for their craft,
so it was exciting enough being in such a place. Then, when I was
shown into his office, he greeted me but was on the phone, his
sleeves rolled up as if he were a big newspaper editor. Out of his
huge window I could see the New York skyline, and through the
glass panel to my side I could see the heads of all the people
working in the office. Lorne was saying, 'Yes, I understand you
can't do it this time but, sure, I'll give your regards to all the kids
on the show – you bet. Thanks. Bye.' Then he hung up and said,
'That was Bob Hope. He's let me down a bit – but what can you
do? He'll come on the show another time, I'm sure.' While he
was saying all this, I kept my face impassive, but was thinking, 'I
like this Lorne Michaels. Bob Hope – what a showbiz world I'm
in. Perhaps I could consider myself one of the kids he was sending
his regards to – in fact, I have spent a lot of time in Eltham, which
is where he comes from: I should have got Lorne to tell him he
was in the room with another south Londoner.' But by now,
Lorne was saying how excited he was about the show, how pleased
he was I was doing it, so I put my mind to that. He told me the
show was going to be sponsored by a beer company and asked if I
had ever promoted any rival beers. I tried not to think about 'Bud's
For You', and said no. He then, being a clever fellow, said that
the important thing was that they were going to keep the show
going until it took off. So many programmes are given six episodes
and then taken off if they don't work. As he realized, it often took

longer than that for a show to find its feet. And, in this case, the beer company was behind it and so was he.

He also said it was important to make a show that I would like to watch myself. It flashed across my mind that the sort of show I would like to watch would be surrealist porno film shot on location in London and the home counties in the 1940s, but I deleted that vision from my mind, since he was saying goodbye. I shook his hand, agreed that we'd meet and have dinner soon, and then I was on the plane back to England once again.

Chord Blimey

I flew out to America again the week of the first show and met with my co-host, David Sanborn, in our rehearsal rooms. He introduced me to the other members of the house band – Hiram Bullock the guitar player, a big jolly fellow who liked cakes, which he and I used to go and buy together, the drummer Omar Hakim, Philip Saisse on keyboards and Marcus Miller, who was the bass player and musical director of the show. You have to be a great musician to get anywhere in the competitive session world in New York City and they all were. I knew that playing with this calibre of musician would raise my own game but, as I sat down at the piano to start, Marcus handed me a piece of paper which appeared at first glance to be covered in coded gibberish. He looked at me suspiciously and said, 'You do read a chord chart, don't you?' I didn't want to appear not to be blending in at this early stage, so I lied and said, 'Yes.' He turned away and I examined it more closely. Then, to my amazement and relief, I saw that the paper actually outlined the bars and the chords and, thanks to my lessons at Shooters Hill, I understood it perfectly. I felt so grateful I almost stood up and cried out, 'Thank you, Mr Pixley.' But I contained myself, and we continued as if I had been using one all my life.

We then moved on to rehearsing on the set, which they were still frantically in the process of building. Being in the middle of all this hustle and bustle gave me a buzz – now I felt as if I was in one of those films in which they throw together a last-minute Broadway show. One of the decisions that day centred round the placing of the sponsor Michelob's brand name within the set. A lot of the American musicians had transformed their lives through the wonder of Alcoholics Anonymous and weren't so keen on having a great big beer sign displayed behind them. I saw people busily conferring and then some blokes took down the huge neon

Michelob signs that had hung there and carried them off. As we continued rehearsing the run, a smaller neon Michelob sign was put up, but that caused a shaking of heads and it was carried out too. The same happened with a Michelob clock. Finally, another clock was brought in, with a very small 'Michelob' written on it, and this was accepted.

At this point, David Sanborn took me aside and said, 'What are we going to say?' in rather a panicky way. He had his own radio show but didn't have much experience on television. However, I was pleased to be able to draw from my huge televisual experience and answer, 'Don't worry – we'll muddle through.' This expression was apparently not one used in American showbiz life, since David looked uncomprehending rather than comforted as we moved on to practise the next section. This involved the simple task of announcing, 'American Airlines. Something special in the air,' a line one of us would say each week on behalf of the second sponsors of the show. However, when I came to take my turn, the American Airline representatives suddenly stopped everything, saying, 'Wait a minute, this is no good – we can't understand a word this English guy is saying.' We could all hear them going on to ask whether the producers weren't skating on thin ice, having a co-host whom no one could understand. But John Head and Lorne Michaels rallied round and said, 'Don't worry about it. It doesn't matter that you can't understand him, it's all about the music,' and, somehow, they went for it.

That night we all went out with some of the corporate bigwigs and, although at this dinner I made an effort to speak as clearly as possible, everyone still looked a bit confused. At one point I heard myself inviting them all over to my house for Christmas, but perhaps they didn't understand that either, because none of then took me up on this.

The first show was broadcast on Friday 23 September 1988. The guests appearing on it were Ivan Neville, George Duke and the great rhythm and blues singer Ruth Brown. This was a very promising start as, whether your tastes lay in the poetry and sexiness of blues or sophisticated jazz harmonies, you were going to be very well catered for. I was very pleased that my friend Brian Clarke was able to be over from England to see it. Being an artist, he understood that it was all about the music and appreciated it for that. And, being English himself, he understood me, which might have helped.

'The Boogie-Woogie Twins'

Up until this point, I'd been staying in a nice hotel with a balcony overlooking Central Park but, having signed up to do twenty-six shows, I knew I'd have to get an apartment, and the producers said they would rent one for me. They then arranged some viewings of apartments they assumed I'd like, groovy loft spaces with stripped floorboards, remote-control lights and state-of-the-art television screens on the walls. We went from one to the next, each one more minimalist and stylish, but none of them appealed to me at all. In the end I found just the one I wanted, belonging to a rather charming elderly gay couple who were away in Palm Springs. Not only did it have a piano, my first consideration, but also cosier decor of a 1960s gay executive variety. I moved in at once and soon after invited some people from the programme round to show it off. As soon as they came in the door, I could see they were at a loss to know what to say about my lovely new place. I suggested to them that it was the sort of apartment Larry, the boss of the husband in *Bewitched*, would have entertained his Westport golfing club buddies in. They agreed it was – but it didn't seem to increase their enthusiasm for it. However, I was very pleased with it and, soon afterwards, Christabel came over to stay. Although she said she liked it, she did point out that it was actually very small, and the owners had got round this by making all the furniture even smaller. She would also have preferred it if the bedroom and toilet had had some partition between them and this I did agree with. On all other counts, I was very happy with my new temporary home. The first night she was there we went out to celebrate her arrival and my first pay cheque at New York's most lavish restaurant, the Quilted Giraffe, after which Christabel had to call the paramedics urgently, because it looked like I was having a heart attack. They arrived within minutes but, to our relief, told me it was just what was known as a wind trap, caused by eating too much rich food.

I had quite a few friends from England living in New York, including Colin Emlyn, Johnson Somerset, his wife Cosima, and the painters Ana Corbero and Tim Steel. They were all very hospitable but, after a while, I did start to worry I wasn't mixing with any of the local people. Ana Corbero was in fact Spanish and Tim Steel was American but from Oklahoma, so he didn't count. New York being a city of immigrants, everyone tends to huddle in their own section, whether it be Spanish Harlem, Little Italy or any of the other ethnic communities. Although I was enjoying my own English immigrant community, I was interested in exploring New York as much as I could.

At that time New York was still quite rough and, on every other corner, there were people fighting one another, being sick or demanding money from anyone who looked as if they might have it. So, in order to go unmolested, I started to dress as much as possible like the street people themselves. I found that if I wore my casual wear from London, I blended in straight away. I was pleased to be able to pass as a genuine New Yorker, stepping over the drunks and having people avoid my eyes. I almost felt that I had become a native – that is, until I opened my mouth. As soon as I said anything, again there were the same blank looks of incomprehension all round as on the show. I now noticed that, whenever an English guest musician appeared on *Sunday Night*, I would be pushed forward by the others to explain everything to them in our shared language.

However, in spite of these little moments of cultural diversity, I began to enjoy life in New York very much. One of the bonuses was that my friend Nell Campbell had opened a club, which I started going to regularly after filming. Nell's was this glamorous place which made you feel you were in a room in Paris before the Second World War; it had long red velvet curtains and gilt-framed mirrors lit by candles. It had a small stage, on which an old jazz trio would play, and all around were these round tables surrounded by squashy red velvet banquettes. All sorts of people would pop in and one night Nell told us that Prince was coming in for dinner, so we sat at her table and waited for him together. Then the word came through – 'Prince is here.' We were all very excited, then we saw this tiny figure about the same size as my daughter Rosie surrounded on either side by these man-mountain minders twice the size of Mike Tyson. As they walked towards our table, they glared around, making sure nobody was going to attempt to buy Prince a drink or say hello or anything of that sort. Nell, being so charming, tried to get a conversation going but, with these two huge minders sitting either side of him, every time any of us tried to have a chat with him, all we could see were these giant arms obscuring our view. But he did do a five-minute gig on the stage there after his dinner which was fantastic. Another person to come and do a great gig at Nell's was my old friend Kim Lesley, one-time member of the Wealthy Tarts, now married and living in New York.

She and I then went to watch Dr John play at the Lone Star Café, and that same week he appeared on *Sunday Night*. For this, he and I decided to do a duet together of a piece in the style of Albert Ammons and Pete Johnson called 'The Boogie-Woogie Twins', which we'd written as our tribute to their genius. I suggested we both adopt the sort of costume Dr John had worn on the cover of *Gumbo* – top hat, morning suit and sash, as if we were dignitaries of a despotic South American state.

The duet we did together was short but there really was something magical about it. You could feel that the crowd in the room was excited and, after it had been on TV, people spoke to me about it and sent letters. It was a sign that we had captured the music properly; had people been indifferent, then we wouldn't have done the business. Just as a concert pianist doesn't try to sound like Beethoven, but interprets his music, so we took the music and made it connect with people, which was our job. And even if the viewers didn't understand what I was saying, if they understood my music, that was the important part to me.

'When I Get Home'

Throughout my time with *Sunday Night*, I would remain in America for three weeks and then fly back to England for a week. Sometimes Mark Smith would meet me at Heathrow in his Rover 3.5 P5B, which made me feel like Edward Heath, since that was the sort of car he was driven in. So much would have happened in the fast-paced life of New York that the three weeks seemed like three years and, whenever I first saw my children on my return, they appeared to have grown considerably. Perhaps, to them, I had shrunk by the same amount.

By now Christabel and I were living together in a house by Greenwich Park and, from there, I used to take George, Fred and Rosie out for different local treats. We would sometimes walk down the towpath to Blackwall Reach and I would let them play on the old industrial sites and disused jetties and piers by the river, which was something I had done as a child, as had my grandfather before me. We also used to visit my friend Trevor, who had a wonderful scrap-metal yard and a vehicle-recovery business next to the river, where the Millennium Dome now stands. When we got home, I would continue with the Naughty Billy stories, which they all still loved. In fact, recently, the three of them all came and told me that, instead of wasting my time writing my lifestory, I should be writing a Naughty Billy book instead. But, with apologies to my children and to my readers, I will return to the subject of me.

My separation from Mary had been expensive and I was busy building my studios. Although I was paid perfectly well in America, by the time I had paid the state tax, the city tax, the Internal Revenue Service and the Inland Revenue here, I seemed to end up just treading water financially. It seemed an odd situation, taking Concorde back to oversee the building works at the end of every third week and the rest of the time having to work non-stop to make sure there was enough money to go round. And, as we were now also in the final editing stages of *The Groovy Fellas*, it began to seem that there was no time to do anything leisurely; every moment there was something happening or something else to think about or deal with. I used to look forward to the three and half hours of peace and quiet on Concorde, paid for by someone else. On one of these flights, the stewardess politely interrupted me to ask if I had the award with me. When I asked, 'What award?', she said, 'Michael Jackson's.' I realized then that she must have seen me on live television the night before, picking one up on his behalf at the BPI awards, as the Brits were then called. When I said that I didn't, she asked, 'Have you left it with Paula then?' And it came to me that she was yet another who assumed that Paula and I lived in this strange television-personality house where Michael Jackson might pop by at any moment to pick up his award, stopping perhaps to join Ronnie Barker and Gordon Honeycombe for a cup of tea.

On the days of filming for *Sunday Night*, we would have a dress rehearsal, with all the musicians giving their full performances. This would give the director a chance to plan the shots. We would then have a very short break and do exactly the same thing again, and that was the show. All the musicians and our guests agreed that everything was better on the dress rehearsal, and this included some of the jokes that I was given. The producers of the show had liked the irreverent tone of *The Tube* and had thought that by supplying me with side-splitting gags, we would create the same atmosphere. The band and I weren't so keen on some of the jokes: when we had Ray Charles' famous side man, the saxophonist David 'Fathead' Newman, as a guest, the writers suggested I interrupt David Sanborn's introduction with, 'Don't be so rude, calling him fathead.' Another top joke was to introduce an a cappella group with, 'I thought "a cappella" meant not wearing trousers until I heard this group.' After a while, we dropped the gag writers.

In December 1988 I flew back to London for Christmas and, during that week, we launched *The Groovy Fellas* in a freezing cold pub in Fleet Street called the Cheddar Cheese. In my opinion, the programme was ahead of its time but, back then, it wasn't altogether well received, although there was much laughter in the Cheddar Cheese. I held the view then, and still do, that it was a great historic document of Britain in the eighties.

As it was Christmas, I now gave myself a bit of time off. The only other thing I agreed to do was to turn on the Christmas lights in Greenwich. Adele Drake, the mother of my friend Torly, had asked me to do this on behalf of her charity, the Drake Music Trust. I was happy to do it as I very much admire and support the charity's work supplying disabled people with the means to make music. Now, through Adele's persistence and hard work, it is a huge organization, with workshops and houses all over the country. It just shows what you can do if you keep at something, and especially something worthwhile like this. However, I was still flapping about with showbiz and, after my short Christmas break, I was on Concorde and back to New York again. I am aware that this might read like a person showing off about his travel schedule, but that was my life then. Nowadays, with Concorde gone and the greater security delays at airports, such an arrangement wouldn't be possible. But at that time, when you arrived in New York, you just had to smile and wave your passport and they welcomed you through.

The reason I'd wanted to do *Sunday Night* was because of its determination to feature great musicians of all genres and generations, some of them famous names, others unsung heroes of American music. Now there are very few of the legendary musicians from the so-called Jazz Age left but, in the late eighties, some of them were still around, even if they were approaching the end of their lives. Dizzy Gillespie had been one of the first guests on the first series, Slim Gaillard another. It was a great honour to work with all these artists, and the standard of integrity and excellence was maintained throughout the second series. For this, the name was changed to *Night Music*, since it was felt that not all countries it was sold to would want to broadcast it on a Sunday. By the time the team had realized that not every country would want to broadcast it at night, it was too late to start thinking again, and that name remained. I was especially delighted that one of our first guests for this series was Willie Dixon, one of the greatest poets music has ever known. He has written so many fantastic songs, including 'I Just Want to Make Love to You', 'I'm Ready' and 'Wang Dang Doodle'. The clarity of his poetry is such that the words he uses go like a dart straight to the centre of your emotions, without a word too many being used. It's the music of men, which I'd always preferred to the music of soppy boys, even when a boy myself. And his bass playing was extraordinary. One evening, when I was having a few light ales with Keith Richards and Ronnie Wood, Keith played me Chuck Berry's 'Little Queenie' and pointed out Willie Dixon's extraordinary bass line on it. It might seem deceptively simple but it jumps to different time signatures and keeps doing what you least expect. We all agreed that the result was the work of a genius.

One of the first people to agree to do a song on my first Friends record, *Small World Big Band*, was Sting, and he said he'd always loved Willie Dixon and particularly his song 'Seventh Son'. Another artist to appear on that same record was Steve Winwood, who did Willie's 'I'm Ready'. I very much hope that Willie was looking down and liking what we did.

I'd been largely out of the recording loop for some years but, inspired by all the great guest performers there'd been on the show, I now decided to start the process off again. I'd begun to think about it in London, but my studio was still all over the place and unfinished, and I was hardly ever there. So I decided to record some songs in New York, for the record that would end up being *A World of His Own*. I booked some time in a recording studio, and the first person I asked to be involved was Kim Lesley. She came along and did a song called 'We're Through', later to be used in the film *The Rachel Papers*. We were both really pleased with how it sounded but, when we stepped outside for a break, we found ourselves in a danger zone. There were people punching one another, what appeared to be a lynch mob on the corner shouting at some unfortunate fellow and another man who had an upturned piece of Tupperware which he was hitting continually with a spoon, which puzzled me for a minute, until I realized that it was his version of busking. We managed to ignore or step over everyone, but I was beginning to feel that it was all a bit much and missed our cosier London studios. However, on the whole, I was still very much enjoying my New York life and there were only a couple of aspects I found I really disliked. These were that there were only about two newspapers and they were both boring and that the beer was undrinkable piss. Now, my readers might well be thinking, 'Hang on a minute, didn't you participate in the "Bud's For You" campaign with Squeeze? And wasn't *Night Music* sponsored by Michelob?' That may well be true, but I can only say that I occasionally missed being able to pop into my local for the best beer in the world.

In the early summer of 1989 we came to the end of the second series and, although there was talk of a third season, which I wanted to do, it hadn't yet been finalized. In the meantime, because I had so many commitments, including the next Squeeze album to work on, I cleared my stuff from the New York apartment and came back to London.

Taking it up the Octave

By now, Squeeze consisted of Chris, Glenn, Gilson, Keith Wilkinson and myself. Because so many of us seemed to be suffering from financial, psychological or domestic stress at this time, the initial suggestion for the title of the new record was 'Angst' but we ended up calling it *Frank*, after Gilson's dog. To save money, instead of the grand Islington studio we had used before, the decision was made to record it at a studio in the Old Kent Road, which was quicker for us all to get to anyway. We had some good songs on *Frank*, and the first recorded version of my song 'Dr Jazz', which had first been heard in *Walking to New Orleans*.

You can never really tell whether a record works until years after it's finished; time changes the way you view it and gives you some perspective. *Frank* received a great deal of critical acclaim but wasn't a big selling success.

All this time I was doing far too much and kept getting ill; being run down, I would come down with anything at the drop of a hat. However, I was still keen to do live shows, not least because when Squeeze weren't touring I had no income. As Miles was so busy with the Police, Malcolm Hardee stepped in and arranged some shows for Gilson and me at the Hackney Empire. However, after we'd done them he explained he hadn't allowed for VAT and handed me three quid in cash. I couldn't hold it against him but it didn't help the state of my health or my bank balance having him act in this way as manager.

Malcolm was probably more than usually preoccupied at this time, as his legendary Tunnel Palladium was due to close following a police raid on the pub in which it was housed. On the sad occasion of its last night I performed there one last time, as did many of the other regulars. Then, as was customary, Malcolm rejoined us on stage, having removed all his clothes, took a bow and walked off, still naked. I followed him and we both went into the garden yard at the side of the pub. It was a drizzly wet evening and, as we stood there together reminiscing about the old days and how sad it was that the club had finished, I couldn't help suggesting Malcolm get some clothes on before he caught cold. He looked at me through his thick spectacles, completely blankly, in the way only Malcolm could and said, 'I can't. Somebody's nicked them.' So I lent him my coat and we went into the bar for a drink.

Malcolm's house was just above my makeshift studio, and one of the benefits of this was that I got to know his lodger better, the great guitarist Mark Flanagan. I was working on the song I'd started writing on tour with Squeeze, 'The Architectural Number', and Mark came down and added a great slide-guitar ending to it. We played together on a few evenings after this, and I realized how absolutely brilliant he was, especially considering how difficult it was for a guitarist to fit in with a busy left hand like mine. He could play the guitar and noodle around without getting in the way of it or play the most sensational solos – perfect. He had performed with us briefly in Edinburgh and now joined up with Gilson and me to play at some of the shows we had lined up.

There was a variety of further shows booked around the country and, at some of them, Mike Paice and Keith Wilkinson also joined us, as did my brother Christopher, to provide the funk and the love interest with his Hammond organ. The group seemed to be growing organically from the rhythm section, which I was very pleased about. But at this stage, to continue calling it the Big Band would have caused our audiences some disappointment. 'Big Band' was a good joke when it had been just Gilson and I but, now, with four or five people, there might have been a few demands for money back, so we just called it Jools Holland's Band.

Despite not having to fly off to New York all the time, life was still hectic because sometimes we would do two shows in a night, driving from one to the other and then arriving back in London at six in the morning. Because I enjoyed playing, it didn't seem to wear me out. If I had been playing for somebody else I wouldn't have liked it so much, but playing your own music is a different thing.

Jukebox Jury

Now that Gilson, Keith and I were touring with the others, Chris and Glenn, quite reasonably, were beginning to complain about our not being able to commit to Squeeze gigs. We had already had to turn down some big European shows that Miles had set up, including a tour with the Bee Gees, because Gilson and I had booked to do our own shows, but another big American tour was planned for the end of the year, which Gilson and I agreed to. And then, in this hectic time, I suddenly got a call from Janet Street Porter telling me that the BBC was thinking of doing a new version of *Jukebox Jury* and asking whether I would be interested in hosting it. I told her that, in theory, it sounded like a good idea but that it was going to be very difficult to find the time. It was to be shot in Newcastle, a place I loved, but this would add to the time needed.

This wasn't the first show I had been offered in England since *The Tube* had ended. Miles was always trying to find other programmes for me and would often set up meetings with television executives. A lot of the time I would find that my heart wasn't in it. They would want something journalistic, which wasn't me, or wacky and sensational, which I didn't feel happy with either. Even Janet, whom I loved, kept talking about making the programme sexy and all these modern ideas – I just thought that it would be whatever it was. But I quite liked the idea of *Jukebox Jury* and said that I would think about it. And then, at this same time, the third series of *Night Music* was confirmed.

Much as I love Miles, I think he would have been quite happy to have me like Frankenstein's monster, taken apart with my piano-playing hands put in one place, my boasting head in another and my feet on the floor of a television studio, just to spread me around. I did say to him that something had to go, I couldn't do it all. And, although it was difficult to decide, we knew that committing to another series of *Night Music* would rule out my own tours, the American tour with Squeeze and *Jukebox Jury*, so Miles was forced to call NBC and tell them I was unable to do the third series. It's a difficult thing, to turn down a major American network show, but we really had little choice.

Just before starting *Jukebox Jury* I bumped into David Jacobs, the presenter of the original programme, and he wished me the best of luck with it. It occurred to me that the producers should have asked him to host it again, since he'd have been much better at remembering the guests' names and is an absolutely erudite and charming presenter. He kindly offered two pieces of advice. The first was to move the front rows of the audience around to the back for the second shoot of the day so it would seem as if there were a different audience for each show – very good advice, and we followed it. The second was to have lots of fun with the show – but I really would have had lots more fun if he had hosted it and I had watched it at home. However, there were some good moments. Ade Edmondson, Jermaine Jackson and Julian Clary came on the first show, and they were all professional and funny, even though the story in the papers the following day was 'Foul Mouth is Back', because there had been a slight swearing incident. However, it's the tabloid writer's job to find an amusing angle and, really, I see them as lovable rogues.

Jennifer Saunders and Dawn French appeared as guests, too, and, after asking her opinion on a record, I apologized to Jennifer for trying to put words into her mouth. Dawn then came in with, 'That's not all you've been trying to put in her mouth!' At once we heard, 'Stop – *Cut*. CUT', and the producer came up and, with a lot of tutting, told us we couldn't have that sort of thing either in the broadcast show or said in front of the audience. So there we were again, the pair of them getting me into trouble with the producers – it felt like old times.

The Blob in Hollywood

In November we all flew out to Chicago for the start of Squeeze's American tour. The Solidarity leader, Lech Wałęsa, was staying in the same hotel on an official visit, so security was tight and it was hard to get in and out. As was the custom for bands on tour, we were all checking in with pseudonyms anyway, presumably to prevent girls coming to sex us in our hotel rooms. Gilson's name on this tour was Justin Time, Keith's B. Lucky, Chris's Shed (which I wished I'd used) and Glenn's Earl Grey. I used Julian Darling because I liked the idea of the manager greeting us in the lobby with 'Justin Time?' 'Yes, thank you'; 'B. Lucky?' 'I will'; and 'Julian Darling?' Yes, my love?'

This particular hotel had followed the horrible contemporary trend of having the bar in the lobby instead of in a separate area, which means there is absolutely no privacy and no cosy atmosphere in which to have a quiet drink. Coincidentally, the actor Dennis Waterman was staying there too and, having bumped into him outside the hotel, we invited him to join us for a drink. We were delighted when he agreed, as we were all long-term admirers. However, we had a lot of bother even getting to the bar, because we had quite a few people with us who security didn't want to allow in. When we did finally manage to get in and had settled down with our drinks, Dennis noticed a piano in the lobby and suggested I give them all a tune. However, the management refused to give us a key to open the piano. We all thought this was daft, so when no one was looking I used an old south London method I knew of opening car doors, got the lid up and started playing the 'Lambeth Walk'. Our little group clustered round, but I think our '*Oy*' at the end of each chorus was a bit too enthusiastic and, by the tenth one, the management came over and told us that Lech Wałęsa was trying to sleep. We were sure he wouldn't have minded this singsong, just as we would have been charmed to hear some Polish folk songs wafting up to our rooms. But then they noticed I'd forced open the piano and suddenly we found ourselves surrounded by armed security men, as if we were criminals, not guests of the hotel. We turned to Dennis Waterman, who was, after all, *Minder* but, rather than chinning them all, he looked a bit stressed himself and persuaded us back to the bar for a calming drink. At that point Matt Irving, our other keyboard player, came in, cheerfully unaware of what had just happened. As the security men had melted away and the piano lid was still open, we said, 'Hey, Matt, we'd love to hear a tune on the piano, mate.' Looking quite pleased, and with a beaming smile, he sat down and started gently tinkling while thinking what he might play to entertain us all. At once, out of nowhere, the security men rushed up and forcefully muscled poor confused Matt off his seat and away from the piano.

After Chicago and for the rest of the tour we found ourselves once again on one of the huge American tour buses but, in this case, one that had airbrushed paintings of cowboys and Indians shooting one another all over the sides. This made us all feel a bit daft, but one of the great aspects of touring with Squeeze was that we were all amused by the same things and made each other laugh. Some bands don't get on at all off stage but, if this had been the case with us, we couldn't have continued. A week into the tour we had a drink with our support band, Katrina and the Waves, who told us that they had been supporting the Beach Boys for a while, a band who were friendly to all outsiders but couldn't stand one another. We assured them that we were the opposite of this.

From time to time, in the middle of this tour, I would have to fulfil my obligations to *Jukebox Jury* and fly back to film the next couple of shows. Because I only had two days to get back, do the filming and then return again, I had to take Concorde to London, then the train up to Newcastle to do the show, then back to London, for about twenty minutes, and then pop back to America again. I also had to cover Squeeze's expenses while I was away so it was not only a bother but also very expensive. I began to wonder who had got me into this situation and, soon afterwards, had a bit of a word with Miles. Really, if you do have a choice, it's best to stick to the things you like doing and, nowadays, that's a policy I'm largely able to follow.

Finally, on 11 December, 1989 we played at the vast Universal Amphitheater in Los Angeles. In the dressing room there was this huge Roman-type bath which had been installed for Frank Sinatra when he played there. It was beautifully tiled and, looking at it before the show, we decided it would be great to try it out together afterwards, like a load of footballers. Squeeze still shared a certain sort of south-east London mentality, and it took over sometimes. John Lay got some Matey bubble bath, which we poured in, along with some champagne to attract the girls, and we all got in and larked about happily. It took me back to the early days of the blob, and we were all rather enjoying it. Suddenly, the dressing-room door opened and our showbiz guests came in.

As we were in Hollywood, these consisted of Matt Dillon, Jamie Lee Curtis and other Los Angeles bigwigs, and they all looked a bit confused at the sight of the blob splashing about enjoying itself. I'd been introduced to Matt Dillon at dinner the night before by my friend Katrina Boorman and I had tried to interest them in oo gauge model railway layouts. I did notice that their eyes had glazed over somewhat. Now I introduced our guests to my bandmates and we made conversation. After a while we wanted to get out of the tub but we were reluctant to appear prudish by asking these filmstars to leave first. In the end, having downed a few more drinks to get rid of any remaining inhibitions, the blob emerged and put its pants on.

Back in England I recorded one more live record with Squeeze at Newcastle Town Hall in January 1990 and then I left Squeeze for good. I knew I was right to leave, since continuing with them would have meant long periods away and not enough time for my own artistic endeavours, but I also knew I would miss a great many of the aspects of being part of Squeeze. I'd miss the music, playing the shows and the amusing times we all used to have on tour. And, perhaps, most of all, I knew I would miss the blob.

The Happening

The dilapidated collection of collapsing buildings and lean-to sheds I had bought in the mid-eighties, with the idea of transforming them into a studio and a little Portmerion-style village, were still far off my original vision. I had one room with basic but usable studio equipment in it, and above it, my small office. The other buildings were rented off us by Mark and Max, who owned Westcombe's, the fireplace business. I was continuing to construct the place bit by bit and, as soon as I could construct a bit more, I did. My friend Eddie Gittings, who had been so astute in warning me about the depressing effect of blue walls in my first studio, came up with the great idea of creating an exterior to look like a Victorian railway station, painted in postwar Southern region livery. This gave me fresh impetus. In order to help this idea along, and because we were constantly short of money, I decided to rent out my office too. My first tenant was Malcolm Hardee, who was by now running a comedy agency and, since his back garden pretty much backed on to my office, it was quite convenient for him. I still used the office too, so we squashed everyone in – myself, Nicky our new secretary, John Lay and Malcolm – and I felt that the comedy and music blended in well together. However, I arrived one day to find cables stretching from the office window up over the roof of the next-door shed, across the garden and in through Malcolm's bedroom window. He assured me they were attached to his phone but, to this day, God rest his soul, I suspect he was pinching my electricity.

He was also a bit messy. I certainly wouldn't pry in to anybody's mail, but he would leave stuff strewn over the desks, including letters along the lines: 'Dear sir, we are so sorry about the incident where you lost your trousers in our venue.' I didn't need to read more to catch the general drift.

One of the other disadvantages was that Malcolm didn't actually ever pay me any rent. I'm sure there was a perfectly good reason for this lapse but, since the arrangement was in order to earn me some much-needed revenue, after a couple of months my friends and Greenwich neighbours Vic Reeves and Bob Mortimer took over as tenants and used the room to write their brilliantly surreal scripts. Even then, Malcolm would often appear, ask if Vic and Bob were in that day and, if they weren't, tell me that he needed to take over the office for a meeting. All their things would be pushed to one side and all his photographs would come out of a drawer, including that of his brother-in-law, who was a police officer. Then Malcolm, his assistant, Potter, and his three-legged dog Tripod would stand there proprietorily, waiting for whomever they were to meet. By 1990, BSkyB had started up, and they needed programmes and had the money to fund them, so one of the meetings was with some of their executives. Without doubt, they were astute and forward-looking because, following this meeting, they proceeded to appoint Malcolm Hardee Head of Entertainment/Comedy. So, what with this office being used by Vic and Bob to write and act out their ideas and by BSkyB's Head of Entertainment/Comedy, and with Mark Flanagan and Ronnie Box, our engineer, living round the corner, it was beginning to feel like a home for our little south-east London artistic community.

One of the first shows Malcolm proposed in his new role was a quiz show, but one in which contestants would bring along some of their own domestic appliances and then, if they answered a question wrongly, have them taken away. The producers didn't think this particular concept would catch on but another idea they did like was a live weekly version of the Tunnel Palladium comedy club but with the addition of music. It was to be called *The Happening* and filmed live each week at the Astoria theatre in Soho. The floodgates were open, with Malcolm getting all his mates work and my band and me booked to appear each week along with the other guests from music or comedy.

Just before the first show we went along to a big hotel in Aldwych to be photographed round the piano with Courtney

Pine, one of the guests of the first *Happening*, to celebrate the launch of BSkyB. Sir Robin Day was also there and he became incredibly sniffy when asked to be in the photograph, saying he didn't want to be part of this showbiz buffoonery. In the back of my mind, I assumed he was talking about Malcolm, who was looking a bit vague and standing around smoking roll-ups in his big shorts, Tripod by his side, but perhaps he meant all of us. Now, looking back, I feel somewhat sympathetic to Sir Robin's view, though at the time some thought he was being a big snob.

Dave Morley and Graham K. Smith did a great job of producing *The Happening*, and the fact that the rehearsals and filming took place at the Astoria rather than in Newcastle or New York made things a great deal easier for me. I began to enjoy the routine of my band playing with some of the great musicians booked to appear, such as Lou Rawls, Eartha Kitt, Slim Gaillard and Mica Paris. The show also introduced me to Eddi Reader and Sam Brown, both of whom now frequently join me on stage with my Big Band.

The Happening lasted for twenty-six weeks. At first, some of the great new comedic talents appeared on it – Steve Coogan, Julian Clary and, of course, Vic and Bob – but towards the end of its run Malcolm found it less easy to persuade the bigger talents to come on as so few people had satellite dishes in those days so everyone knew that the audience would be small. He was reduced to booking such acts as Dave Dud and His Dead Dad, a ventriloquist whose dummy was his decomposing father, an idea that worked well on paper but less well in reality. Malcolm also appeared himself occasionally, one time blacking up as Nelson Mandela. Again, this didn't raise quite the laughs he'd hoped for.

While this was going on I finished the album *A World of His Own*, which I'd been working on since my time in New York. To coincide with its release on Miles's independent label, we decided to make a video for 'Holy Cow', an Allen Toussaint song featured on the record. My idea for this video was to film my rather tired Jaguar XJ6 being crushed, and to put a dummy inside it so it looked as if I were being crushed too. I also told Vic and

Bob that they could have a month's free rent if they would appear in it. They agreed, but added rather sneeringly, 'But only if we can be in a bathtub filled with mud, naked apart from great plumed hats and frilly Elizabethan ruffs. I just nodded and, when they turned up to do it, there it was, all laid on for them. I didn't feel the slightest bit guilty about seeing them squashed uncomfortably, naked in this mudbath in their Elizabethan ruffs, because I was only acceding to their demands.

This video was shown a lot and the record sold very well. It received a lot of coverage and very good reviews, including one from the *Guardian* which called it 'a record of kaleidoscopic beauty'. I've never gone along with the theory that you can't believe the good reviews unless you also believe the bad. I think the good ones are absolutely accurate and perfect journalism and the bad ones are rubbish and I don't buy that paper again for a month.

Mr Roadrunner

By now Andrea Wonfor had raised the money we needed to make the follow-on to *Walking to New Orleans*, which was to be called *Mr Roadrunner*. This was to be a more ambitious film, as it was to focus on the music and musicians of two cities, Memphis and Nashville. Director Geoff Wonfor and I flew out there to research some of the locations and meet the musical legends we wanted to film. We had a lovely time exploring Nashville and driving through the lush, rolling countryside of Tennessee. Moving on to Memphis, one of the places I was most excited to visit was Sun Studios, where legendary records by Howlin' Wolf, Charlie Rich, Jerry Lee Lewis, Carl Perkins, Elvis Presley and Johnny Cash had been made. I personally felt as if I were in a holy place, but I did feel that this aura would be very hard to capture on film because, without any of those legends being there, it would just be a room, without any of the mystique. There are some things you can't experience through television.

One of the artists we wanted to be in the film was Jerry Lee Lewis, and we met up with him a few times and became very friendly with his family. He invited us to a fundraising dinner being held at a hotel just outside Memphis to help re-elect the local sheriff. When we arrived, the venue was covered in huge posters saying, 'Re-elect Sheriff Gene Barksdale', and the sheriff himself was there greeting people, this huge man with a beaming face and sideburns. As we went in we were given Re-elect Sheriff Barksdale stetsons, and Geoff had a big sash put on him which said, 'The evangeline preacher prays for victory. Gene Barksdale.' Sitting there, in our stetsons and sashes, we hoped we were blending in.

Jerry Lee then played and blew this tough crowd away. Afterwards, Phoebe, his daughter, took us up to the 1970s-style presidential suite where Jerry Lee and his new young wife and family were gathered. He said he'd love to sing something by Hank Williams in the film, and we talked about how much we loved his songs. He then added, 'But, you know, that's why I've not written many songs, because that's what killed Hank Williams. Writing all those songs. He couldn't have all those songs inside him and it not kill him.' What he was saying was all interesting but it was hard to concentrate because his skeletal uncle was sitting with us and he looked a bit like Hank Williams might have looked had he not written any songs and lived to be 105. He wore a pale blue seersucker suit with huge lapels and a great big cowboy hat, and had dyed jet-black hair. Every time I tried to chat, he started coughing so hard I thought he was going to die. Jerry Lee said, 'Sorry about my uncle there, he's not so well,' and I said, 'Please don't worry at all.' Then I said, 'Jerry Lee, have you ever run for sheriff?', and he laughed and said, 'Run for sheriff? I've never run for sheriff, I just ran *from* the sheriff.' We all roared with laughter, but this just brought on another deafening coughing fit from the uncle.

Coming to the end of this initial research trip, I was feeling quite buoyed up because of all the great locations and the people who had agreed to be in it, and because I had thought of a narrative that could run through the whole film. However, just as I was preparing to return to England, Christabel rang me with the terrifying news that my stepson Fred had been in a very bad car crash. I caught the next flight home and, when I saw him, the little five-year-old Fred I knew was completely unrecognizable; he had broken his jaw in three places and his face had blown up like a balloon. However, since he'd been told that his mother, his grandmothers and I had also been in car crashes, he assumed that everyone had to go through one in their lives and his view was that he was glad to have got his out of the way. He seemed somehow to be infused with the same spirit of positive thinking that had characterized my mother. I'm glad to say that he recovered fully soon afterwards and no lasting damage had been done.

Soon after this, we went back to Memphis to begin filming the various artists and locations. Charlie Rich singing Duke Ellington's 'Mood Indigo' was the best version I have ever heard. However, one of my biggest artistic regrets is that I didn't then know of his own song, 'Feel Like Going Home'. If I had I would have asked him to sing that; it would have been perfect. We also filmed Betty Wright singing 'Clean Up Woman' and Rufus Thomas singing 'Walking the Dog.'

Returning from Memphis, we were very fortunate, as a lot of heavyweight British stars wanted to lend their support to the film, which they felt would help shine the spotlight on some of the lesser known musical greats from that area. One of these British stars was Robert Palmer. Not only was he dashingly handsome and gifted with an amazing voice, he also had a huge and deep knowledge of a lot of roots music, which we would stay up till five in the morning discussing and playing. I hoped at one time that Robert Palmer and myself were going to record together. His untimely death in 2003 sadly meant this was not to be.

The other person who was very generous with his time and contribution of ideas was the guitar giant David Gilmour. When you hear his playing with Pink Floyd or his solo work, it should be obvious he's been heavily inspired by the blues. When I told him about the theme running through my film – a witch casting a spell on me – he rang me the next day and said, 'We've got to do "I Put a Spell on You" and get Mica Paris to sing it.' This idea of David's turned out to be a really good one and was my first realization that, by putting one and one together, you often come up with three. We performed the song, as we did Robert Palmer's number, in what appeared to be the interior of a blue and yellow tent, the exterior of which we had already filmed in a location just outside Memphis to make it seem that our British artists were playing there. We were actually playing in a studio in London – another showbiz lie revealed for you.

So many people wrote in to ask where they could get a copy of Mica and David's brilliant performance that eventually we recorded it. It appeared on the first volume of my *Small World Big Band*. It remains one of the best live performances of guitar and vocal I've ever had the privilege of being involved with.

★

I used to meet up with George Harrison from time to time and, soon after recording Mica and David, had dinner with him. I told him about the film and the narrative I had now developed, based on the theme of a lost chord, a story not dissimilar to Robert Johnson selling his soul to the devil at the crossroads in exchange for musical gifts. However, I told him I was worried I might be making the whole film too weird with this whole allegorical theme and having a devil and an angel both being played by the same actress, the talented Tanya Coleridge. But he was really encouraging and said, 'No, man – that's great, you've got to make things interesting,' and then he asked if I wanted him to do a song for it. I was delighted – having George in it would immediately lift it up a level. He didn't want any money, just wanted to help, and I suddenly realized what a great friend he was.

The following very snowy Saturday I went out to see him to figure out the song he was going to do for the film. His house had an incredible garden, which was very beautiful in the snow. His wife, Olivia, met me and, with many apologies, said, 'George is doing an interview for *Time* magazine and he's going to be an hour or so. I've got to dash out, so can I leave you alone for a while?' I assured her that was fine and, giving me some sandwiches to eat, she added, 'The thing is, Bob Dylan's going to pop in for tea. Could you let him in and give him a cup of tea and explain what's happening, because I've got to run.'

So I was left there and, since George had a particularly beautiful Steinway upright piano, I started playing that. Suddenly I felt these hands on my shoulder and heard this unmistakable voice saying, 'Hey, that sounds like Sister Rosetta Tharpe.' I turned and, although I shouldn't have been, was startled to see Bob Dylan. He asked me if I was playing 'Up above My Head', and how I knew it. I told him that my mum had had a 78 record of Sister Rosetta Tharpe and it was one of the first records I'd really loved, with Sammy Price's piano and Sister Rosetta's machine-gun-style guitar. Bob said, 'Wow, an original 78 – have you still got that?' Still unable to believe I was having this conversation with one of my heroes, one of the world's all-time great songwriters, I said, 'No, sadly, a family friend called Reardon sat on it.'

With Olivia's message in mind, I got up to offer him a cup of tea. We got chatting in the kitchen and I asked him where he'd been. He said, 'I've been to Stonehenge. It's quite a thing.' I explained that, twenty years earlier, he'd have been able to sit and have his sandwiches on the stones and we both agreed it was a shame it wasn't like that any more. Then I told him I'd managed to buy a miniature version of Stonehenge, which was constructed to the scale of approximately 4mm to a foot, the same as my oo gauge model railway. However, when I turned from making the tea to provide further details, I realized that he had left the room half-way through my explanation. Perhaps the subject of model railways didn't provide such a connection as Sister Rosetta Tharpe had done.

At that point George turned up, having had his photograph taken for the front of *Time* magazine. Apart from his many other great gifts, George always had the ability to make everybody feel at ease and was happy to share whatever he had with his friends, including his enthusiasms. We all had lunch and it was very jolly. George explained to Bob about the film I was doing and continued to be very encouraging. Then he said in his gentle voice, 'Well, everybody, you know what the best thing after a nice lunch is?' We were wondering what it could be – a cigar, a cup of coffee, a country walk? – and George said, 'A George Formby film. Do you know of him, Bob?' Bob said, 'I don't think I do know him. No. Is he kind of like one of the blues people from Memphis that Jools is filming?', and George said, 'No. He was from Wigan and was one of the first British pop stars.' Bob looked quite interested at this but, for the benefit of the younger readers who might, like Bob, have trouble placing him, George Formby was a working-class 1930s singer who starred in a series of prewar British films in which he would sing cheerful music-hall songs such as 'When I'm Cleaning Windows', accompanying himself on the ukulele, with a beaming, cheeky smile. His catchphrase was 'It's turned out nice again.' George explained they'd queued round the block to see these films in Russia.

He drew the curtains on this wintry afternoon, and we all sat back ready to watch as George selected his favourites from the numerous videotapes in a large box marked 'Formby'. I'd had no idea George Formby had made so many films.

Bob seemed a bit confused and bewildered by George Formby. At one point, after the sixth or seventh selection, he got closer to the large television and, squinting, stared at one of the performances, shook his head and said, 'Wow, we really never had anything like this in America.' Sensing enthusiasm, George explained that he often played these songs of an evening with his great friend Joe Brown and he'd let Bob know the next time. Then he fast-forwarded through for more of the best songs. After a few more, Bob started saying, 'I've got to kind of get back to London soon,' adding that it was only because he had a gig, not because he wasn't enjoying the films.

George, Olivia and I then wandered out to Bob's van which had tinted windows. George said, 'John's psychedelic Rolls-Royce had blacked-out windows like this and, when it was picking us all up from our homes in Surrey, we'd all be car sick by the time we got to London because we couldn't see out of the windows. Now, you're not going to be car sick, are you, Bob?' Bob smiled and said he hoped not. He then thanked George and they gave each other a big hug.

Then, just as the van was leaving, the wheels started spinning and George said, 'Oh, I think he's going to come back in. Good, I'll show him some more George Formby.' But the wheels seemed to catch a bit of purchase and Bob sped back to London. George went to see him play that night at the Royal Albert Hall and gave him a video cassette of George Formby to enjoy on his tour bus.

The song George wanted to do in my film was 'Between the Devil and the Deep Blue Sea', not only because he loved it but also because it fitted in with the theme of the film, being torn between the devil and an angel. We recorded it in Air Studios in Oxford Street, with Mark Flanagan, Ray Cooper, Joe Brown, and Herbie Flowers dressed as Noddy, which was George's idea, because he said that Herbie Flowers always played especially well when dressed as Noddy. George's own playing and singing were beautiful, and I was delighted and honoured that he wanted to be in the film.

Mr Roadrunner was well received and was even nominated for a prize in the Cannes Festival of Music, which meant a glamorous trip for Geoff and me, dressed up in our bow-ties. It didn't win so, sadly for the Cannes audience, I didn't get to make another acceptance speech.

'Able Mabel'

In April 1990 Christabel and I were really delighted to discover
that she was going to have a baby, due in January of the following
year. However, in November, on the day I was due to film another
episode of *Jukebox Jury* – which I was making simultaneously with
The Happening at the Astoria – she suddenly woke up, saying I had
to rush her to the hospital. Terrified, and with the hazard lights
on, I drove through the rush-hour traffic to the Portland Hospital
on the other side of London. I drove as fast as I could, simultaneously trying not to shake her up. We then waited in the
hospital, watching the drama of Margaret Thatcher resigning on
the television in between contractions. The baby was definitely
ready to come out and, after two days, poor Christabel was so
delirious she thought that John Major had delivered the baby. In
fact, the consultant who did deliver Mabel was a great expert. He
arrived after a big lunch, still smoking his cigar, and delivered her
superbly, in the most relaxed manner. However, in the middle of
the delivery the other doctors and nurses seemed to get in a
kerfuffle about something and the room became very hot. One
of them said in a slightly strained voice, 'Can someone open a
window?' As I was nearest, I went over, opened the window and,
glancing down into the alley below, I saw my silver Jaguar XJ12
saloon being loaded on to the back of a trailer to be towed away.
Under normal circumstances, I would have been annoyed, but
now it hardly seemed to matter: they could keep the car.

Mabel was born on 22 November, St Cecilia's Day, the patron
saint of music. She was the size of a human hand, and I just didn't
know if she could stay alive being that small. The nurses took her
off to an incubator and, leaving the sedated Christabel with
Margaret Thatcher again, I went to watch over her.

A nurse came up to me and told me not to worry, that babies

were born even smaller than Mabel, she would be fine. I did think that this really must be one of the great things of modern life – such advances in medical technology. As I was thinking this, 10 per cent of my mind moved on to what I should do about picking my car up from the pound. Just then, someone bumped into me, and I turned to see Lonnie Donnegan, whose premature twins were in the incubator next to Mabel's. I'd last seen him when he appeared on *The Happening*. On leaving the show that night, he'd answered my cheerful 'See you!' with 'Who knows when I'm going to see you. I may never see you again, or I might see you very soon.' And here he was. We gave each other a warm pat on the back and went back to watching over our babies.

Eventually, I had to go off to the Astoria to film *Jukebox Jury*, my mind still on Mabel and Christabel in the hospital. Vic and Bob came on and were very funny, but we also had a mystery guest called Glenn Medeiros, who had to listen behind the scenes while his record was savaged. He was so upset by this that he burst into tears. That was the last thing I wanted; I hate the sort of television where people are horrible to each other. I tried to give him a prize of a Nicolas Poussin reproduction, but he didn't want it. Of course, the papers all had stories about 'Cruel Programme Makes Lad Cry' and, in this case, they may have had a point. Soon after this, the BBC decided that *Jukebox Jury* was no longer the sort of programme it wanted but, before it ended, and soon after this incident, there appeared a picture of me in the papers with the headline, 'It's a Miss for Jools'. I assumed it was a bad review of *Jukebox Jury* but, when I looked closer, it was a nice story about Mabel being born.

Mabel and Christabel remained in the hospital until Mabel was strong enough to come home. They were with us for Christmas dinner and we celebrated at Frank's café, with Nicky Keller, Vic and Bob, our wonderful engineer Ron Burrow, John Lay, my old friend Andy Morse, Fred the builder and, of course, George, Fred and Rosie. I'd been worried the children might feel resentful of this much younger child, but they loved her at once. So the inner sanctum of the Greenwich artistic community had a splendid meal, with party hats and all the trimmings, to celebrate a successful end to the first year of the last decade of the twentieth century.

Perfect Pitch

At the beginning of 1991, I was approached by the boss of Apple, Neil Aspinall, on behalf of the Beatles, to ask if I would be interested in interviewing them in a film they were planning, *The Beatles Anthology*, which was to recount their history, as remembered and told by them.

I was very much fascinated by the prospect of learning more about their story. Their impact was so great they can be considered the most important group in the history of popular music. John Peel told me that, when he first went to America, he managed to make a modest living out of just being a person who had once interviewed the Beatles. It did occur to me that I too could fall back on that career option if things turned bad.

The Beatles could have chosen anyone to direct their anthology but unanimously chose Geoff Wonfor, as they trusted him more than anyone to capture the essence of what they were. After a few preliminary meetings with Apple, we all realized that this was going to be a huge, worldwide show. It wasn't a case of whether an American network would screen it prime-time but which one. At one point Neil Aspinall asked Geoff and me to attend a meeting with himself, the Beatles' publicist, Derek Taylor, and one of the chief executives from ABC in America. If ABC was going to spend millions, the high-powered executive wanted to know exact details of the planned format as well as the overall ethos and philosophy of the show. The meeting was slightly tense: there was a lot at stake here. Then the executive asked Geoff what exactly our approach was going to be. Geoff paused, looked out the window a bit vaguely and said in his matter-of-fact Geordie voice, 'Well, I'll go with my camera,' – long pause – and the executive said, 'Yes . . .'

'Then Jools'll ask them questions.'

'Yes.'

'And I'll film it.'

Afterwards Neil said, 'Thanks, mate, you seemed to have clinched the deal there.' Geoff and I weren't asked to any more of these high-powered meetings, but Derek Taylor subsequently became a great friend. He had been the Beatles' publicist and right-hand man from their earliest days and was one of the most charming and funny people I've ever met. He had a big video library and one of the best films he showed me was his favourite: *The King's Stamp*, a ten-minute information film from about 1939 of how the stamp came into being and how we use it. He gave me a copy and I still watch it. All I can say is there's nothing to it but at the same time it's got everything. Sadly, Derek is no longer with us, but every time I watch *The King's Stamp*, I think of him.

The plan for *The Beatles Anthology* was to take each year the group were together and interview them individually about that year for a couple of hours. This would form the basis of the film and it would be edited together with archive footage.

The first person I went to interview was Paul, and Linda was there, always making sure we had sandwiches and cups of tea. She was one of the gentlest, kindest people I've ever met. She always thought the best of people. I then moved on to George, and then Ringo. At one point all of them individually mentioned a van they all hated travelling in, but each of them remembered the make and colour of the van differently. I brought this up with Chips Chipperfield, the producer, and he said, 'Silly detail. Doesn't matter.' But my policeman's mind had already gone to work and I was thinking, 'Well, it might be a silly detail to you but, if they're not remembering the same facts about this one horrid van, it might cast a shadow over their memories of other matters.' And this was borne out throughout the course of the *Anthology*.

When I asked them about meeting Elvis, Paul said, 'Oh yeah, I'll never forget it. It was quite an event, this, because we were in Memphis and it was like our gang meeting his gang. He was in his house with his band, we were with our crew. Elvis was in front of his TV, he had, like, this remote control and he was changing the channels and we had never seen this before. Then Priscilla came in, wearing this red and white gingham dress. She was like the perfect sort of American sweetheart and she brought us all apple pie and we all had that and it was really great.'

Then I talked to Ringo and he said, 'Oh, yeah. It was really lovely because we went there and Elvis was sitting on top of some cushions, playing a twelve-string guitar and he had a bank of televisions and somebody was changing the channels for him, which we thought was funny. Priscilla came in and she was dressed all in black, like a Spanish woman going to a funeral.'

So then I asked George about it. I said, 'How was it?' He said, 'Well, I remember Elvis was sitting there and I think he might have had a ukulele, but Priscilla couldn't be there, she was on holiday, which was sad because we were all hoping to meet her.'

Occasionally I would say, 'Can I just compare your evidence to the evidence put forward by your co-members?' But they all found their differing memories amusing.

This was a fascinating time for me, but this is not the Beatles' story, it's mine, and my own career was about to reach a turning point. Throughout 1991 I was also touring and playing live shows and I managed to make *The Full Complement*, a follow-up LP to *World of His Own*. However, the gigs weren't big and, since the small label which had paid for the record had been sold to EMI, *The Full Complement* was lost in the takeover and sank without trace.

Although I was making a living at this time, my outgoings were continuing to rise and, since I had a family to support, I considered I had a responsibility to think of further ways to earn money. Some people I'd known had set up television production companies and suggested I do the same, but that wasn't for me. However, Christabel's ex-husband, Ned, Laurie Latham and I did start to form our own record label. What with my musical experience, Laurie Latham's production skills and Ned's brilliant and original mind, we thought we might be on to a good thing. Miles Copeland kindly came down to advise us, but his first piece of advice was:

'Why are you even thinking of doing this? It's a big headache.'
We tried it for a little bit, and he was right: it was a big headache.
We folded it after a while. Really, I preferred to concentrate on
my own music, not to have to think about which aspects of other
people's would please a commercial audience.

I had started to write songs based on old poetry, including a
song called 'The Maiden's Lament', which is an anonymous poem
from the eighteenth century. I needed some horn arrangements
written out to add to this and it suddenly occurred to me that the
horn players from the Deptford Dance Orchestra, a local band I'd
been to see play some months earlier and had loved, would be
perfect. They lived down the road, were semi-professional, loved
the music and often played for no money or whatever they could
collect in a hat at the end of the night. Some of them came and
laid down the horn arrangements, and it sounded so good it
occurred to me that this could be the start of something – and it
was. Not only did we join up and play gigs with the Deptford
Dance Orchestra from time to time but also the four horns from
it, Jon Scott, Phil Veacock, Paul Bartholomew and Roger Goslyn,
regularly joined my line-up. Apart from Gilson and myself, Keith
Wilkinson was still on bass, Mark Flanagan on guitar and my
brother Christopher on the Hammond organ.

However, this added line-up increased my expenses. At first, I
was worried I didn't have enough money to continue with it
in this form. Then I had this tremendous realization that this
didn't matter; throughout my life I'd always obeyed my instinct
to follow the path of the music I loved. Now I felt I was getting
on the right track, the lack of money should be and was a secondary
issue.

I had a lovely turn-of-the-century showman's living wagon in
the studio yard, and it came to me that we could live and move
around in that if it came to it. I'd be playing the music I loved, I'd
be able to have a big band and I'd be following the spiritual
principle that the less you have, the less you need. After all,
St Simeon Stylites the Elder lived on top of a column for a while,
doing very little himself, and people threw food up to him to keep

him alive. I didn't quite want to go that far but I thought it would be all right to be in a spiritual space where you could be without needs and ready for more enlightenment.

But something was starting to happen that meant it wasn't necessary to make this change in lifestyle. With our bigger line-up, we began to be incredibly busy and increasingly popular. As soon as we booked one venue it would sell out and we would wish we'd booked a bigger one. As it turned out, Christabel and the children didn't have to live in a caravan parked next to JB's Club in Dudley and a succession of other welcoming venues. And this unexpected turnaround in fortune was thanks to the people who in many ways I love the best, and that is the people who pay to come and see us at our shows.

The irony was, having reconciled myself to the fact I was going to be more hard-up by sticking to the activities I enjoyed, those very activities ended up bringing me in much more than the ones I'd thought about doing for money. I've been incredibly lucky, but it's something I'd recommend to everybody: stick with your dream.

Later with Jools Holland

Then, just as my fortunes were starting to improve, they improved further still. In the autumn of 1991, while we were playing a sold-out run at the Edinburgh Festival, I received a call from Mark Cooper at the BBC, to discuss the possibility of a weekly music show. I'd known Mark Cooper from when he'd written on the *Record Mirror* with Paula. He'd always been a brilliant journalist and his interests had never diverted away from music.

The BBC hadn't done any music shows since *The Old Grey Whistle Test*, except for *The Oxford Road Show*, which had been pushed off by *The Tube*. Channel Four had tried one or two music programmes, all of which had lasted about five minutes. Music shows are expensive to produce and never get huge ratings, compared to other types of television programme. However, music being a genuine art form, the BBC felt it was their responsibility to reflect good quality music of all genres from all over the world and that they needed a vehicle for this.

Michael Jackson (not to be confused with the self-styled King of Pop) was Controller of BBC2 at the time. He had worked as assistant to Jeremy Isaacs, who had always supported me. Not only did Michael appreciate that a show such as this would fulfil the BBC's remit to 'educate, entertain and inform' but he was enthusiastic about my hosting it, because he had liked what I'd done with *The Tube* and *Night Music* in America. Between us, Mark and I had knowledge of a wide range of music, and it was felt we might be an interesting combination.

After this initial call Mark and I got together with Janet Fraser Crook, who was going to direct the programme. The first thing we all agreed was that we didn't want anything to get in the way of the fans' appreciation of the music. We decided that the rational thing was to have me in the middle of the set and the bands around the outside. The show would be called *Later with Jools Holland*, as it was going to be aired after *The Late Show* and was made by the same department. We all felt excited to be starting with a clean palette in this way. The only drawback was that there was no money in the budget and therefore no set or lighting to speak of, but we knew Janet was so skilled and resourceful, she could make tuppence look like a thousand guineas. So having agreed everything, we were given the go-ahead for an initial six shows; we would see how it went.

What we wanted to achieve from the start was a programme that would reflect all elements of music and appeal to varied musical tastes. In the first series we had the Neville Brothers, D'Influence, Morrissey, Shane MacGowan and Smokey Robinson, among others. Off camera, I talked to Art Neville of the Neville Brothers about the organ player Bill Doggett, and he showed me a technique Bill had used on the organ, punching it with the palm of his hand to make it sound like a beating drum. Discovering a detail like this was, for me, one of the brilliant things about the programme; for the viewers it might have been the great excitement of managing to secure an exclusive with the marvellous k d Lang. The point was, the show was brilliant and illuminating in many different ways.

People have asked me a number of questions about the show over the years so, for the curious, I will answer the three most frequent.

How do people get to perform on the show?
There are only a limited number of shows made every year. As each show is only an hour long, time is at a premium and there is a great deal of music competing to get on. Most of the artists who do appear are established and successful in their own field already, even if they are not mainstream performers. Often an appearance will coincide with the artist being on tour in Britain.

It's also important to get a balance between different generic styles. We showcase important record releases by established or sometimes new performers. When we do have new performers on, they generally already have experience of performing live, a following or a record out. Although I am very proud that the show has helped break a number of new artists, it is not a talent show.

Mark Cooper, Alison Howe, the series' producer, Janet Fraser Crook and I discuss who we would like to appear. We go to the ends of the earth to achieve the right balance. Occasionally, when necessary, I'll ring up an artist to try and give an extra bit of persuasion. However, being immersed in my own music, mostly I leave the business of the final booking to Mark, Alison and the *Later* team, and they do a super job. All of the performers are paid the same Musicians Union rates, whether it be Roland (drums and percussion) or Paul McCartney (bass).

How is it decided who I play with?
Well, there are a number of possibilities. If I have already success-fully recorded with an artist or played with them live, it's good to try to replicate that in the studio. Sometimes another artist may feel my piano style is either sympathetic or will add another dimen-sion to their music. Occasionally, a singer will be doing a pro-motional tour but without a band. We don't have people miming to tracks on our show and, if there isn't the time or space to get a band in for one of these performers, then I'll accompany them. At other times, it's better to tacit – one of the keys to the art of music which I hope I've learned by now is knowing when to be quiet and listen.

Whatever the situation, I've had the honour and privilege to have some of the best views in music over the lid of the grand piano in the *Later with Jools Holland* studio.

Why is the show on so late?
I think there's a general view in television's upstairs that only ghosts, lunatics and insomniacs enjoy music programmes and that the time best suited to them is late at night. However, for those readers who are none of the above, you can relive the excitement of any of the shows first thing in the morning if you like, by buying

one of the many DVDs from the BBC shop or taping it yourself. The other alternative is to emigrate to Venezuela or Paris, where the show is broadcast at a different time of day.

Having started with the simple premise of getting good and varied music in, we have made changes along the way. After each series, we discuss how we can improve things for the next. After the first series, we added an audience, to get the feeling of a live gig and, after the second, we decided we needed some tables and chairs on the set so that I could talk to a few of the guests each week, and a special area for my piano.

Then, in October 1993, while my band and I were driving from Aberdeen to Newcastle, the car phone rang. It was Mark Cooper, to say that the BBC was also interested in doing the New Year's Eve show he and I had talked about, and Michael Jackson wanted to call it *The Hootenanny*. I was very pleased with this and, just as I put down the phone, I heard a traffic warning on the radio advising motorists to avoid Arbroath because of the likely queues for Andy Stewart's memorial service. At once I remembered watching Andy Stewart's New Year shows as a child, with the pipers and lovely displays of Scottish dancing. I felt that, with Mark's call, I had just been passed his New Year's Eve baton. I looked at Steve Taylor, my tour manager. There was no need for me to say anything. Steve glanced at me and said, 'Arbroath?' I nodded, and the car left the main road to speed off in that direction. Once there, we joined the long procession of vehicles and, at the church, we all got out of the car, taking our hats off as a mark of respect.

I am incredibly proud of the two hundred shows we've made up till now. The other people who must be credited are all the technicians and the production team who work in the studio and behind the scenes. Mike Felton and his sound men, Gerry Tivers and the cameramen, Antonia Castle, Mel, and Sam Ribeck on the floor, and the whole team, who always want to do their very best for the musicians on the show. It's a show that could only be made in Britain because of the luxury of having a huge public broadcaster like the BBC to support it. It's now watched by millions of people around the world and has captured music at the end of the twentieth and beginning of the twenty-first centuries like no other programme before or since.

As we aren't making a commercial programme, we don't have to cater rigidly to a generic audience. We can have the Arctic Monkeys and Sonny Rollins on together, or Abdullah Ibrahim and Lily Allen. And, unlike many music shows, in which the artists perform their piece and then go off to a backstage room for the rest of the show, on *Later* the artists all remain and respond to each other and each other's performances, which adds to the energy. No matter how different people's music might seem to be, the bands always share something in common. Willie Nelson, for example, was very struck with the music of the Cure, who were on the same night as he was.

Funnily enough, in the 1960s there was a music show with similarities to ours; it was called *Hullabaloo* and was hosted by my late father-in-law, Rory McEwen. It had a house band, Cyril Davis Rhythm and Blues All-Stars with Long John Baldry, and guests such as the Spinners, Sonny Boy Williamson, Martin Carthy, Fitzroy Coleman and many other folk and world music stars, all in the same room at the same time. Rory would play the guitar sometimes with his brother Eck in the middle of the show, in between introducing the acts. Recently, when Paul Simon was on *Later*, we were all having dinner after the show and Paul was sitting next to Christabel. She was telling him about having recently discovered *Hullabaloo*, which he remembered. They both agreed that it was the first music show on television to feature non-mainstream music and that its great strength was that Rory could both introduce and play with the guests. At this, Christabel suddenly paused and said, 'That's odd, I think I've married my dad.' Paul shrugged in a very philosophical New York Jewish way, and said, 'You wouldn't be the first girl to do that.'

The A–Z of the Piano

In 1992 the line-up of my band changed again. The bass player
Keith Wilkinson left and was replaced by the extraordinary Dave
Swift. Dave could improvise brilliantly and play both upright and
electric bass. He could transcribe exactly the bass parts from records,
often correcting music books when they hadn't paid enough attention to the detail. With music, sometimes the most important
aspect is the small detail. That can be the thing that makes you
want to dance or cry. I didn't realize it then but, soon, Dave's
talent for being able to play such a broad range of music exactly
right was going to come in very handy.

Around this time we were touring and promoting my album,
The A–Z Geographer's Guide to the Piano, which consisted of piano
pieces inspired by different parts of London. Despite the fact that
it was an instrumental record, it was still played on the radio and
TV. One of the first people to pick up on it were Richard and
Judy, whose morning TV show was then broadcast live from the
Albert Dock in Liverpool. Their show didn't really feature music
and the studio didn't have the facilities to fit in a band, but I was
so pleased they liked our record I agreed that a slimmed-down
band of Mark, Gilson and I would do the show. Fred the weatherman was a feature of their show back then and he would give the
weather forecast while skipping about on a giant cut-out map of
the British Isles which was about twenty-five feet long and floated
on the water in the dock. I always enjoyed this surreal sight and
was delighted when Richard and Judy agreed to let us perform on
top of this floating miniature Britain.

Mark Flanagan's family all live in Liverpool and, having been
up till the wee hours with them in the Adelphi hotel, we had
slightly fat heads when we arrived to do the show first thing in the
morning. Dear Fred the weatherman noticed this and said, 'Mind

how you go on my island – it can be a bit slippery.' It was quite cold that morning but we performed my composition 'Temple Bar' on our floating stage without mishap. It was a little tricky climbing off but Fred gave us a hand and said, 'Well done for not falling in.' The show was live and, as we'd finished our bit, we went to the Green Room, where you could watch the show being broadcast. Richard and Judy introduced the weather, and Fred started darting about miniature Britain, giving his forecast. Regrettably, Graeme, our roadie, hadn't finished clearing away all our electrical cabling. Fred didn't spot this, and probably mistook one of our cables for the M1 motorway. Whilst hopping from London to Wales, he caught his foot and went straight into the Irish Sea. There was silence in the Green Room, until Fred emerged from the Albert Dock like a bedraggled Neptune colossus and we all breathed a sigh of relief. I'm pleased to say that Fred was all right about the whole thing and, amazingly, we were asked back.

Another show where we used to perform live was Chris Evans' radio show on GLR. In early 1993 Chris contacted me, as he had now been offered his own mainstream television show for ITV, and wanted to know if I would be interested in being involved. Chris is incredibly talented and has so many great ideas. *Don't Forget Your Toothbrush* was basically a game show with music in which contestants would work towards winning a holiday. It would have a musical guest each week and, since Chris was obsessed with quizzing, the musical guest would also participate in the quiz.

Chris's first suggestion was that I come on and play the piano solo each week. Flattered though I was at being asked, I explained that I now had a whole band to support and couldn't really afford to take the time away from doing shows with them. Chris then suggested it would be great fun to have them on the show too. I felt I had to tell him that my band was quite big – and it had recently grown still further with the fabulous inclusion of Rico Rodriguez, who had joined us after calling me to say he liked the sound of what we were doing. Chris generously reiterated, 'No, that's great – let's get you all on.' And so we set to work.

Some of the older musicians in the band had done TV but some of the younger ones hadn't and it was a whole new world to them. And this mainstream world of ITV was a whole new world to me. I was used to Channel Four's laidback approach and the BBC's old-fashioned Auntie approach. But the difference between ITV1 and BBC2, say, is that ITV1 has a vast audience whereas BBC2 has a more selective minority watching. With this huge audience, ITV producers have to be very hard-nosed about what they're doing; they can't afford to have anyone turning off. They would have endless committee meetings, fussing about each individual thing. *Later*'s main criterion is sincere artistic endeavour but, with *Toothbrush*, they wanted a big hit.

Being on *Toothbrush* galvanized us as a band, since each week we would have to learn new songs quickly and make them sound good on the live show. This is where Dave's skill would often save the day. We always knew the bass part was going to be right and could build up from there. Also, it brought Phil Veacock, Jon Scott and Roger Goslyn to the fore because we had to start writing out arrangements. For example, when Barry White came on, we had to get in a big string section and draw up the score. It made me realize what an incredible pool of talent there was in the band. There was the odd moment of tetchiness between the band and the world of commercial television – the band weren't used to all the hanging around and officialdom. There was also the occasional clash over the smoking and drinking and arguments over parking but, with the income from this mainstream show, a lot of the band members were now able to buy their own homes for the first time, so that more than made up for it.

Toothbrush had a great many celebrity guests, such as Cher, Paul Young, Neil Sedaka and Ray Davies, all of whom were famous because of their genuine talent. Barry White was such an amazing singer and so beautifully dressed: he wore a black suit, a cross between a zoot suit and a morning suit, with one huge button halfway down the jacket, and his lovely lady wife had such long nails that they curled right round. After the show he said he wanted a word with me, which worried me at first. But, in fact, it was to tell me that he loved the band, and the performer he loved best was 'that drummer. Tell him to do more, not less. His shit really gets me going.' That really made me happy, but I didn't tell Gilson about his shit getting Barry going – he would only have got big-headed.

The person who made the most impact on me doing these shows was Lulu. I hadn't worked with her before and I didn't realize what an amazing and belting voice she has. She enjoyed singing with the band and we agreed that some time in the future we had to do more together.

Later carried on as usual, and I was especially delighted when we had Johnny Cash and Pops Staples as guests one evening. Johnny Cash had always been a musical hero of mine; aged twelve, I'd been taken to see him play at the Albert Hall by Alan Mills, a family friend. I'd always loved the music from Sun Records; the truth within that music really did something to me. It made me want to dance; I didn't need to think about it, I felt it.

June Carter Cash was there too, and they both knew Pops Staples. Off camera they would have lengthy discussions about Old Testament texts and then howl with laughter. I interviewed Johnny on the show and at one point he said, 'It's kind of fantastic, because they're gonna put June on a stamp – and that really is a first for the US post office. You usually have to be dead to get on a stamp.' I was then given a signal to wind up the interview, and said, 'Well, we'll be looking forward to that – thanks very much.' Johnny roared with laughter because it seemed as if I was saying I was looking forward to June dropping dead.

Then he sang Nick Lowe's 'The Beast in Me' and he was great. He had the inner wisdom of a man who had spent his life on the road. In fact, all three of them were how I imagine Chaucerian pilgrims would have been in England seven hundred years ago – absolutely charming God-fearing folk. At the end of the show, they all performed 'Will the Circle be Unbroken?' And, of course, none of them is here any longer.

The Rhythm and Blues Orchestra

Some people believe that creativity springs from a chaotic lifestyle but, in my life, I have often found the reverse to be true. By the mid-nineties Christabel and I had moved to a more comfortable home, which had a library. Having all the records, books and a piano in one area was far more conducive to writing and thinking about music. I was able to return from the hectic world of touring to a settled home life, a house from which I could walk to the local pub, see my old friends, and a garden where I could play with the children. For the first time in a while, this brought a much welcome feeling of stability.

Professionally, John Lay had emigrated to America, and Miles Copeland's main focus was now on Sting, so the brilliant Paul Loasby, who'd been working with John Lay, stepped in and has worked as my agent and manager ever since. At first, Paul was eager to show how hands on he was so not only would he drive us to the shows but he would simultaneously be on the phone and reading a number of contracts, his briefcase propped up against the steering wheel. After a short while, we all realized it was just too much of a job for one man. We had then recruited the supremely efficient Stephen Taylor, who has been tour manager for myself and the Rhythm and Blues Orchestra ever since. Nicky, my secretary, left because she and Gilson married and she wanted to spend more time looking after their wonderful son, Little Gilson. I was worried she'd be hard to replace but we've been incredibly fortunate in that my mother's cousin Valerie McCartney took over the job, and she too has been with me ever since. Her sunny nature and kindly disposition are the perfect counterpoint to Paul Loasby's more hard-nosed approach. Finally, for more than a decade, Andy Salmon and his brilliant crew have worked tirelessly as our touring technicians. Sometimes people ask me how I manage a Big Band

and organize all the transport, hotels, staging and individual requirements, bedtime stories, etc. The short answer is: I don't. It's all arranged by the aforementioned team and this allows me to focus on the part I love, which is the music. I'm indebted to them.

1994 saw the beginning of this team working together when the Big Band released a live record. Coinciding with its release, the name of my band was changed to The Rhythm and Blues Orchestra. This was at least partly in honour of my Uncle David's band, the Planets, and the lovely wooden sign that proclaimed them London's top rhythm and blues band – an early family boast. By the time we recorded the 1996 LP *Sex and Jazz and Rock and Roll*, we were almost a fully blown Big Band. Then, as we needed an additional tenor saxophone, Rico introduced me to the amazing Michael 'Bammi' Rose. Bammi is so handsome that his wife, Blossom, insists he keeps his hat on when we perform, as removing it to reveal his full beauty would cause the women in the audience to throw themselves at him. Rico and Bammi had come to England together from Kingston in 1962. It was a privilege for my orchestra to feature their authentic Jamaican sound. Not long after, Winston Rollins, who was from a gifted family of jazz musicians, joined us on trombone. Our line-up consisted of four sax, three trombones and the two trumpets of Jon Scott and Jason McDermid, and a rhythm section of piano, bass, drums, guitar and organ. In this configuration, we recorded a couple of covers, one by Count Basie and one by Charles Mingus, but it was on our own songs, such as 'Hamster's Wheel' or 'Lonesome Joe', that I was starting to learn how to use our wonderful Big Band sound.

When we recorded the single 'Waiting Game', which I'd written with Chris Difford, we invited Eddi Reader to come and sing it. I realized we were reaching popular consciousness when I was walking through Soho one afternoon and heard the piano intro, followed by the falling horns and Eddi's first line, 'You keep me waiting . . .', booming out of an underground club. A striptease artist had selected the music to accompany her performance. Regrettably, I didn't have time to go in to see how the artist's footwork would synchronize with the syncopation of Gilson's drumbeat.

The other thing working with Eddi made me realize was that introducing a female singer to our band performances could lift the whole thing up another gear. Throughout the nineties we invited other female singers to tour with us, such as Marianne Faithful, Sam Brown, Carmel, Carleen Anderson and Ruby Turner. All these singers were very different in their style but when they sang with us, the whole band would focus on playing better, as they could hear what a great performance the singer was giving. In turn, the singers would raise their game because of the size of the band and the excitement it created. It was the opposite of a vicious circle – a circle of love. Sam and Ruby have since become the mainstay of my orchestra. They are, without question, two of the greatest singers I've ever worked with.

I also wrote pieces specifically for the soloists. One song was inspired by seeing my two small daughters dance around while I played skank piano. This song became 'Able Mabel' and it also turned out to be the perfect way of showing off Rico's talents. I was later delighted to be told that 'Able Mabel' had become an anthem in gay women's clubs, where they would all chant the backing vocal: 'Are you able, Mabel? What you say, Rosie May? Are you able, Mabel, to rock my blues away?' That's sex and jazz and rock and roll for you.

I would sometimes receive offers to do TV series, but I would always turn them down, explaining that I had my band and I enjoyed working with them too much to find time to do anything else. An exception was *Name That Tune* which, like *Toothbrush*, was prepared to employ the whole band. At first, I didn't quite get the point of the game but then, one afternoon, Dave Morley, the producer, came to our smoke-filled rehearsal room in Bermondsey and got the band playing it, and it was not only entertaining but instructive. Perhaps you, the reader, would like to try it too. Think of a famous or well-loved tune and hum the first two bars to your neighbour, relative or friend. I expect you'll find, firstly, that it's not that easy for them to spot what the song actually is and, if you played back the notes you hummed against the original recording, there would no doubt be some discrepancies, as there were for us that afternoon in Bermondsey. We recorded the whole series in two weeks in Leeds and, afterwards, the members of the band were able to furnish the flats or houses they'd been able to buy after *Toothbrush*.

My only other forays into TV were *The History of the Piano*, a personal two-part view of some of the pianists I've loved over the ages; *Beat Route*, a series of six travel programmes and an accompanying book about music and culture around the world; and a one-off programme about the late film and TV composer Ted Astley.

I have few regrets but one of them is certainly that I wasn't able to use Ted Astley as a string arranger on the Millionaires album, as Glynn Johns had suggested. I was saying this to his son, Jon Astley, who masters all our records at his London studio. Jon then went to the cellar and got a dusty box of tapes and singles of his father's. Playing these back in my library on a summer's afternoon, with the French doors open and the birds singing, I was struck by the tremendous beauty of his writing. I then asked the BBC if I could make a film about him. It was no longer as it was at *The Tube*, when you'd ring up Andrea Wonfor and say, 'I want to make a film about bees and their pelts,' to which she would answer, 'That's fine – what time do you want the crew?' The BBC was far keener on treatments and prepared written work. This was quite a specialized subject and one the BBC felt might be difficult to communicate to a mainstream audience. However, in the end they gave me the go-ahead. The two things that helped with this were an interview with Ted Astley's son-in-law, Pete Townshend, and the participation of my dear friend Kate Moss. Kate and I were filmed having a formal dinner. We played the film back three times, each time accompanied by a piece of Ted's music, the first a romantic *adagio*, then dissonant dramatic music and, finally, something comedic. We hoped this would illustrate how brilliant Ted Astley's music was at dictating the viewer's feelings towards the pictures they see. Kate's presence brought glamour and romantic interest to what would have been a rather dry film even to me, a Ted Astley admirer.

One of the things that I really have enjoyed doing is my Radio 2 programme, which I've been presenting now for almost a decade. On this, I've been able to focus on a guest at length, and share with the listeners some of the rare gems from my personal record collection. I've been amazed and delighted at the success of this show, which has a larger audience than *Later*.

In being more selective with things that didn't have anything to do with my band, I had more time to do what I really wanted to do. My piano playing was more in demand. Paul Weller invited me to perform with him at a number of big summer arena events. Performing with him on stage is like being next to a nuclear reactor. After the London show with Paul, we all went back to the flat of Brendan Lynch, Paul's producer, for a party. He told me he'd been producing Primal Scream and had let them all stay in his flat. Somehow, they'd managed to get barred from the local pub and from the cornershop, but the great outrage was that they'd left a huge sinkful of dirty washing-up. I couldn't help but feel that he'd got off rather lightly. Coincidentally, one of the biggest fans of my band is Bobby Gillespie's mum, Wilma. I quizzed her over this business and she said that washing up had always been one of his weaker points.

One of the phone calls I was most pleased to get at this time was an invitation to perform on a duets record BB King was making. BB King really is the true king of the blues. I headed off to the studio, not knowing what to expect or who would be there. I felt some nervous anticipation, as I hadn't met him before. When I got to the control room, the producer, John Porter, introduced me to B – as his friends call him. He told me he had heard my version of his song 'Bad Luck Blues' and was a huge boogie-woogie-piano fan. When I got to the piano, I was delighted to see my old friend Pino on bass, and Paul Carrack on the organ. B came in, followed by a smaller man of a similar age who I'd been told had been working with B since the 1940s. Apparently, every six weeks or so, this trusted manservant and valet, Gomer, would let B or himself down in some way and be sacked. I got the feeling it was getting near to sacking time again, as B was becoming rather

gently exasperated with Gomer's desperate-to-please but vaguely
incompetent ways. When Pino asked B how many records
he'd made, B asked Gomer, 'Gomer – how many records have
I made?'

'I don't know, boss – how many records have you made?'

B rolled his eyes and focused his attention back on Pino, and
said, 'I did my first record just after the war, and I do one once a
year, like birthdays.' Paul then chipped in that it was actually his
birthday that day and Gomer wondered if there was going to be a
party with womenfolk present. Ignoring this, B said, 'Right, Jools,
what we going to do?'

I said, 'I don't know, B, what do you want to do?'

'I want to boogie and I'd like you to start.'

Through a loudspeaker a crackling voice announced, 'Tapes
running' and, like a greyhound out of the trap, I started to play.
Then B began to boogie over the top of us. I caught a glimpse of
him sitting there, banging his foot and moving his neck involun-
tarily to the guitar boogie he was laying down. We got to the end
and a voice said, 'That's a take.' B asked me what the piece was
called and, when I said I didn't know, he paused and said, 'That's
"Pauly's Birthday Boogie".'

B asked, 'What you going to sing for us Paul?'

Paul thought for a moment and then suggested, '"Bring It on
Home to Me", B flat? Piano solo then guitar solo?'

Five minutes later we had a wonderful rendition of this song
which, again, had been made in one take. I felt delighted and
euphoric. By now, I assumed we'd done our day's work and
was just about to close the piano lid when Gomer came in looking a little flustered, and said, 'He's here – he's here – but he
doesn't want me to take his coat. What do I do about his coat,
boss?'

B said, 'Don't worry about the coat – who's here?'

I looked round from the piano and, in the doorway, with his
coat on, was one of the greatest singer-songwriters in the world:
Van Morrison. Van then played through this song he'd written so
we could figure out the changes, and we went for it. Unbelievably,

once more in just one take, it sounded fantastic and, in fact, to this day I think it's one of the most beautiful pieces of music I've had the privilege to be part of. 'Pauly's Birthday Boogie', 'Bring It on Home to Me' and Van's 'If You Love Me' all ended up on the UK release of BB's record *Deuces Wild*.

Later, BB King was to tell a newspaper reporter that he hadn't heard a left hand like mine since Pete Johnson passed away. This is the greatest compliment of my entire musical career and the perfect boogie-woogie boast with which to end this chapter.

Small World Big Band

By the end of the 1990s my orchestra had become the most hardworking and popular of its kind. We'd been joined by fantastic soul serenader Lisa Grahame on alto and rockabilly Nick Lunt on baritone. Peter Long would make marvellous arrangements and we now featured Chris Storr on trumpet. We also added Fayyaz Virji on trombone. Not only were we booked for festivals and by theatres, we were now brought to the attention of the Prime Minister and his fellow world leaders. In 1998 Britain chaired the summit of the G8 nations at the Symphony Hall in Birmingham; the most powerful countries in the Western world were gathering to discuss shared issues regarding the future. The promoter Harvey Goldsmith had been asked to arrange some entertainment to show off how good we British were at that sort of thing. It was arranged that we would play and be the house band. The other artists would include All Saints, Mick Hucknall, Sam Brown, Ruby Turner, Chris Rea and the Voice of Gospel.

There was a lot more security than any of us were used to and, by the end of rehearsals in the theatre, we had come to assume that every tea urn and vending machine was a disguised CIA operative. For the show, the world leaders were to have a whole balcony to the left of the stage. Members of the public and under-cover secret-service men filled the rest of the auditorium. Harvey Goldsmith asked me to go on and do a twenty-minute set for all the people in the hall and then leave the stage while the world leaders took their seats. The crowd really appreciated this first short set so, at the end of it, I thanked them, explained that we'd be back in a minute and, if they could act surprised and applaud very loudly when we came back on, it would help with loosening up the atmosphere. The world leaders took their seats, and we re-entered the stage. The audience had taken me at my word and were letting out theatrical gasps of surprise and applauding hysterically. It certainly had the desired effect as, when we started, the world leaders too had been drawn into this vortex of good humour.

We played a storming set and even Mr Yeltsin, who had been inadvertently over-served, seemed to be happily wagging his finger in time to the music. I found it hard to believe that we were having the same effect on the most powerful people in the world as we did on the beautiful men and women in the street who come to see us play.

Mick Hucknall and I had agreed that 'All You Need is Love' would be a great last number to do all together, both because of its sentiment and also as an example of the best of British music. We started playing the first few bars and Jacques Chirac, beaming and bristling with pride, stood up, thinking it was 'La Marseillaise'. Out of respect to Mr Chirac, and to save his embarrassment, the other politicians stood up too. By the time it had evolved into the Beatles song, the main audience were on their feet as well and the music weaved its magic on them all.

After the performance we were all invited to meet the G8 leaders. We stood in a line and were introduced one by one to the various prime ministers and presidents. The charismatic President Clinton was introduced to us last. He spent some time talking to Sam Brown and handed her something. Then he focused his attention on me and said clearly and kindly, 'Thanks, Jools, we really enjoyed that – it was a great show.' I told him it had been an honour for us all to represent our country like this. The whole time he was talking to me I felt as if he was concentrating entirely on me and interested in everything I had to say. I asked him what he'd given Sam Brown and he beamed and said, 'A pressed flower – is that OK?' I said it was fine as long as I could have one too. We laughed and he started talking to Jason McDermid, our trumpet player, and after a short while he was surrounded by my entire sax section. They were all busily chatting until the room had emptied of all the other world leaders, and this talk then went on for another twenty minutes. I stood next to Dave, our bass player, and we wondered what on earth they could be talking about.

Eventually, after what seemed like an age of them being in a huddle, Mr Clinton left. We said to the horn section, 'This is amazing – you've just had a half-hour audience with the most powerful man in the world. People would pay thousands to have such a long private audience with the President of the United States. Did you challenge him on climate change, global poverty – did you ask about the Roswell alien?' No. None of this. All they had done was discuss the saxophone with him. Being a keen amateur player, the President had enjoyed discussing what reeds they used and embouchure. They'd all agreed that they loved Junior Walker. He thanked them and, as he was leaving, Sam accidentally dropped the flower he had given her and he bent down to pick it up for her. President Clinton is physically a large and impressive figure. When he bent over, it emphasized his huge arse, which was contained in a perfectly cut pair of presidential trousers. Dave Swift said to me, 'I'm really tempted to go and give him a comedy kick up the arse. It's not that I don't like him, it's just an arse that wide is so inviting.' It was just as well Dave didn't give in to this babyish impulse. It would have displayed a side to British culture that is best kept to ourselves.

Somebody must have judged this show a great success, since I was then asked to be one of the musical directors for the Millennium celebration at the Dome built on part of my friend Trevor's scrapyard on Blackwall Reach, or the Greenwich Peninsula, as it is now called. Although I was looking forward to welcoming in the new Millennium and saying my fond farewells to the departing century, New Year's Eve and the following day would prove to be rather turbulent. Myself and Paul Daniel, the conductor and leader of the English National Opera, were to guide everyone through the music and, at first, I thought that after midnight my band could play and get everybody dancing and having a nice time like we do on our hootenannies. As it drew nearer to the date, more politicians seemed to become involved and the likelihood of us doing simply this diminished. Eventually, we were all gathered backstage, waiting to perform before Her Majesty the Queen, the Blairs, the Cabinet and the fifteen thousand people in the arena –

plus a worldwide TV audience of a billion viewers. Just before Stephen Fry was to introduce Paul Daniel and myself I decided to check my shoelaces to avoid any mishaps. As I did this, I heard a noise like an ocean liner crashing into an iceberg; I had torn my trousers at the back, thus completely revealing my underpants. Then I heard Stephen Fry's voice saying, 'Ladies and gentlemen – please welcome to the stage your musical directors for the evening, Mr Jools Holland and Mr Paul Daniel.' I walked on as quickly as I could and sat down on the piano stool, too nervous to move in case I revealed my pants to the world. It really rather marred the whole evening for me and, although Ruby Turner, Mick Hucknall, Willard White and all the other singers performed beautifully, the pants incident had taken away something of my optimism for the turn of the century. I went home and had an early night.

The next morning the headlines, instead of saying 'Happy 2000 – welcome to a new age of love and understanding', were announcing, 'Mr and Mrs George Harrison Attacked in Home'. I immediately drove to the hospital to see them. On the surface, although badly injured, they were trying to smile, and offered me tea. I could see, however, how upsetting it all was. I was briefly left alone with the policewoman, who had been taking notes. I asked her what had happened, but all she would say was, 'I think that Mrs Harrison is one of the bravest people I've ever met.' I don't think any of the readers would like to contemplate fighting for their lives in their own home with a knife-wielding maniac for seventeen very long minutes. George had been badly stabbed, which was horrible to see. He said that after he'd got to the hospital and regained consciousness, he'd seen a little of our show at the Dome. He said he saw John Prescott looking gloomy and a lot of flouncy Brazilian-style dancers salsa-ing, and he'd thought to himself, 'Where are the marching bands, the pearly kings and queens, and why isn't Jools being allowed to get everyone going with the boogie?' Then he had gone back to sleep, disappointed. I felt that the big build-up to the Millennium Eve had ended in a let-down, and this horrible awakening on the first day of 2000 took away any remaining high spirits.

Dissonance

George and Olivia survived, but there were other friends who didn't make it. One of the frustrating and sad things is that they were often people I was saving for later on. I'd think, 'I'm busy now, but when I'm older, it will be great – we'll be able go on holiday together, on tours of British leylines or stone circles in Normandy.' And, with their death, apart from the tragedy for all concerned, came the frustration that these pleasant plans would never be fulfilled and that my friends would have to remain living in my memory alone.

In September 2000 I was at the Goodwood Festival of Speed, an incredible spectacle of motor racing which Lord March hosts. I was in a box, standing next to Netty Mason, Nick Mason's wife, and we were looking at a race of 1950s sports racing cars, one of which was driven by my friend and BRDC member Valentine Lindsay. The noise grew louder and louder as they revved up to start and, just at that moment, my phone rang. I went inside to be able to hear, and it was Christabel saying she'd just heard that Paula had died. She said, 'I'm ringing you straight away to tell you in case you suddenly get someone from the press coming up to you and asking for your views.' I was shocked and all I could say at that moment was, 'Oh.' I went back into the box and Netty asked whether I was OK. I said, 'Well, I've just had a bit of bad news.' When I told her what it was, she said, 'Oh, I'm so sorry – perhaps you should come and sit down?' I said, 'I think I will, then I think I'll drive back to London, I don't think I want to stay here now.' I did, in fact, watch another race after that; it was what Paula would have wanted. It was the race featuring the Jaguar D-types.

I drove back to London and had to pull into a petrol station on the way. It was the time of the petrol shortage and, as in wartime

England, you almost had to resort to intimidation or bribery to get petrol. The sign in this station said, 'Only £10 worth of petrol allowed.' I started putting the petrol in, thinking about poor Paula. And, thinking about her, I ended up filling my tank. The proprietor came out, shouting at me, 'What are you doing? You've helped yourself to all this petrol,' and I replied, 'Well, I don't care about that. My friend's just died and I'm thinking about her.' At once the anger dropped out of him and he said, 'Oh, I'm sorry to hear that.' I thought what a kindly and gentle race the English are underneath our petty-bourgeois shopkeeper front.

Back on the road, as people do in these circumstances, I went back in my mind's eye, wondering if there was anything I could have done. I thought what a frustrating and awful thing it would be for Bob and all the children and how, when Paula was with Michael Hutchence, they'd been quite wild. I like a night out and a light ale but, when I went out with them of an evening, they would want to go just that little bit further than everybody else. Really, when it came down to it, I had found it quite stressful seeing her with Michael. It was hard to get them to concentrate on one of my interesting stories or any of those things. There was a dark side to him, and she was drinking, which changed her personality. Some people can consume all sorts of things and it doesn't seem to change their personality but, with Paula, it did. She wasn't herself – not the sharp, amusing, lively and attentive, doting mother I'd known.

Around the time of Michael's death I went round to see her in her house and I could see what a mess she was in; she wasn't looking after herself. I was concerned for the children too and, although it's not for me to presume things, I think that it was a terrible worry for Bob, and I think he did brilliantly.

I said to her, 'You'd better come and stay. You can stay with us or, if you'd prefer some privacy, there's a shed at the end of the garden you can stay in.' Paula did have moments of being her old self. I remember her looking at me and saying, 'You're going to dump me in a shed at the end of the garden?? You fucker. Thanks a lot – after all I've been through.' And I said, trying to make it seem more interesting and inviting, 'No, it's nice there – I've got a model railway and everything.'

She did come to stay, and she was fine for a bit. It was a busy time for me and I was playing at the Royal Albert Hall, but I got *Wuthering Heights* out on video, and said, 'I've got this old film, shall we watch it?' But, rather uncomfortably, it seemed to be all about obsessive love leading to madness and death. Again, this was the old Paula: she looked at me and said, 'I can't believe it – this is the worst possible taste. What are you doing putting this on?' We were both amused by the inappropriate nature of my choice of film.

The following day she had to meet some high-powered lawyers to discuss some matter to do with Michael's affairs. They were meeting her at our house but, before they arrived, she found some wine and started drinking. Seeing the effect it had on her was terrifying. I was worried that she was going to meet all these lawyers in this state and, although I felt it wasn't my job to interfere in her affairs, I did feel I should be doing something – it was a very difficult position to be in. The doorbell rang and it was a very dear friend of Christabel's called Margaret Canty-Shepherd, one of the kindliest and most gentle of people. I let her in and she headed towards the kitchen, where Paula was. I didn't want nice Margaret to see Paula in that state and, as it was all getting too much and I couldn't bear it, I hid in the larder cupboard and shut the door. I knew I had to play at the Royal Albert Hall that night and I just couldn't think about it all. But when I came out, Margaret was cuddling Paula and trying to make her feel better – which of course is what I should have been doing instead of hiding in the cupboard.

I told Paula she was welcome to stay for as long as she liked but she didn't really want to stay. I saw her from time to time after that and she seemed to be improving and getting herself back together.

All these things were going through my mind on that drive back to London. Then, of course, back in London, the phone was ringing and everyone was trying to organize everything. Poor Bob had to sort out a great deal, and he did brilliantly, as he always does.

There were many people who wanted to sing at Paula's funeral, including Kevin Godley and Nick Cave. Bono wanted to do something too, in spite of the fact that he was in the middle of a tour. Apart from being an amazing singer, Bono is one of those people who is absolutely loyal to his friends – in situations like this he will have no regard for his own schedule but will put his friends first. He came to our house with Ali, his wife, and we rehearsed round my piano. It's very difficult to sing at a funeral. Your voice just goes if you're upset, so it's hard to do. We all sang her favourite songs. And it was a shame she wasn't there, because she would have enjoyed it. I'm sure she would have liked it even more if we had recorded the service and turned it into a Tribute to Paula record: we should have done that – it would have been a winner.

The only other thing I have to say is that I was pleased that she died on a day when nothing much else was happening because her death made headline news. My mind went back to doing *The Tube* and having a laugh together. I remembered flying back from Newcastle one time with Elton John, who had been one of the guests, the rest of the cast of the show and my father and Martin Pugh too. The turbulence had been so bad that nobody could even hold a glass and everything was crashing about everywhere. I thought I'd better reassure poor Paula, who was looking really worried. I told her that planes were built to withstand anything, you could bend the two wing-tips up till they touched and still it wouldn't crash. She said, 'I'm not worried about that – I'm worried about the billing.' When I asked what she meant she said, as if addressing a simpleton, 'If the plane goes down, the headlines will be "Elton Killed in Plane Crash, turn to page two for others." We will just be the others.'

In this instance, she was front page, and she would have been happiest with that.

Crescendo

This new century has produced a number of amazing twists in my life. One of the most important is the fact that my music became a success in terms of record sales. I had always loved touring and would have made records anyway but now I was delighted to find that they moved to another level both artistically and commercially. Remembering my hard work with the Millionaires back in the early eighties, I felt all the more grateful to providence that success should come in my fifth decade. From the early nineties each record sold more than its predecessor and finally our LP *Hop the Wag* went gold in 2000 – my first solo work to achieve this.

One of the tracks on the record was a collaboration with Jay Kay from Jamiroquai, which we had made at the suggestion of Harry Enfield, who wanted to use it in his *Kevin and Perry Go Large* film. It had been a success and was great fun to do, so it was decided that the next record would be one of collaborations. The first person I rang up was Sting, who agreed immediately and enthusiastically and, after that, the whole thing snowballed. I was very touched by the way people wanted to help; people I'd known in music over the years all seemed to rally round.

The artists I invited all came at it from a different angle. Eric Clapton, Van Morrison, Taj Mahal, Mick Hucknall, Steve Winwood and Sting all elected to cut some of their favourite blues songs with us. In other instances, some of the artists wanted to capture on record the magic of songs they'd performed with my orchestra at concerts or on the television. Paul Weller, Mica Paris and David Gilmour were great examples of this. Other songs on the record were written by myself or co-written with the featured artists. It's curious how some songs come about; I'll give you a couple of examples. Christabel and I had a wonderful dinner with the Boyle family, the famous artists who live in Greenwich. The

other guests at this dinner included self-help guru and know-it-all
Edward de Bono and the dazzlingly gifted author Blake Morrison.
As we left, Edward de Bono was still pontificating but Blake
paused, pointed to the moon and said, 'What a beautiful moon to
see on Valentine's night.' The following morning I spoke to Sam
Brown and she too remarked on the extraordinary moon the night
before. From this came our joint composition 'Valentine Moon'.

Another example: I have an upright piano in my *Later* dressing
room on which I can rehearse or learn songs with the performers.
I was alone and started trying to figure out a new riff. My concen-
tration was suddenly jarred by a thuggish kicking at the door.
Preparing for a row, I opened the door but, instead of being
confronted by an angry complainer, there was Joe Strummer, eager
to get in. I was so startled I didn't know what to say to Gentleman
Joe, but he said impatiently, 'I have got just the words for that riff,
let me in – we're writing a song.' 'The Return of the Blues
Cowboy' was born.

I also went on to write with Dr John, Paul Carrack and my
brothers, Chris Difford, Eric Bibb and Suggs. Finally, a couple of
artists had written songs they thought might suit my style of
playing. Mark Knopfler was one of these and the other was George
Harrison.

When George sent me a cassette of his song I became very
excited – it was brilliant. However, by the time it came to recording it, he'd become quite ill. I spoke to him on the phone and told
him not to worry about the music, as he clearly wasn't in a good
state of health. But he was determined and said that playing music
made him feel better. He wasn't feeling strong enough to put the
guitar on, but said, 'Get your Mark Flanagan to do it, I trust him
more than anyone to make a good job of it, because he's a nice
boy from Bootle.' 'Horse to the Water' is probably one of the
most powerful pieces my orchestra has ever recorded.

The LP *Small World Big Band* was released in early November
2001 and was a phenomenal success. This success, however, will
always be overshadowed for me by my grief at George's death, on
29 November. In my mind, George's illness was accelerated by

the traumatic attack in his home. George and Olivia had been such good friends, and I had imagined us all going to gardens and Grand Prixs together as we grew older. I still see Olivia but I miss George, and still feel grateful to him for contributing to this first Friends record.

There were so many more things we wanted to record that we ended up making three records in the series. These sold more than all those I'd made in the last century put together. It was wonderful to be able to record with people from different generations – to record with the Blind Boys of Alabama one week and Norah Jones the next is quite an extraordinary feeling. We'd be recording and on tour and at the same time writing for the next record. While doing some shows in Europe, we took a suite with a piano in Amsterdam, and Sam and I wrote for Nick Cave, Sam Moore and Chrissie Hynde. Back in England we wrote for Edwin Starr and Dionne Warwick. It felt like a dream come true.

Most of all, it was the generosity of my fellow artists I appreciated. Before Bono came to cut 'If You Wear That Velvet Dress' he said to me, 'It's great, because your orchestra will make it sound like a Frank Sinatra or Duke Ellington arrangement, and so completely different to the U2 version.' He flew in specially to do it but the traffic jam was so bad coming from the airport that he got out of his stationary car, flagged down a passing motorcyclist, who happened to have a spare crash helmet, and persuaded him to give him a lift to Greenwich.

Mark Cooper had introduced me to the King of Soul, Solomon Burke. We wrote together and set a date to record. But that day Mark Flanagan was taking his mother to the doctor's and so couldn't make it. We therefore needed a guitar player for the session. It was a long shot, but on the off chance I rang Eric Clapton, who not only came and did it, delivering one of the greatest solos I've ever heard him do, but he also helped us rewrite the song. In addition, there wasn't a single word of complaint when I knocked the wing mirror off his Ferrari when opening the gate to let him in.

In the 1980s I'd met Ray Charles and had asked him what he'd liké written on his tombstone. He said, 'People can like me or dislike me, people can like my music or dislike my music, I don't care, so long as they know I told the truth.' I said to him, 'That's amazing, you should make a song out of that.' He replied, 'Hey, son – why don't you?' Twenty years later, Sam and I did. We let Ray hear it and he wanted to do it. Sadly, he became too ill. But when Paul Rodgers heard it, he said he thought it could have been written for him so he cut it and it sounded brilliant.

It's particularly touching when a great songwriter wants to sing something you've written yourself. This also happened when Shane MacGowan sang 'Just to be Home with You'.

The success of the series of *Small World Big Band* records made it clear that people loved the Big Band sound. Equally, I loved the chance it gave me to play with musicians I'd always admired. When Tom Jones recorded 'Don't You Kiss My Cheek', which we'd written together, we discovered we had a shared love of the same music. Like me, Tom refused to recognize any barriers between soul, country, blues, jazz and rock and roll – he was only interested in whether the music got you going or not. We decided to make a whole record together. Tom is one of the musical greats who gets songs down in one take. Getting to know him during this process I found him to be one of the most modest, kind and amusing people I've ever met. All he really cares about is the music and making it feel right. I was pleased that our record was a bestseller.

In 2005 we put out our first instrumental Big Band record, *Swinging the Blues and Dancing the Ska*. Warner Brothers didn't feel very optimistic about its chances, as instrumental records of swing and ska music don't usually feature in the charts. They were delighted when it proved to be an unexpectedly big success. On my side, I was just as delighted that it introduced the music not only of artists such as Count Basie, T-Bone Walker, Rico Rodriguez and Dinah Washington but also my childhood piano heroes Albert Ammons and Pete Johnson to a mainstream contemporary audience.

Perfect Cadence

Buoyed by all this success, I now wrote to Christabel's mother, Romana, explaining that my prospects had improved and asking whether she would consider letting me take her daughter's hand in marriage. I had a very nice note back saying, 'Yes, of course – which daughter?' I then explained it was her youngest, Christabel, and everything was settled. My next hurdle was to get Christabel to agree. I was so thrilled when she accepted my proposal, but it then became hard to decide on a date for the wedding, as I was still so busy working.

However, I am delighted to say that on Tuesday 30 August 2005 I found myself sitting in a small country church packed with our relatives and friends. I was only sad not to be able to see some of my dear departed friends there too – George Harrison, Rob Hesketh, Max Barker, Paula, and Malcolm Hardee, who had tragically drowned in the Thames earlier that year. I thought again of how much I missed them and how much I would have enjoyed seeing them all at the wedding. Although it did cross my mind that, in Malcolm's case, it's likely he would have let me down in some way.

Mick Talbot had brought in his Hammond organ and Leslie Cabinet in order to accompany Ruby Turner, and there was some of the most beautiful singing I've ever heard. Sam Brown arranged a choir of heavenly voices, then Jon Scott, Jason McDermid and Chris Storr, the trumpet section of my orchestra, played a wonderful anthem John had written entitled 'The Arrival of the Bride'. We all stood up and I turned to see my intended looking even more ravishing than ever before.

After the King James service, impeccably delivered by the Reverend Wright, we left and came back for a big lunch in our garden. I felt so happy, it was the most beautiful day and, looking around,

I could see many of the characters who have featured in this book – my loved ones, friends, relatives, people I'd worked with – and the people I'd forgotten to invite, I imagined to be there. I thought momentarily that it was a shame I couldn't stay longer and spend more time with them all. But we had arranged to drive off on our honeymoon at five o'clock sharp in order to be in Europe by eight o'clock. There's no point letting any party, however good, spoil your dinner.

As Christabel and I drove off we could hear the happy sounds from the garden. Christabel said, 'I almost wish we could have stayed longer,' but here I was able to give her my first spousal piece of wisdom – and my last showbiz tip to the reader: 'Enjoy the time you have, no big goodbyes, and leave 'em wanting more.' We drove contently off towards the Continent.

Index

Rockin' Dopsie 235, 236, 237, 238
Rod (roadie) 100
Rodriguez, Rico 152, 171, 331, 335, 352
Rogers, Harry 79
Rogers, Paul 352
Rollins, Sonny 329
Rollins, Winston 335
Ron (muscle man) 117
Rose, Michael (Bammi) 335
Rosie (JH's grandmother, 'Nan') 6–7, 23–6, 29, 170, 216, 279–80
Rossiter, Leonard 217, 219
Roxy Music, 'Virginia Plain' 104
Roz (family friend) 21–2
Ruspoli, Dadoa 248
Russ (roadie) 113, 115

'St Louis Blues' 12
Saisse, Philip 287
Salmon, Andy 334
Sanborn, David 279, 284, 287–8
Sanders, Mr (teacher) 20
Sandra (landlady) 69
'Saturday Night' (Roy Brown) 50
Saunders, Jennifer 200, 213, 302
Scott, Jon 323, 332, 335, 353
Scott, Selena 217
Sedaka, Neil 332
Seth Smith, Alex 58–9
'Seventh Son' (Willie Dixon) 296
Sex and Jazz and Rock and Roll 80, 335
Sex Pistols 102
'Shake, Rattle and Roll' 63
Shanghai Surprise (George Harrison) 250
Shaw, Sandie 25
'Sheik of Araby' 152
'Should Have Known Better' 107
'Shout for Joy' (Joe Turner) 28
'Shutting the Door' 171

Simon, Paul 329
Sinatra at the Sands 39–40
Sinatra, Frank 39
Small World Big Band 296, 312, 350
Smith, Bessie 13, 280
Smith, Graham K. 308
Smith, Mark 48, 67, 163, 216, 222, 282, 293
Somerset, Johnson 279, 291
Songs in the Key of Life (Stevie Wonder) 118
Speed Freaks 43–5
Springham, Steve 36–7, 104
Squeeze
    albums: *Babylon and On* 266, 277; *Cool for Cats* 118–20; *Cosi Fan Tutti Frutti* 245–6; *Frank* 298; *Packet of Three* 99; *Squeeze* 103, 106, 136
    history: A40 court case 72–6; appears on *The Tube* 247; band reforms 234, 245, 298; bubble bath episode 305; choice of name 53; early days 47–50, 54, 59, 67–70, 78–83; first managers 51–3, 61, 65; JH leaves 141, 305; success 84–9, 98–9, 102, 108–13
    singles: '853–5937' 276; 'Annie Oakley' 63; 'Backtrack' 99; 'Broadway Boogie' 106–7; 'Buick 48' 106; 'Call, The' 103; 'Cat on a Wall' 99; 'Cool for Cats' 119, 120, 121, 144; 'Dr Jazz' 135; 'Foolish I Know' 142–3; 'Heartbreaking World' 163; 'Hop, Skip and Jump' 119; 'Hourglass' 266; 'Knack, The' 119; 'Lonesome Joe' 80; 'Monkey On You' 63, 78; 'Night Ride' 78, 99; 'Raymond'

He just wanted a decent book to read ...

Not too much to ask, is it? It was in 1935 when Allen Lane, Managing Director of Bodley Head Publishers, stood on a platform at Exeter railway station looking for something good to read on his journey back to London. His choice was limited to popular magazines and poor-quality paperbacks – the same choice faced every day by the vast majority of readers, few of whom could afford hardbacks. Lane's disappointment and subsequent anger at the range of books generally available led him to found a company – and change the world.

'We believed in the existence in this country of a vast reading public for intelligent books at a low price, and staked everything on it'
Sir Allen Lane, 1902–1970, founder of Penguin Books

The quality paperback had arrived – and not just in bookshops. Lane was adamant that his Penguins should appear in chain stores and tobacconists, and should cost no more than a packet of cigarettes.

Reading habits (and cigarette prices) have changed since 1935, but Penguin still believes in publishing the best books for everybody to enjoy. We still believe that good design costs no more than bad design, and we still believe that quality books published passionately and responsibly make the world a better place.

So wherever you see the little bird – whether it's on a piece of prize-winning literary fiction or a celebrity autobiography, political tour de force or historical masterpiece, a serial-killer thriller, reference book, world classic or a piece of pure escapism – you can bet that it represents the very best that the genre has to offer.

Whatever you like to read – trust Penguin.